A Forest Farm

James Walter Gozzard (1861–1926), *The Forest Farm* (detail), date unknown

A Forest Farm

The History of Tickeridge Farm, Kingscote, West Sussex

Kim Bayne

UNICORN

Published in 2026 by Unicorn
an imprint of Unicorn Publishing Group
Charleston Studio
Meadow Business Centre
Lewes
BN8 5RW
www.unicornpublishing.org

Text © Kim Bayne
Photographs © Kim Bayne, except where individually credited
Diagrams on pp.14, 25, 44, 63, 81, 86, 87, 93, 95, 109, 125 and 133 © Paul Hewitt, Battlefield Design, based on originals by Kim Bayne

All rights reserved. No part of the contents of this book may be reproduced, stored in or introduced into a retrieval system, or transmitted, in any form or by any means (electronic, mechanical, photocopying, recording or otherwise), without the prior written permission of the copyright holder and the above publisher of this book.

Every effort has been made to trace copyright holders and to obtain their permission for the use of copyright material. The publisher apologises for any errors or omissions and would be grateful if notified of any corrections that should be incorporated in future reprints or editions of this book.

ISBN 978-1-917458-55-9
10 9 8 7 6 5 4 3 2 1

Design by Felicity Price-Smith
Printed in Turkey by Özlemprint

Editor's note
This book includes variant spellings of names due to inconsistencies in historical record keeping.
Dates written with a / between two years are a result of the change from Julian to Gregorian calendar in 1752.

Contents

	Preface	7
	Introduction	9
1	The Wealden Forest	11
2	First Human Influence Drovers' Routes	13
3	Iron and the Romans	18
4	Origin of the Name	19
5	William de Teggeherugge and his Sheep	22
6	The Medieval House is Built	24
7	The Black Death (1348–51) and its Aftermath	30
8	The Benke Family	33
9	The Tudor Extension to the House	37
10	Hanna Banks and Timber Extraction	42
11	The Slany Family, Exploration and Shipbuilding	44
12	Robert Mills and John Chisman, Tenant Farmers	53
13	The Hamlin Family, Part I	55
14	Simon Eaton – The First Civil War, the Irish Problem and the Rise of Puritanism	57
15	The Hamlin Family, Part II – The House and Farm Refurbished	66
16	Francis Tully, Tenant Farmer – His Life and Times	69
17	Edward Paine and John Browning – Agriculture Dominates	72
18	The Woodman Family – Tenants to Owners	80
19	The Longley Family	90
20	The Impact of the Railway	95
21	Tenant Farmers and Two World Wars	101
22	The House and Farm Part Company	122
23	Progress in the 20th Century	130
24	Design Changes in the 21st Century	136
	In Conclusion	151
	Bibliography and References	152
	Appendix 1 Will of John Kempe	161
	Appendix 2 Waldingfield Family Tree	162
	Appendix 3 Hamlin Family Tree	164
	Appendix 4 Slany Family Tree	166
	Appendix 5 Warner and Eaton Family Tree	168
	Appendix 6 Eaton and Mathew Family Tree	170
	Appendix 7 Tassell and Eaton Family Tree	172
	Appendix 8 Boakes, Gilbert and Still Family Tree	174
	Appendix 9 Tully Documents, 1687–8	176
	Appendix 10 *The Gypsy*, Edward Thomas	181
	Index	182

Preface

As an enthusiastic amateur historian, for many years I have been delving into the history of the Kingscote area near East Grinstead in West Sussex, and particularly that of our farm at Tickeridge. It has proved to be a fascinating study of a remarkable place, and I hope that this book will do justice to its story.

Along the way, I have been most fortunate to meet, or have contact with, many people whose kindness, encouragement and expertise have helped me to progress this project, and I should like to express my heartfelt thanks and gratitude to them all. They include Michael and Maggi Amos, Sir Robert Aske, Arthur Bowers, John Carver of Arun Pumps, Jeremy Clarke and John Crane of the Wealden Buildings Study Group, Paul Coulson and members of the Sussex Historical Search Society, Charles Doble of Green & Carter Ltd, Joan Dutton, Elizabeth Furber, Andy Gammon, Paul Gould, Vinnie Grosjean, Jeremy Hodgkinson, Herbert and Magdalena Kean, David Knight, Michael Longley, Doris Moody, Dr John Ralph, Alan Reed, Gilbert Reed, Heather Sargent, Paul and Jackie Spinks, John Vince and Geraldine Warren.

Most of the photos are from my own collection; for others, I have indicated their source in the text. The internet has provided some of the other illustrations.

I have made every effort to identify copyright owners and to ensure that the information given in the Bibliography and References is accurate. I apologise for any errors and if, inadvertently, any copyright which I have been unable to trace has been infringed.

Finally, my warmest thanks must go to my dear husband for his kind support and endless patience, which have enabled me to complete this book.

Kim Bayne
2026

Introduction

People and things pass away, but not places.
DAPHNE DU MAURIER

IN THE HIGH WEALD OF SUSSEX lies an ancient farm. It occupies land on the Forest Ridge of the Hastings Beds of Tunbridge Wells Sand and Grinstead Clay; separating the sand from the clay is a seam of Ardingly Sandstone, running from Sandhill in Crawley Down south-eastwards through the farm. In places the sandstone rock is exposed, like the stunning feature of Big-Upon-Little in West Hoathly. Where the sandstone lies just below the soil, landslips have occurred where the clay has slumped off the underlying rock.

Located just two and a half miles to the south-west of the historic town of East Grinstead, in the hamlet of Kingscote, is Tickeridge Farm, its farmhouse standing on an imposing outcrop of the sandstone. To an altitude of around 400ft at its highest point, the farm extends westwards from the farmhouse and buildings which overlook the attractive valley of a tributary of the River Medway, the Stone Brook, its own waters augmented by several Wealden gills. The land is heavy but grass grows well, making excellent grazing for livestock.

Fig.1: Exposed sandstone rock

Figs.2 and 3: Landslips

Historically, Tickeridge lay in the Hundred of Streat and the Rape of Lewes. Within an outlying woodland area of the Weald belonging to the Manor of Plumpton Boscage, its land extended into the adjoining Manor of Imberhorne. Today, Tickeridge Farm straddles the parish boundary between West Hoathly and East Grinstead.

Tickeridge was once one of the largest farms in the area, at around 350 acres, and extended westwards towards Selsfield, down to the main channel of the River Medway in the east, and across Vowels Lane into what is now the Gravetye Estate in the south. Over the years, land sales have reduced its area, but almost 14 acres of it remains as ancient woodland, Hazel coppices and spinneys.

Using documentary, cartographic and verbal evidence, I have endeavoured to unravel the dynamic history and development of the farm, which has inevitably been greatly influenced by its people. We know something of the owners, tenant farmers and farm bailiffs and their families, but I should like to pay tribute to the unsung heroes of this story, those courageous early settlers who ventured into the wildwood, then later the toilers and tillers of the soil such as the agricultural labourers, woodsmen and servants without whose backbreaking work Tickeridge Farm could not have functioned. The lodgers too will have contributed with their rental payments.

Before the 19th century, it is rarely possible to identify these individuals; being then of lowly status, their names do not often appear in documents. Later, thanks to better and more universal records, we can at least get to know some of them and give due recognition to the vital role they all played, so what follows is not only the history of a Wealden farmstead, but also of the people whose lives played their part in shaping that history. I have adopted the spellings of names as they appear in the documents I have used for research, and, as different scribes would have chosen their preferred version, there may be variations within the text.

Chapter 1
The Wealden Forest

About 8,000 years ago the primeval forests of the Weald began to be transformed, evolving into the mixed deciduous woodland we know today. Oak, Hazel and Beech became the dominant arboreal species and others soon followed.

The strong soils of the Weald provided the ideal habitat for the English Oak to flourish and the sandstone base enabled their roots to gain a good hold in the cracks and crevices.

The Beech trees were a valuable partner, providing leaves rich in fertilising properties.

At Tickeridge, the Hazel coppices, now hundreds of years old, provided the wood for hurdles to enclose sheep flocks, wattles for building, fence stakes, and charcoal for the local ironworks. Today, in the spring, their woodland floors are awash with lapis lakes of fragrant native Bluebells.

A limited tree survey at Tickeridge carried out in 2016 recorded that, besides the Oak and coppiced Hazel, which dominate, are Beech, Ash, Holly, Field Maple, Crab Apple, Cherry, Alder, Hawthorn, Blackthorn, Elder, Yew and the occasional Aspen tree. Many of the trees are parasitised by Ivy, or entwined with Honeysuckle, with Roses, Brambles and Bracken forming the thicket beneath them.

This woodland type is known as 'The English Oak, Honeysuckle, Bracken and Bramble Community of NVC W10', the British National Vegetation Classification of mixed deciduous woodlands.

There are two hedges with ditches on the farm; one is a ditch topped on its western side by a row of Field Maples which appear to be of considerable age and may date from Tudor times when they were a popular hedging plant.

There are five surviving trees, the largest with a base girth of 10ft. The short main trunk of each tree divides into four or five trunks, some of them with distinct right-angles. This might indicate that, as young

Fig.4: Bluebells in Hazel coppice

Fig.5: Oak tree parasitised with Ivy. Image courtesy of Vecteezy

Fig.6: Field Maple

trees, their main trunks were cut back to about one metre above ground, a process called 'stubbing', with the new growth perhaps laid to form a hedge or barrier which, combined with the ditch, defined the boundary of woodland or enclosed land.

The other ditch and hedge run in a straight line from the farm down to the brook. This hedge produced an interesting mixture of Hawthorn, Hazel, Holly and Blackthorn, with an undergrowth of Ivy, Honeysuckle and Brambles. The Hawthorns are spaced at regular intervals, apparently planted to mark a boundary or enclose livestock pasture, perhaps in the 18th century during the Enclosure Movement.

All the woodland shaws and spinneys at Tickeridge are categorised as 'Ancient Semi-natural Woodland' (ASNW), meaning that they are believed to have been continuous woodland cover since at least 1600 and have arisen from natural regeneration or coppice re-growth.

The woodland provides habitats for a number of indicator plant species, among them the native Bluebell and Yellow Archangel; Wood Anemone flourishes near the brook, as does Wild Garlic in great profusion. Wood Sorrel, Dog Violet, Cuckoo Flower, Common Star of Bethlehem, Field Chickweed, Lesser Celandine, Lords and Ladies, Ground Ivy, Primroses, Wild Strawberry, Foxgloves and Common Spotted Orchid grow well in the dappled shade of overhanging trees, and the rarer Spotted Hawkweed has also been found here.

There are two further sites of woodland which historically belonged to the farm – sharing its western boundary is Holstein Wood, presently owned by the Balcombe Estate, and on the Gravetye Estate is Minepit Wood. In both cases, the native tree cover has been felled and replaced with planted stock.

Fig.7: Yellow Archangel.
Image courtesy of Teun Spaans

Chapter 2

First Human Influence Drovers' Routes

The history of Tickeridge Farm begins soon after Neolithic farmers came to Britain from Europe in about 4100 BC. They brought with them their technique of land clearance – the 'slash and burn' method of clearing woodland. Their arrival heralded something of an agricultural revolution, for they abandoned their previously nomadic existence as hunter-gatherers and instead turned to agriculture and a settled way of life. In Sussex, the most fertile land was near the coast and close to the foot of the South Downs, so this was where their earliest settlements were established. Once land was cleared, Wheat, Oats and Barley were grown, dogs were kept and wild animals were domesticated and selectively bred to produce pigs, cattle, sheep and goats.

In time, as the herds of livestock grew, so did their food consumption, so these early farmers would have sought to supplement their winter feed where they could. To this end, they were drawn to the forests of the High Weald, then an expanse of dense woodland, mostly of Oak and Beech, interspersed with bogs, and later called by the Romans 'Anderida', meaning an unfrequented or untrodden spot. This ancient Wealden forest, which extended from north-west Hampshire through northern Sussex to Kent, included the forests of Worth and Ashdown Forest which from the 14th to 17th century was included in the portfolio of land known as Lancaster Great Park.

In the forest was to be found the food supply the farmers needed – the harvest of Acorns, Beech Mast, fruits and berries, known collectively as pannage. But this strange and mystical place was not without danger, for wolves and wild boar freely roamed there, and it must have taken great courage and great need to penetrate its depths.

Eventually, a network of tracks from the foot of the South Downs northwards into the forest became established. Historian Ivan Margary studied these ancient trackways and concluded that the one relevant to

In Britain, the Neolithic Period extended from around 4100 to 2500 BC.

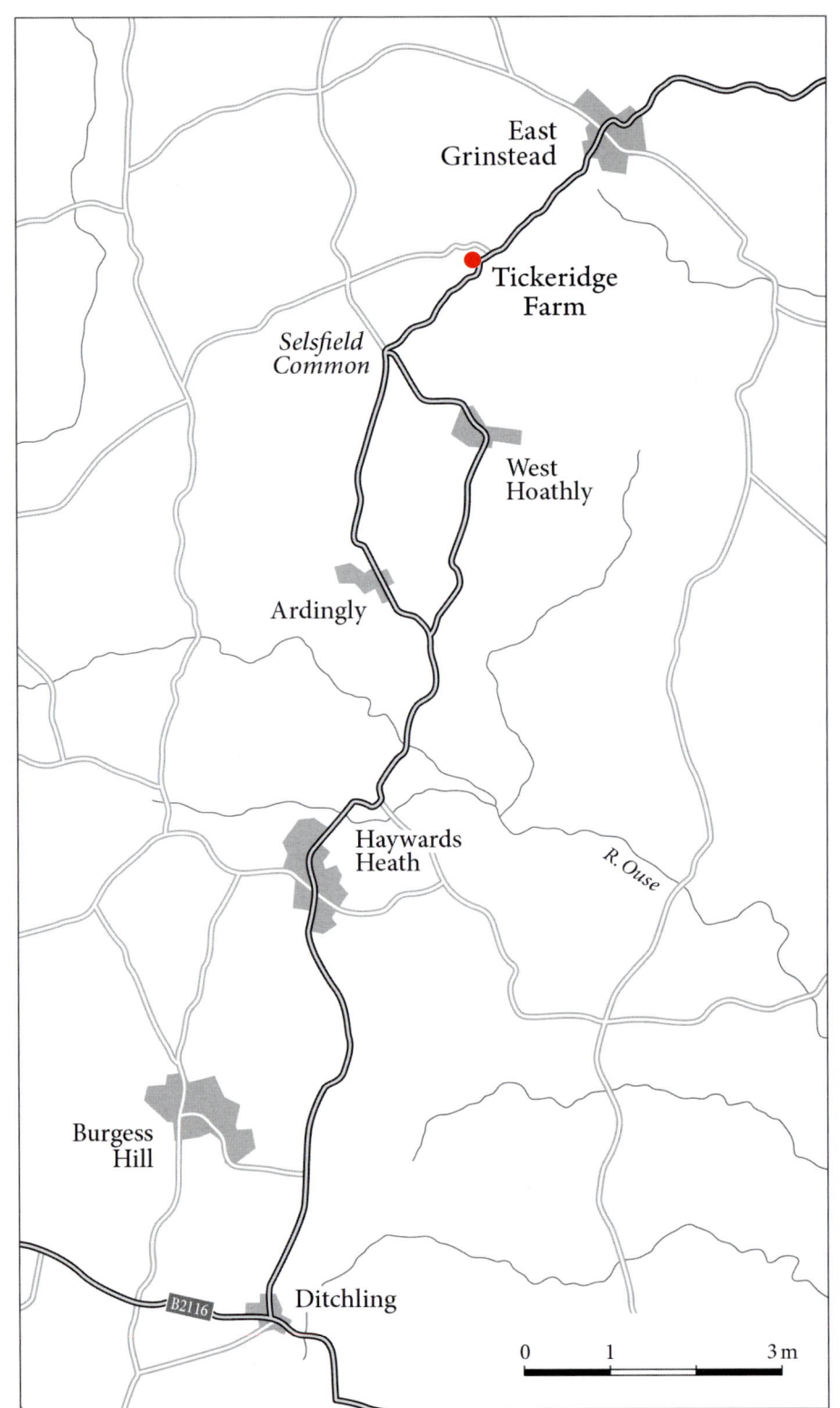

Fig.8: Map of the drovers' route, with the location of Tickeridge Farm marked in red

Tickeridge came northwards from Ditchling, past Burgess Hill, through Haywards Heath and Town House Farm, Ardingly, with a choice of alternative routes to arrive at Selsfield Common, then down what is now Vowels Lane to the farm, and onwards to the north.

Along these routes, livestock – predominantly pigs, but also sheep and cattle – were driven each autumn, arriving in early September. For the four months they would spend in the forest, the drovers would have had mules to carry enough provisions for their stay, and dogs to help them control the pigs, the herding of which was said to be a most difficult and exasperating task. Travelling up to six miles a day, it would have taken several days to complete their journey. On the way they would have needed overnight shelter and a safe area for their livestock, which in time led to the establishment of hostels and inns at regular intervals along the route.

Its prominent sandstone outcrop, and the proximity of a reliable source of water, must have been an appealing location for some drovers to make their den or winter camp at Tickeridge, erecting an enclosure for their livestock, and for themselves, a shieling, or simple, one-roomed shelter.

Fig.9: Drover's hut by Sue Linton, with her kind permision

The shelters had to be sturdy and weatherproof, and the enclosure substantial enough to contain and protect the animals at night. Once the den was established, the drovers would have returned to it each year, repairing and refurbishing their shelters on each visit.

Fig.10: Harvesting Acorns, illustration from the *Luttrell Psalter*, courtesy of the British Library

In January, once the Acorns hardened and were no longer edible, the animals and their drovers had to make the arduous return journey south through the wet clay soils of the Weald.

The tracks thus created are known as droves or drovers' routes and the system of seasonally moving animals this way was known as transhumance. Thousands of animals were involved each year.

Fig.11: Top/south end of Vowels Lane – ancient droveway. Here you can clearly see how all those thousands of trotters, hooves and feet wore down the track, leaving high banks on either side.

Fig.12: First edition Ordnance Survey map, *c.* 1792–1805. The red line marks the original track from Selsfield, the blue line marks the river.

In Britain, the Bronze Age began c.1900 BC, to be followed by the Iron Age which began in about 800 BC and lasted until the Romans arrived in AD 43.

The droves survive today as the north–south road network of Sussex. They are very wide in places and easily identifiable where ancient hedges are some distance from the present roadside, maybe 30 to 40ft apart. They often have high banks running alongside the road, evidence of the effect of all those trotters, hooves and feet wearing away the surface of the track; these are the sunken roads of the Weald. One of them was the drove route from the foot of the Downs which ran through Haywards Heath to West Hoathly; another ran through Ardingly, arriving at Selsfield and either may have provided access to Tickeridge down what is now Vowels Lane.

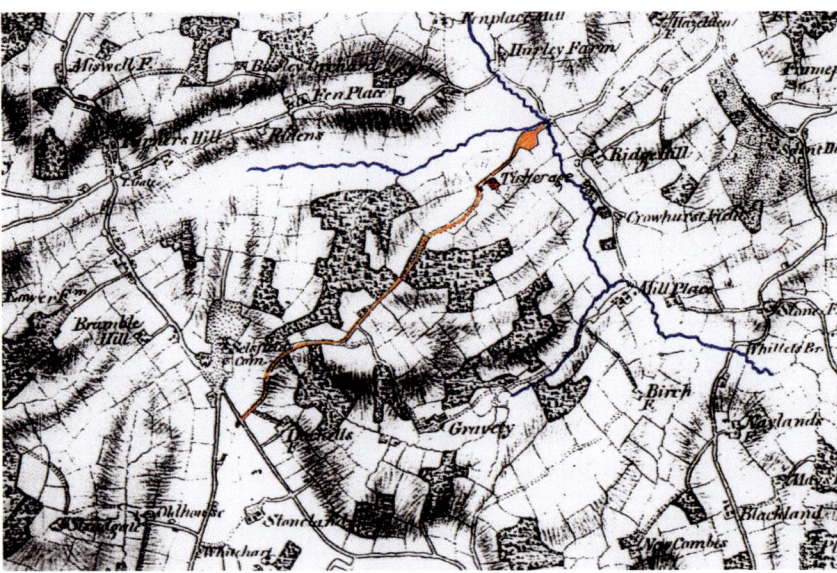

Skirting round the enclosure, the ancient track continued along the edge of the fields and beside the river towards the Turners Hill/East Grinstead road, near its present junction with Vowels Lane. Here, there would have been a ford or simple bridge across the river to enable access to and from the route north.

The condition of the droves in the winter made them difficult and hazardous to traverse so that, gradually, the temporary homesteads in the Weald became more permanent and, by the 5th century, agriculture had developed and the process of settlement had begun. Over the next 500 years, droving gradually declined as many of the isolated Wealden farmsteads were established though, in 1086, the Domesday Book records that around 150,000 pigs were still being driven from pastures in the south of Sussex to the forests of the Weald.

To the practice of pannage and the bounty of Acorns and Beech Mast can be given the credit for the preservation of much of the woodland at

Fig.13: Last remnant of the ancient track through Tickeridge

this time, for to fell too many trees would have deprived the livestock of these valuable food sources.

The necessity to access the Wealden harvest and the establishment of the droves led to a system of land division whereby the Manors in the south of the county were each allotted parcels of land located directly northwards of them in the Weald. These were the detached outlying woodland areas of the Manors, of which the Boscage was the outlier of the Manor of Plumpton in the Hundred of Streat, later held by the Bardolf family.

Chapter 3

Iron and the Romans

Phalera: A bronze decorative feature of a Roman Legionnaire's uniform, dated to around AD 200.

BENEATH THE LITTER OF THE FOREST FLOOR lay a valuable resource; iron ore. By the 5th century BC the Celts in the Weald were producing iron implements and weapons.

Soon after their invasion in AD 43, the Romans came to the forest and found a well-established local tradition of iron making, using small, clay bloomery furnaces. They valued the local deposits of iron ore, extracted from the Wadhurst Clay, and the timber, once converted to charcoal, was an essential ingredient for smelting it. It is said that the Romans obtained nearly all their iron from Sussex and to access it they built roads into the forest, one of which passes nearby across Selsfield Common, where remnants of the agger[1] still survive. This particular route, from the foot of the South Downs near Pyecombe, has been numbered 150 by Ivan Margary.[2] From the Common, through the farm, runs a track which was apparently known to the Romans, since their pottery, a coin, a buckle and a phalera have been found near it.

About 450 yards away to the east of the farm, on the left bank of the River Medway on land belonging to Ridge Hill, are the remains of the most northern Roman bloomery yet found in Sussex.

Fig.14: Roman phalera, *c.* AD 200, diameter 4.5cm, found on the farm by Paul Coulson of the Sussex Historical Search Society of metal detectorists (SHSS)

---

1. An agger is a ridge or embankment.
2. Historian Ivan Margary developed a catalogue system for Roman roads, known as the Margary numbers.

Chapter 4

Origin of the Name

During the medieval period (476–1485), when Tickeridge acquired its name, sheep – and particularly their fleeces – were the mainstay of England's wealth and foreign trade, much of the best English wool being exported to Flanders in northern Belgium.

By 1100, England's sheep numbers were already 3 million and rising and sheep husbandry was an important part of the national economy. By 1300, wool exports had reached a peak of around 12 million fleeces per year and the country's sheep flock was nearly 20 million animals. (The present English flock is around 11 million.) In Sussex alone the flock exceeded 110,000, and around 300 of these were in the local area. At Tickeridge, meadows on cleared land would have provided grazing, and hay for winter feed.

The earliest occurrence I have found of a name for the place we now call Tickeridge is *Teggeherugge* in the 13th century, the period of our language development known as Middle English, which extended from 1151 to about 1500. Middle English itself had developed from the earlier Anglo Saxon, or Old English, dating from around AD 500.

The name comprises two elements, *tegge* and *herugge*. According to Mawer and Stenton[1] the name means "a ridge of land with an enclosure" on it. They propose that the second element comes from the Old English *hrycg*, meaning a ridge. The Middle English version of this word was *rigge*, and the 13th-century example above appears to demonstrate the progression from the Old to the Middle English, becoming *regge* by the 14th century.

The first element, *tegge*, is indeed a Middle English word from the Old English *tegga*, meaning a teg or tye, an enclosure for livestock, but this itself derives from the Old Swedish *takka* or *tackae*, meaning a ewe. Today,

Old English: Dating from the Anglo-Saxon settlement in Britain, c. 450, to about 1150.

---

1. See Bibliography and References.

Fig.15: 14th-century sheep pen as illustrated in the *Luttrell Psalter*; on the left is a woman milking a ewe. Image courtesy of Wikimedia Commons

Fig.16: 14th-century shepherd. Image courtesy of the Institute for Research and History of Texts

we would use the word 'teg' to describe a sheep or ewe in its second year.

Piecing together the two elements, we may arrive more specifically at 'Sheep Ridge', indicating that the main purpose of the enclosure by the 13th century was to enfold sheep. These would have been short-woolled sheep, with a white staple length[2] of only 3–4in, and of a small, stocky build. Known as 'the golden hoof', sheep were good for the land, providing valuable manure without damaging the soil structure. Though they were kept primarily for their fleeces, their milk and meat were also important.

The earliest forms of the name vary, and it continued to evolve until 1592 when its present form is first noted and, apart from occasional minor spelling variations, has remained constant to the present day.

However, originally, this name referred only to the portion of the farm which lay in the parish of West Hoathly. During the period from the 12th to 16th centuries, this was held by the Priory of St Pancras, Lewes. The farm's land in the parish of East Grinstead, which lay on the right bank of the River Medway, was known by various versions of 'Meadows and Shelves' and was administered by the Canons of South Malling. This area comprised woodland and water meadows, swampy in nature and extending many metres beyond the river bank. The definition of the word 'meadow' describes this area exactly, being "moist low-lying, usually level grassland".[3] Its derivation is from the Middle English *medwe*, from the Old English *maedwe*. For Jessup,[4] the word 'medway' is of Celtic origin (*c.* 750 BC – AD 43).

The Romans called the river *Fluminus Meduwaeias*, said by Penn[5] to

---

2. The staple length is the size of the wool fibres.
3. Definition from the Merriam-Webster Dictionary.
4. See Bibliography and References.
5. See Bibliography and References.

mean "river with sweet water". By the 9th century it was *Medwaeg*, in the 13th it was known as *Aqua de Medewey,* in the 14th it was *Medewaye* and in the 16th, William Lambarde[6] suggested that the name of the Medway meant "a fruitful medowe".

Fig.17: Meadows and Shelves, photographed on 29 April 2010

Today, the verdant meadows are less marshy, thanks to drainage work carried out by teams of Italian and German prisoners during World War II from their camp at Rowfant, whose hand-dug ditches eventually improved the land. Formerly, the slope beyond them continued up to the parish boundary which is delineated by the road to Mill Place, but the embankments of the railway have greatly distorted the lie of the land here. The definition of 'to shelve' is "to slope gently".[7] The Middle English form was *scylfe*, akin to the Latin *sculpere*, to carve, and the Old English *sciell*, shell. In an article for the East Grinstead Society, M.J. Leppard cites the theory of Prof. Coates who proposes that *scylfe* refers to a "rather flat-bottomed valley". The name appears as 'Shellvys' in 1564 and 'Shells' in 1579. The name 'Meadows and Shelves' in its latter form surely reflects its topographical origins and referred specifically to those lands which, before the railway, were adjacent to and, historically, often held as part of Tickeridge Farm.

---

6. See Bibliography and References.
7. Longman Concise English Dictionary, 1985.

Chapter 5

William de Teggeherugge and his Sheep

The farm's occupants adopted its name as their own, and the first of these whom we can identify is William de Teggeherugge, a Carpenter/Builder who, in 1257, witnessed a grant of land to the parish church of West Hoathly.

Wealden settlements were flourishing and their demand for timber for building or burning, and the corresponding need for land to graze livestock or grow crops, led to the land clearances of the 13th and 14th centuries. William or one of his ancestors would have been part of this process, building a simple dwelling of timber harvested from the woodland around him, and using the cleared or *assarted* land on which to graze his livestock and grow crops. These included Peas (additional feed for the sheep) but mainly Barley, Oats and Wheat, the latter of which he could take to the water-driven corn mill at nearby Mill Place to have the grains ground into flour.

Figs.18 and 19: Medieval Carpenters – since buildings were constructed using timber framing at this time, carpenters were also builders.
Left image courtesy of Wikimedia Commons, right image courtesy of the Metropolitan Museum of Art

The straw provided bedding for his animals and at the market in East Grinstead he could buy provisions and sell his own produce. His fleeces may have been simply packed and sold or spun and woven into cloth locally.

There is perhaps additional evidence that large numbers of sheep were on the ridge at that time, for a few years later, in the 1265–6 Court Rolls of the Rape of Lewes, Simonem Tith/le Tyer /le Teyere or le Teghere, and Thomam le Teyer or Teghere are mentioned, all of which appear to be mutated forms of the original first element, *tegge*, to denote 'the sheep keeper' or, as we might say, Simon or Thomas 'the Sheep'. According to Crossingham Gower, this was the origin of the surname Teague.[1]

In 1289, an inquisition was held at West Hoathly following the death of William Bardolf who had died seized[2] of a tenement there and 50 acres of arable land, half an acre of meadow, some pasture and woodland, in total valued at 12s.4d. His heir was his adult son, Hugh, so I am assuming this refers to the lands of Tickeridge since, seven years later, we know that their tenant was Simon de Thegheregg, a villein of Hugh Bardolf.

---

1. *Sussex Family Historian*, December 1996, Vol.12, No.4, pp.146-148.
2. Meaning 'having ownership of'.

Chapter 6
The Medieval House is Built

Probably William's son, Simon de Thegheregg paid 3s.0d. of the Sussex Subsidy taken in 1296. As a manorial tenant, he owed agricultural work service to his overlord, Hugh Bardolf. Hugh was Lord of the Manor of Plumpton, and held the Manor in chief of[1] John de Warrenne, Earl of Surrey, by knight service. By 1321, Thomas Bardolf, Hugh's son, had inherited the Manor of Plumpton and held 40 acres of land and 10 acres of meadow there.

In 1327, the first year of the reign of King Edward III, the subsidy under the "Hundred of Strete and Villata de Hothleigh" again lists Simon de Thegheregg. Since he is believed to have been a Carpenter and Builder and the oldest surviving portion of the present house, the open hall, is said to date from around that time, in Simon de Thegheregg we have a potential candidate for its builder.

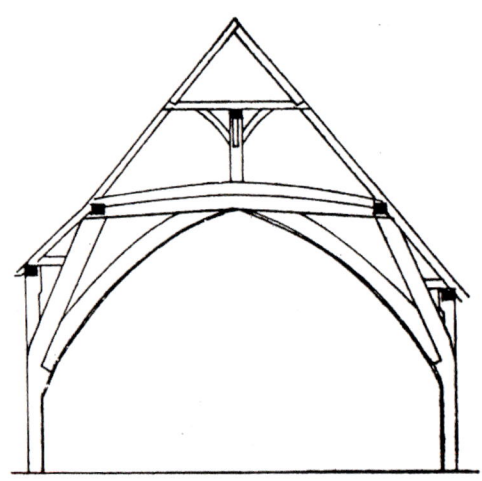 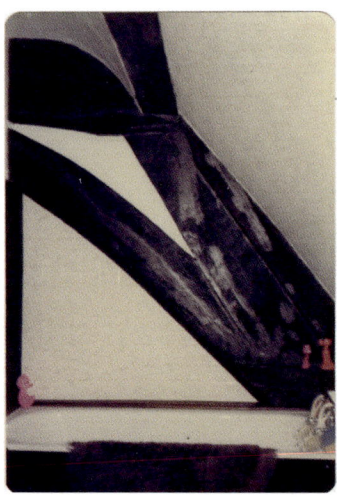

Fig.20: On the left, an illustration of base crucked trusses in Tickeridge. As a pair, they supported the roof of a building. *Source: Framed Buildings of the Weald,* by R.T. Mason, 2nd edn., 1969, p.11

Fig.21: On the right, one of the base crucks at Tickeridge, photographed by Joan Dutton, 1979

1. Meaning 'directly from'.

Carpenters were skilled artisans, learning their craft as apprentices, and taking several years to hone their skills in the use of the tools, reading the plans, and the design and construction of buildings. On completion of his apprenticeship, a Carpenter became a Journeyman, working on different projects until he was competent enough to submit one to the Guild of Carpenters; if it was approved, he was then able to establish his own business. The work was demanding, not only physically but also intellectually, since an understanding of geometry and mathematics was required in order to create complex structures.

Benefitting from the timber sourced from his own woodland, and prospering from the income generated by his sheep flock and his crops, which were now of the greater value, Simon was of a status to erect for himself a splendid quasi-aisled base crucked hall.

It is not uncommon in the Weald to find timber-framed houses but Tickeridge is one of the oldest and finest of them.

Following a visit to Tickeridge farmhouse in 2002, a report by the Wealden Buildings Study Group concluded that the Hall was some 40ft long and 15 ft wide, comprising two bays, with a two-storied Solar wing at the south end, overlooking what is now Vowels Lane. This wing accommodated the private chambers of the resident family.

Fig.22: Ground floor plan after R.T. Mason, 1942 and *Sussex Archaeological Collections*, vol.82, 1942

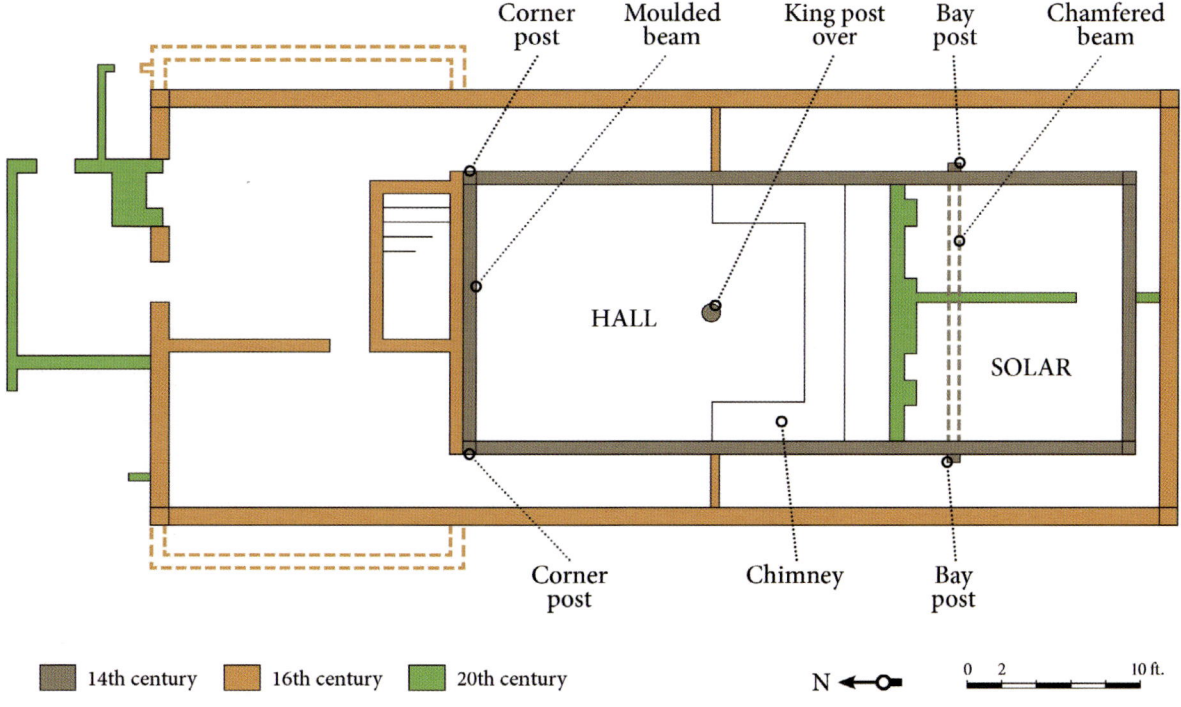

THE MEDIEVAL HOUSE IS BUILT

25

Solar: The name derived from the Latin word, solus, meaning 'alone'.

Buttery: Said to derive from the French word bouteille, *meaning bottle. However, my own theory, based on the definition for boite in the Cambridge Dictionary, is that the word 'Buttery' comes from the French word* boite, *meaning "a box, or a bin, a container used for storing corn" such as Barley, the essential ingredient for making beer, which was made in a Buttery. Hence our modern usage of the word 'butt', meaning a large barrel for collecting or storing liquid.*

However, current architectural thinking is that the south end of the house was not the Solar but was instead the Services Bay, comprising a Buttery, for brewing and storing beer and ale, a Pantry above for the storage of dry foodstuffs, and some servant accommodation.

Part of the original building survives within its present structure, as illustrated below in 1942.

At Tickeridge, the Solar is thought to have been an additional bay on the north end of the house, with a parlour on the ground floor and stairs to a bedroom above, accessed by a door at the west end of the dais beam. Part of this theory is supported by the fact that, today, beams in the 16th-century northern crosswing appear to be recycled from an earlier building.

But it begs the question, why was the Solar accommodation located at the northern end, bearing in mind that this would inevitably have been the coldest portion, exposed as it is to the prevailing wind, especially at a time when windows were usually unglazed and shutters provided the only protection from the elements? The Services Bay and Buttery, placed in that location, would have better served the storage and preservation of foodstuffs. Security might also be considered; the southern end of the house rises immediately above a virtual cliff of sandstone which would make it difficult for any intruders to enter there.

The north of the house, from whence the cellar was accessed and where the well was located, would also have been convenient for domestic staff to obtain their water supply and access their working and living accommodation in the Services Bay.

Spanning the width of the Hall at its northern end is the magnificent moulded or carved dais beam, a testament to its creator's skill and a symbol of Simon's wealth. At the beam's western end is the doorway,

Fig.23: On the left, outline of the moulded beam, from R.T. Mason, *Sussex Archaelogical Collections*, vol.82, 1942, p.69

Fig.24: On the right, photo of moulded beam taken by Joan Dutton in July 1979

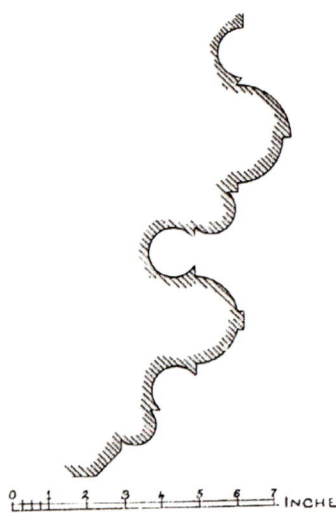

mentioned above, whose alternative purpose could have been to give access to and from the Services Bay located at the northern end of the house, which would have been convenient for the servants bringing food and refreshments to those in the Hall.

Beneath the beam at Tickeridge were the remains of pressure mark and peghole evidence on studs, indicating fixing points for a long bench on which Simon would have sat with his family at a long Oak trestle table. Being on trestles, the table top could be easily removed if the occasion arose when more space was needed within the Hall.

Fig.25: Medieval dining, illustration from the *Luttrell Psalter*, courtesy of the British Library

With the impressive beam behind them, Simon's family were warmed by the glowing embers of the fire in a stone hearth on the floor nearby, its smoke curling slowly upwards, the soot blackening the impressive crown post, shown to the right, before escaping through the roof.

The medieval Hall at Tickeridge was built on one of two neighbouring outcrops of Ardingly Sandstone, overlooking its land, at about 350ft above sea level. Today, the other outcrop is occupied by the huge old weather-boarded barn (of much later date), with 20th-century agricultural buildings a short distance away. The cleft between the two outcrops enables access to the farm and the fields beyond, and through it runs the parish boundary between East Grinstead and West Hoathly.

The larger part of the farm, extending westwards up the valley from the house, lay in the parish of West Hoathly and was called Tickeridge (or variations) and held by copyhold – that is, held in tenure of the mesne Lord of the Manor[2] in return for agricultural services.

The remainder, Meadows and Shelves lying in East Grinstead, was held freehold, a secure tenure where an annual payment was made

Fig.26: Photo of crown post by Joan Dutton, July 1979

2. A lord who held land belonging to a superior lord and let that land to tenants.

THE MEDIEVAL HOUSE IS BUILT

Fig.27: Andy Gammon's impression of an open Hall like Tickeridge, with his kind permission

instead of work service. It is unclear whether the field to the north of the buildings, which also lies in East Grinstead, formed part of the Meadows and Shelves holding.

By what means the farm changed hands I cannot say for certain, since evidence is lacking, but, on 15 December 1329, Sir Thomas Bardolf died seized of Plumpton Manor, including a messuage,[3] 88 acres of land and 40 acres of wood and heath in 'Hothleigh'. Since Hugh Bardolf, Thomas's father, had held this land in 1296 when Simon de Thegheregg was one of his villeins, I am inclined to believe that at least some, if not all, of these 128 acres belonged to Tickeridge. In 1330, the tenant of the messuage and

---

3. Main house.

its garden was bound to work on the lord's land, reaping his corn instead of paying a money rent, a custom known as *Gavelrip*.

In 1332, there are no entries for 'Hothleigh' under the Rape of Lewes, and Tegherugg family members are recorded only in 'Horsted Kaynes', 'Burle' and 'Lyndefeld', the latter listed under the Hundred of Strete and apparently relevant to Tickeridge since, besides Richard de Thegheregge, it also includes the Gravetye family nearby. Ursula Ridley suggests that this Richard, a Carpenter, Timber Merchant and Builder, inherited the farm from his father, Simon, and subsequently 'acquired' the surname of Benke. However, in the 1332 Subsidy, also for Lyndefeld, there is mention of Agn' and Rico (Richard) le Benek(e), obviously a local family, and my alternative suggestion is that at some point, a daughter of the Thegheregge family married a son of the Benek family to whom the farm eventually passed.

Confirmation that much land had been cleared locally and brought into arable production by this time may be found in the tithe records for West Hoathly, taken in 1340, when one ninth of the value of sheaves produced in the parish was valued at £7.16s.8d., making their total value some £70.10s. By comparison, the parish's total wool output was valued at only 18s. and its lambs at 12s.

Chapter 7
The Black Death (1348–51) and its Aftermath

In June 1348, The Plague – or Black Death – arrived in Dorset from the Continent and by summer the following year had spread to the whole country; its effect was devastating, decimating the population, creating a shortage of farm labour and a consequent demand for higher wages. By 1351, however, the rate of infection had begun to decline and life slowly returned to something approaching normality; in East Grinstead, thoughts turned to the construction of new houses.

Writing in 1957, R.T. Mason compared the workmanship at Tickeridge with that of other early 14th-century houses in the area and came to the conclusion that the quality of their moulded oak beams suggests that they may all have been created by the same hand. In 1955, Ursula Ridley compared the quality of the construction of Tickeridge with the open Hall of Wilmington House, 48 High Street, East Grinstead which also dates from the early 14th century, and is one of only three open Halls of this antiquity in the town; another is Amherst House at numbers 66 and 68 High Street.

The third of these ancient houses is 38 and 40 High Street which formed part of the Broadleys clothing store, closed in June 2024. Studies have shown that this is a high status four-bay hall, with three open and one floored bay, an integral cart way, plus a four-bay crosswing. A dendrochronology date confirms that at least one of its timbers was felled in the winter of 1351 or spring of 1352, the latter being the more likely date since Oak trees were usually felled in the spring, the optimum time to harvest their bark, when the tannin was at its strongest. The bark was stripped from the tree trunk and branches, and stored under cover to dry out. It was an important by-product, used in the tanning industry, and tons of it were sent to London from the Weald.

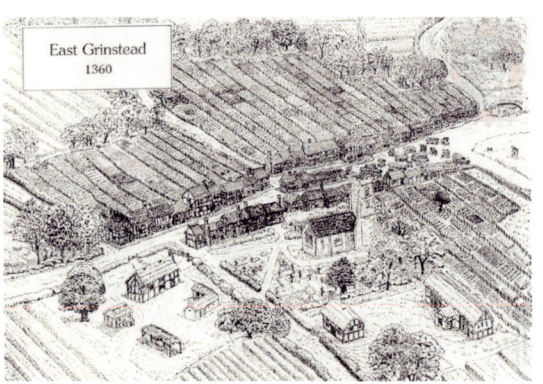

Fig.28: Sketch of East Grinstead, 1360. Original source unknown.

Fig.29: Middle Row, south side of High Street, East Grinstead, photographed in 1883 but still retaining its Medieval appearance. Image reproduced courtesy of East Grinstead Museum

These three properties are all on the south side of the High Street. Though taken more than 400 years later, the photograph above provides a glimpse of what the area looked like before modern renovations had taken place.

Illustrated below are the profiles of their moulded beams, in each example of which its similarity to the beam at Tickeridge and the signature design is clearly evident.

Figs.30, 31 and 32: Outlines of moulded beams of 14th-century houses in East Grinstead. *Source: Framed Buildings of the Weald*, by R.T. Mason, 2nd edn., 1969

left – 38 High Street
centre – 48 High Street
right – 66/68 High Street

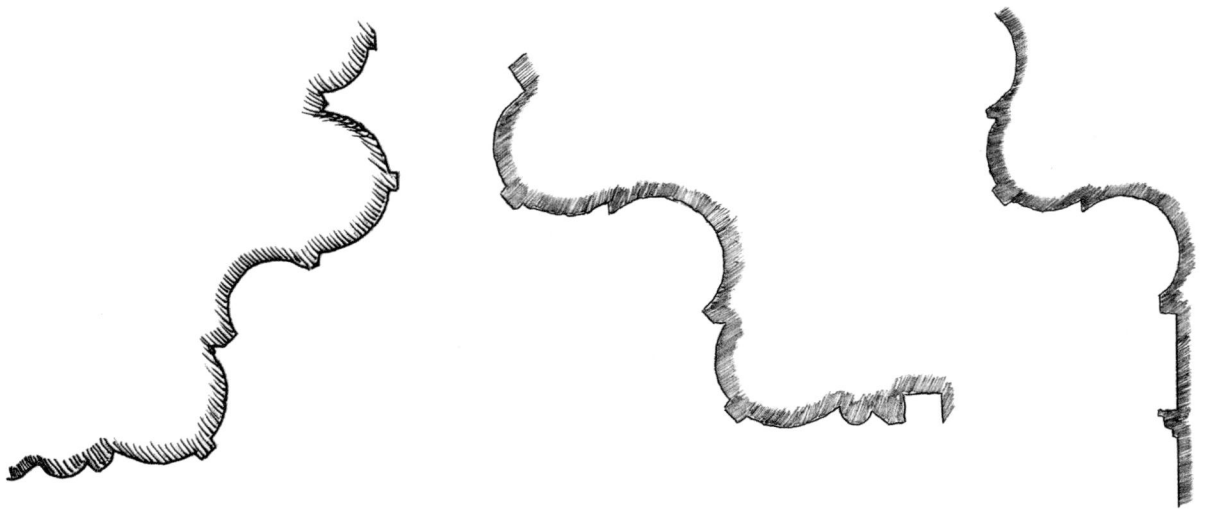

THE BLACK DEATH (1348-51) AND ITS AFTERMATH

Figs.33, 34 and 35: Assembly marks, formerly "Carpenter's marks", on beams in the 14th-century hall at Tickeridge

The Carpenter who built all these medieval halls in East Grinstead would have felled the trees using an axe. The tree trunk was split into beams whilst still green; once seasoned, they were fashioned into something like a kit, using an adze and numerous other tools. On some of the beams he would have scored assembly marks, formerly known as 'Carpenter's marks', to indicate the order in which the timber frame structure should be put together. Above are some of the marks found on 14th-century beams at Tickeridge.

Once the site in the town had been prepared, the beams would be transported there in batches, on a large cart drawn by a team of several oxen.

Chapter 8
The Benke Family

Over time, the name *Benek* morphed into *Benke* for, a century later in 1440/1, Thomas Benke is mentioned in an agreement concerning land in West Hoathly, but nothing is known of his immediate descent since documentary evidence is lacking. It seems likely that he was the copyholder of Tickeridge, the West Hoathly portion, but it is not possible to know whether he also held the freehold portion comprising Meadows and Shelves and the 9-acre parcel of land north of the farm buildings, which might have been owned by another family.

There may be a clue as to who this was, for in later years, the name of this field was *Jenkin's Mead*, first mentioned in 1564. Five years previously, Edmund Jenkyne of Westhothlye had made his will, leaving various bequests to his siblings Thomas, Joyce, Dorothy, Alyce and Ann. He was apparently a man of substance, for at the time he wrote his will at least two people were indebted to him, and one of these was Edmund Benke of Tickeridge. The two men obviously knew each other well. The field is mentioned again in 1607, when local Yeoman John Haselden, of the farm of that name, made his will bequeathing to his wife Margaret, "Jenkyns Meade with all the greate woods and trees thereon growinge".

In 1496, the blast furnace had been introduced into England from the Continent and this new technology meant that the production of iron could be increased. Within a few years, a furnace had been built at nearby Mill Place and iron ore was mined locally. In 1510, the conflict with France, Spain and the Netherlands generated the demand for ordnance, cannon and shot, which was cast at Mill Place, supervised by its ironmaster, Richard Infield of Gravetye. With extensive woodland at Tickeridge, charcoal production would have been an additional lucrative enterprise for its tenant, since regular supplies would have been needed for the furnace.

The wealth and lands of Lewes Priory had been surrendered to the Crown in 1537 and granted to Thomas Cromwell.

Fig.36: Thomas Cromwell (*c*. 1485–1540). Image courtesy of Wikimedia Commons

Fig.37: Charcoal burning, original source unknown.

From Cromwell, the Manor of Plumpton Buskage was acquired by the Carewe family in 1539. In 1555, Edmund Benke was their tenant, living at Tickeridge with his wife Jane and their five young daughters: Jane, Susan, Sara, Rebecka and Phebe.

In that year, John Mascall of Plumpton purchased from Francis Carewe of Beddington, Surrey, the rents of daywork due from his tenants. Amongst those named in the document is Edmund Benke, liable for the rent on one copyhold yardland (estimated to have been at least 30 acres) called "Tekeredge" and committed to "employing one man for six days at harvest time or else pay 18 pence".

On the assarted land, crops of Wheat, Oats and Peas were grown and for these, Edmund ploughed and worked his land with teams of oxen, perhaps using a wrought-iron ploughshare made locally. Important too were the meadows beside the river where livestock grazed and hay was made.

From other evidence, we know that Shelfyes extended to around 33 acres and, with his copyhold yardland of Tickeridge, Edmund's land holding exceeded 60 acres so he was obliged to grow a quarter of an acre of either hemp or flax, under penalty of a fine. The hemp was to be used to make fishing nets and ropes. Flax was spun into linen thread and woven into cloth used to make clothing, and sails to rig the ships.

The Benkes were a staunchly Protestant family on whom the religious upheavals of Mary Tudor's reign had a profound effect.

As soon as she came to the throne, Mary attempted to reverse the English Reformation of the Church instigated by her father, Henry VIII. Her fanatical Catholicism touched every community in England, and

Fig.38: Flax plant, image courtesy of Wikimedia Commons

West Hoathly was no exception. In July 1556 Ann Tree, an elderly village resident, was interrogated by the Catholic authorities, convicted of heresy, and carted away along the rutted and bumpy road to East Grinstead, to be imprisoned in the cellar of what would become the Broadleys store, before being burned alive at the stake in the High Street, together with Thomas Dungate and John Forman.

A brass memorial plaque on the south wall in St Margaret's Church, West Hoathly, reads "Ann Tree of this parish who for her faith was burnt at the stake in the High Street of East Grinstead on 18 July 1556. The plaque was made by George Friend."

Only their discretion and good fortune will have saved the Benkes from a similar fate.

Not long after these events, Edmund's health began to fail and, anticipating death, he made his will which bears the date 25 October 1559. A year earlier, Mary Tudor had died and the Protestant Queen Elizabeth I was now on the throne of England, so Edmund could freely express his faith, which he chose to do by leaving to the poorest of his local fellow believers the sum of 40s. to be distributed amongst them.

Edmund died a few months later and was buried in West Hoathly churchyard. From his will, which was proved on 25 May 1560, we learn everything else we know about Edmund. In it, he bequeathed £10 to each of his five daughters, to be paid to them when they married, or reached the age of 21 years. To his wife he left his "freehold lands and woodde called Shelfyes lying and being in the parish of East Grinstead", and "all the residue of [his] moveable goods". We already know that Edmund held the West Hoathly copyhold portion of the farm called Tekeredge. His will confirms that he also freely held the East Grinstead, wooded portion, Shelfyes (Meadows and Shelves).

As Overseers of his will, Edmund chose Andrew, John and Thomas Browne, whose job it was to supervise and assist the Executor, Edmund's widow, Jane. In addition, Henry Browne was one of the witnesses. These gentlemen are known to have had a sister called Jane so, being intimately involved in the settlement of Edmund's estate strongly suggests that they were siblings of Jane Benke, appointed because they had a vested interest in looking after her fortunes and the welfare of her children, and Edmund trusted them to be diligent in this task.

Like Edmund and his family, the Brownes were Protestants and in 1559 Thomas Browne was a member of the commission to deal with complaints about wrongs done in Mary's reign to those accused of heresy. Residing in the Priest House, they were a prominent West Hoathly family, descended from John who had died in 1546, leaving his widow Jone, six

Fig.39: Hemp, the *Cannabis sativa* plant

Fig.40: Mary Tudor, Queen of England from July 1553 until her death on 17 November 1558

Fig.41: Elizabeth I, Queen of England, r. 1558–1603

All images on this page courtesy of Wikimedia Commons

Fig.42: The Priest House, West Hoathly, from the archives, with the kind permission of the Sussex Archaeological Society

sons and three daughters of whom Jane, I believe, became the wife of Edmund Benke.

Contemporary with Edmund Benke was John Benke, who worked for the Mill Place Ironmaster, Richard Infield of Gravetye, and was mentioned in Richard's will of 1571 as "my servant John Benke" to whom he left 5s., suggesting that John's role was an important one. Perhaps he was in charge of the day-to-day running of the furnace and lived in the house at Mill Place. There is no direct evidence to connect John with Tickeridge, but it seems very likely that he was at least related to Edmund.

Chapter 9
The Tudor Extension to the House

The wealth generated by the iron works and the farm's crops would have financially benefitted Edmund and Jane and started the process of redesigning and upgrading the house to provide separate accommodation for their family and the farm workers. Reusing some timbers derived from an earlier structure, the northern end of the Hall was rebuilt, and glazed windows incorporated, for cheaper, good-quality glass was now available after glass-making techniques were improved by immigrant French glassmakers. Where once had burned the central hearth, a chimney was built to serve an inglenook fireplace. Some 11ft wide, it included a bread oven, a salt cupboard and a spit for roasting joints of meat. It was also a natural place for seats on either side of the alcove to provide somewhere warm to sit close to the fire.

In the inglenook fireplace was installed a large cast-iron fireback, some 5ft wide and nearly 30in high, decorated with square and round

Fig.43: Stained-glass windows in the 16th-century extension. Photograph, taken 2006, with kind permission of Robert Leech, Estate Agents

medallions, depicting fleur-de-lis and large birds, around which flowed a vine motif border. This vine decoration originated from the house of Cleves and is said to have been introduced by Anne of Cleves in 1540 when she married Henry VIII. Later that year, on the annulment of the marriage, she was granted several Manors, including West Hoathly.

Fig.44: Illustration of the fireback, with the kind permission of Jeremy Hodgkinson, Wealden Iron Research Group

The fireback was cast at John Harvo's Pounsley furnace in Framfield, which operated from the mid-16th century. Jeremy Hodgkinson described it as follows: "Rectangular; undulating vine tendril edging (top and upper sides); eight circular, fleur-de-lys butter mould stamps alternating (except at left end) with six rectangular, fleur-de-lys and leaf shortbread or gingerbread stamps, in a line along the top; six bird stamps (wings displayed and inverted) alternating with five pairs of butter mould stamps, as above; continuous line of horizontal vine strips; six descending vine strips, interspaced unevenly with eight butter mould stamps, in pairs except for rightmost two."[1]

The large birds are believed to represent swans, an heraldic device of both the house of Cleves and the Duchy of Lancaster of which Ashdown Forest formed a part, and the fleur-de-lis was a symbol of purity. It was recorded at Tickeridge in 1868 and was still there in 1941, but was sold sometime later, and can now be seen in the Garden Hall at Nymans, Handcross, Sussex.

This extension, and the portion of the hall warmed by the fire in the inglenook, were lofted over to create first floor rooms, and thenceforth became the main accommodation.

Described in a document of the 1620s,[2] this Tudor extension comprised

---

1. https://hodgers.com/firebacks
2. National Archives C3/365/33_001

Fig.45: Apotropaic mark in the form of a butterfly, on a beam on the first floor of the 16th-century crosswing. Formerly known as a "Witches' mark", an apotropaic mark was intended to ward off evil.

a parlour, with a cellar beneath it. Above the parlour was a bedchamber with an adjoining closet, used as a cupboard or a quiet place for prayer and contemplation, with a garret or attic room above that. Adjoining the attic space was a small dovecot, housing breeding pairs of domesticated pigeons or doves whose dung was used by tanners to remove hair from animal skins. It also contained saltpetre, which, combined with charcoal and sulphur, was used to make gunpowder. Their feathers stuffed mattresses and the flesh of their *squabs*, or unfledged chicks, formed an important part of the winter diet.

Near the house, by the track, was a barn with adjoining yards and orchards with fields surrounding them. There was also a brewhouse and a 'bark house', a shed for storing and drying the Oak bark.

Having moved the Services accommodation into purpose-built outbuildings and the cellar, the self-contained unit at the southern end, with its own hearth, was available to provide housing for farm labourers or be rented to another family. Tickeridge farmhouse was now divided into two dwellings.

By 1577, the 'Great Rebuilding Movement' was in full swing and many homes like Tickeridge were being rebuilt, extended or modified, often providing separate accommodation for two or more families.

Surveys of the boundaries of the Hundred of East Grinstead, taken in 1564 and 1579, provide evidence of the Benke family's continuing presence at Tickeridge. After Richard Infield's land at Gravetye, the surveyors headed north past "a parcel of land called the Shells and so

Fig.46: "Coat of Arms of the Worshipful Company of Grocers. The arms: Argent, a chevron gules between nine cloves sable. The Crest, granted in 1532: On a wreath of the colours, camel statant or bridled sable, on his back two bags of pepper argent powdered with cloves and corded sable. Mantled azure, doubled argent. On either side a griffin per fesse gules and Or, the underwing azure, beaked and clawed Or. Motto: God grant grace."
Source: heraldry-wiki.com

The griffin supporters symbolise strength, courage and protection, combining, as they do, the attributes of the lion, the King of the Beasts, and the wings and head of an eagle, the King of the Air.

forth to a whapple way leading to 'Benke's [or Banckes'] Gate' and so thro' Jenkins Mead to a brook called Stone Brook".

The next recorded occupier of Tickeridge was Thomas Benke, who was born in about 1554. Neither Thomas Benke nor the copyhold land of Tickeridge is mentioned in Edmund's will of 1559, when Thomas would have been about five years old. This is not surprising however, since Edmund did not own that land, so it was not his to bequeath. Instead, it was the custom of the Manor for the eldest son automatically to inherit the copyhold, which appears to have been the case here.

In mid-summer 1567, young Thomas was apprenticed to Humphrey Sloughe of London and, in 1576, after serving his full eight years, was made a Freeman of the City of London and of the Worshipful Company of Grocers, then based in Conningshop-Lane, Poultry, London. He could now trade on his own, joining the ranks of eminent and wealthy merchants, mainly dealing in quantities of exotic spices and other foodstuffs, wool and cloth.

In time, the status of the holding of Tickeridge changed from copyhold to freehold, so that in 1575, Thomas Benke, then aged 21, was one of the Freeholders of the Manor, holding "one yard of lande and all those lands called Sykridge [sic] in West hoytlygeh late holden by copy of Court Roll and now be granted by Dede payenge yerely 12s.6d." – the payment he would make to his overlord.

In the spring of 1578, wood from Tickeridge was being supplied to Ralph Hogge's ironworks in Buxted, at four shillings a cord, confirmation of the timber trade generated on the farm.

On 3 July 1581, now an established merchant and receiving income for felled timber, Thomas Benkes was married to Hanna Kemp at Freshwater on the Isle of Wight. She was a daughter of John and Agnes Kemp(e), he the owner of property in Godstone, Surrey, and the parson of Freshwater. A reformed 'free-will man', during Mary Tudor's reign John narrowly escaped execution for his unorthodox beliefs and the undesirable topics of his sermons, dealing as they did with predestiny and freedom of thought. The preamble to his will, dated 15 July 1579 and proved six months later, gives an interesting insight into his religious fervour.[3]

Thomas and Hanna made their home in Gresham Street, London, in the parish of St Lawrence Jewry, where their daughter, Eunice, was baptised in 1584 and their son, Samuel, was born three years later.

But on 22 October 1587, just three months after his baby son's baptism, Thomas Benke died, aged about 34. A week before his death,

---

3. See Appendix 1. National Archives ref. PROB 11/70/212

he had made his will, leaving Tickeridge in the hands of his wife until his son reached his 21st birthday. His daughter was next in line, followed by Thomas' sister, Phebe, and his cousin, Bartholmewe Banks. Finally was mentioned John Bancks, "nowe or late serving and dwelling in or aboute Hodley" who was to inherit if all the other beneficiaries had died, but there is still no clue as to John's relationship to Thomas. One of the witnesses to Thomas' will was Caleb Kempe, Hanna's brother, Deacon at Lincoln and later Vicar of Bradford. The will was proved the following month.

After Thomas' death, Hanna remained in London, so a tenant would have run Tickeridge Farm.

It took nearly five more years before the Inquisition Post Mortem was held to determine and settle the details of Thomas' estate. During this time, as was the custom of Plumpton Boscage, Hanna as Thomas' widow retained Tickeridge for her natural life. Five years more, in 1597, the heriot of 'best beast', equivalent to 12s.6d., was paid to the Lord of the Manor as an early form of estate duty. That same year, John Hazelden the younger held the 33 acres of "Midwaies, parcel of Sellers", and the nine acres of Jenkins Mead, which was now recorded as "land called Benkes als Bankes".

Chapter 10

Hanna Banks and Timber Extraction

As a young widow, and still of child-bearing age, it is not surprising to find Hanna Banks getting married for the second time. Her new husband was Thomas Lovell, whom she married on 13 July 1589 in her local church of St Lawrence Jewry. Thomas was Minister of the Gospel at Great Waldingfield, Suffolk.

Thomas and Hanna Lovell had a family of two daughters (Sara and Margaret – the latter married Edward Newman in 1607) and five sons (Isaac, born 1590; Timothy, born 1594; Titus, born 1595; Stephen and Thomas), baptised in Great Waldingfield. Titus was to spend much of his youth in the household of Sara Venables (née Browne), a village resident whose husband, Richard, had died in 1598. Eunice and Samuel Banks completed the family. (For the families of Great Waldingfield, see Appendix 2.)

In May 1609, Thomas Lovell purchased the advowson[1] of Great Waldingfield Church and three-quarters of an acre of land for his own use. Just a year later, on 8 June 1610, aged 64, he died, leaving to his son Timothy all his houses, lands and orchards in Little Waldingfield. To his son Stephen he left his two copper houses, to his other sons and two daughters some money and to Eunice and Samuel Banks, a Bible each worth 6s. Hanna is mentioned only as one of his executors.

During Samuel Banks' minority, his mother Hanna had benefitted from the timber resources of the farm. When he reached his majority in 1608 and inherited Tickeridge, she persuaded him to appoint a tenant for the farm and for the next 13 years, at a rent of £72 per year, John and then Thomas Jenner were in residence, but I know no more about them.

After Thomas Lovell's death, Hanna instigated a bill in the Court of Chancery claiming jointure rights; she claimed that before her marriage

5 November 1605: Gunpowder Plot – to kill King James I, end persecution of Roman Catholics by the English government and replace the Protestant government with Catholic leadership. It failed and eight of the conspirators, including Guy Fawkes, were hanged, drawn and quartered in the churchyard of St Paul's Cathedral.

---
1. The right to appoint or recommend a clergyman to a paid post.

to Thomas Benkes in 1581, he had conveyed Tickeridge to her father, John Kempe, by way of a jointure, or guaranteed widow's income, to the value of £15 per annum.

But when Hanna's father died, he left a will written in January 1586/7 in which he states, "to Caleb my sonne my land at Hodely which is his already as appeareth by the copye". Perhaps this refers to Tickeridge but, if so, I cannot explain this statement since by the time of the marriage between Thomas Benkes and Hanna in 1581, the farm was freely held by Thomas and after his death, in July 1587, was held by Hanna on behalf of their son, Samuel.

Hanna also stated that when Samuel turned 21 in 1608, she relinquished her jointure in exchange for the rent of the Tudor portion of Tickeridge farmhouse together with some of its buildings and fields.

In 1612, Samuel Banks was mentioned in a bill concerning various loans and bonds which suggest that he was having financial problems. In 1621 he was accused by his mother of colluding with John Slany, Citizen and Merchant Taylor of London, to whom he had first mortgaged and then, unable to redeem it, relinquished Tickeridge.

An acrimonious exchange developed between Hanna and John Slany culminating in Slany's reply to the accusation, denying knowledge of the jointure and instead accusing Hanna of stripping the assets of Samuel's inheritance by cutting down all the mature timber at Tickeridge and taking the proceeds. In 1624, after these hostile exchanges in which John Slany sought to confirm the legitimacy of his acquisition from Samuel Banks, he eventually emerged as the new owner of Tickeridge Farm. This meant that he had access to any remaining timber for his shipbuilding enterprise, and income from renting out the farm.

At some point in all these proceedings, Samuel Banks had gone to fight as a soldier, perhaps in Spain, and nothing more is known of him.

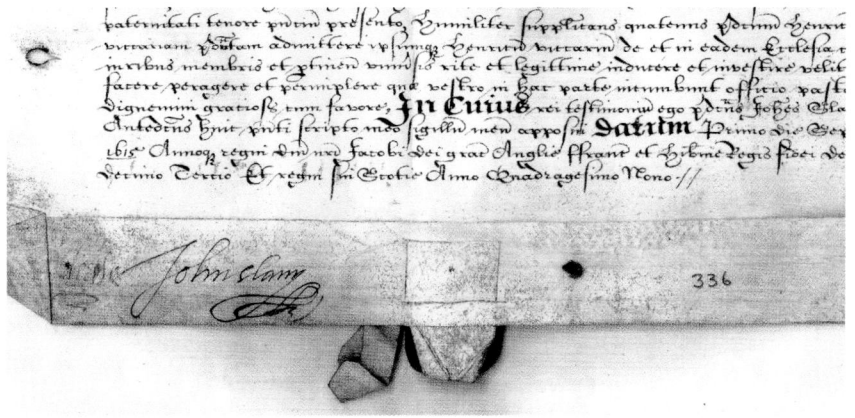

Fig.47: John Slany's signature. *Source:* Document ref. Ep/I/6/336, dated 1 September 1615, by courtesy of the Rt Revd The Bishop of Chichester, and with acknowledgements to the County Archivist, West Sussex Record Office.

Chapter 11

The Slany Family, Exploration and Shipbuilding

Fig.48: Coat of arms of Slane of Ireland

Fig.49: Coat of arms of Ralph Slaney.

THE LARGE, INFLUENTIAL AND WEALTHY FAMILY of Slany (also Slanie, Slaney, Slaynne, Slaynie), whose members enjoyed the zenith of their power during the 16th and 17th centuries, epitomised the golden age in which they flourished, for they enthusiastically embraced the Tudor and Elizabethan ideals of trade and colonisation.

According to the Heralds' Visitation of Shropshire in 1623, the ancestor of this great dynasty was Ralph Slaney, who was born in about 1460. He is said to have arrived in this country from the Bohemian town of Slaney, about 18 miles north-west of Prague in the Czech Republic. However, it is alternatively suggested that the surname originated in Ireland. There was much antagonism towards the Irish in the early 17th century, and it was not uncommon for the Heralds at that time to manipulate pedigrees, so perhaps the Slanys thought it politic to distance themselves from their Irish ancestry. It is, however, impossible to ignore the similarity of the coats of arms of the Irish Slane family and those of Ralph Slaney, shown here.

Whatever his origins, Ralph Slaney established himself in Yardley, Worcestershire, and fathered four sons, namely Stephen of Yardley, Ralph and Thomas who both died without issue, and John who was born in about 1490, settled at Mitton, Penkridge in Staffordshire, and married in about 1520.

This John Slaney I also had sons, including John II (of whom little is known), William (who had a son called Robert), and Henry and Stephen (later Sir Stephen Slaney), the only two still living in 1598.

Stephen Slaney was born in about 1524 and on 22 January 1559/60, as Stephen Slanie, was married to Margaret Fesant (aka Pheasant) of Tottenham. He was soon flourishing as a businessman, and rose in the ranks of the Skinners' Company to become an eminent citizen of London, as Alderman, then Sheriff from 1584–6, before becoming Lord Mayor in

Fig.50: Portrait of Sir Stephen Slaney, by kind permission of the Worshipful Company of Skinners, at Skinners' Hall, London

Fig.51: "Coat of Arms of Worshipful Company of Skinners. Arms, granted in 1550: Ermine, on a chief gules three caps of the first tasselled and enfiled with coronets Or. Crest: On a wreath Or and gules, a lynx statant proper, about the neck a wreath leaved vert purified Or. Mantled azure doubled argent. Supporters: On the dexter side a lynx proper and on the sinister side a marten sable, about the neck of each a wreath leaved vert. Motto: To God only be all glory."
Source: heraldry-wiki.com

1595, the same year in which he was knighted and granted the right to bear arms, *Gules, a bend between three martlets, two and one, Or,* as Slaney of Mitton. The family motto translates as "God being my guide, Industry my companion".

Sir Stephen Slany had five children; Jasper, Mary, Elizabeth, Anne and Stephen. Of these, his daughter, Mary, was betrothed in 1569 and then married to Richard Bradgate (also Brudgate, Brodgate), Citizen and Skinner of London, until his death in 1589. Mary's second husband was Humphrey Welde of Holdwell, Hertfordshire, whom she married in about 1592. Humphrey was a Freeman of the Grocers' Company, became Sheriff in 1599 and was made Lord Mayor in 1608.

Humphrey and Mary had a son called John Welde, a Brewer and a lover of the lute, and for that instrument he accumulated a renowned collection of music which, after his death in 1623, was preserved by his daughter, Dorothy Welde, in *The Welde Lute Book.*

Fig.52: The lute; a plucked, stringed musical instrument, image courtesy of the Metropolitan Museum of Art

Sir Stephen Slany's country seat was at Norton in the coal-rich vicinity of Eccleshall in Staffordshire, a property which he purchased from Lord Sheffield, but his business was conducted from his London base in the parish of St Swithin's.

Sir Stephen's wealth came from various sources, including coalmines and ironworks, and in 1566 he had collaborated in the purchase of some land in Chatham, near London, which was later most advantageously sold to the Navy, then in the process of developing the dockyard there. But perhaps most importantly, he was a Levant (or Turkey) Trader, competing with the Venetians for the exotic goods such as wine, fruits and spices available in the eastern Mediterranean, a lucrative trade which enabled him to amass a huge fortune. This enterprise was not without risk, however, for the story is told of his capture by Turkish pirates who held him for a ransom so large that only the sale of his property of Norton and the sacrifice of his entire fortune at the time could secure his release. Though some sources say that it was his son, Stephen, who was deprived of his liberty, the story serves to illustrate the hazards regularly faced by seafarers at this time.

Whatever was the case, Sir Stephen Slany survived in prosperous comfort to the great age of 84 years. His will, written on 2 August 1598 when he was still in rude health, was proved some ten years later following his death on 27 December 1608. He was buried in a vault beneath St Swithin's Church, London, where there was a commemorative stone in the east end of the north isle, with a dedication in Latin, confirming that he performed his duties with faith and prudence, and that his wife Margaret bore him five sons and six daughters. The church was destroyed in World War II.

In his will, Sir Stephen mentions two of his brothers: William, who had already died, and Henry, to whose son John he bequeathed the house where Henry was living. Henry Slaney was also mentioned in the will of Sir Stephen's widow, Lady Margaret (dated 1612), and that of their daughter, Mary Welde (dated 1622), Humphrey Welde's widow, but little more is known of him. He probably married in about 1555 and resided at Willey, near Barrow, Shropshire.

We know that Henry Slany had three sons – Richard Slany I, John Slany III, and Humphrey – and six daughters, including Elizabeth. His eldest son, Richard I, was born in 1560 and was later of The Hem, Shiffnal, Shropshire. At Worfield, Shropshire, in 1595, this Richard married Mary Rowley and they had six children, including Richard Slany II, born c. 1596, John Slany IV and Moses. Richard I died in 1620, soon followed to the grave by his own eldest son, Richard II, who had married Elizabeth

Fig.53: Church of St John the Baptist, Willey, Shropshire

and fathered his own sons: John, born in 1621, and Richard Slany III, who will feature again later.

Henry Slaney's daughters all married, but of particular note for the purposes of this account is his daughter, Elizabeth, who was married to John Eton/Eaton in 1582.

It is Elizabeth's brother, Henry Slany's second son, John Slany III, born at Willey, near Barrow, Shropshire around 1572, who now becomes the focus of my story. (For the Slany family tree, see Appendix 4.)

On 1 December 1593, having served his apprenticeship, John Slanie was made a Freeman of the Merchant Taylor's Company.

His friends included Robert Bradgate (also Brodgat, Brvdgat, Brodgate) and his wife, Margery. Robert was a fellow Merchant Taylor and brother of Richard Bradgate, mentioned earlier. His wife, Margery, was baptised on 10 April 1569, a daughter of Joan and Thomas Langton, he another Merchant Taylor of Cornhill, London. In the summer of 1593, Margery's husband, Robert, was drowned whilst on a voyage to Middelburg in the Netherlands, leaving her and a baby daughter called Mary, who had been baptised on 19 November 1592 in the little church of St Martin Pomeroy, Ironmonger Lane, Cheapside, London, which was destroyed several decades later in the Great Fire of London.

On 15 January 1593/4, in his early twenties, John Slany married Margery Bradgate, his friend's widow, in the same church. Two sons were soon born, John Slany junior in 1594/5, and Thomas Slany in April 1596, followed by a daughter, Mary, born in June 1597. But Margery did not

Fig.54: "Coat of Arms of the Worshipful Company of Merchant Taylors: On a wreath argent and azure, On a mount vert a lamb argent in sunbeams Or. Mantled gules, doubled argent. Arms: Argent, a pavilion imperial purple garnished Or, lined ermine, between two mantles also imperial purple, lined ermine. On a chief azure a lion passant, guardant Or. Supporters: On either side a camel Or. Motto, In harmony, small things grow while with discord the mightiest are ruined." Source: heraldry-wiki.com

The two Arabian camel supporters are said to have symbolised Patience, Discretion and Prudence, indicating a man expeditious and always ready for business; they may also have referenced the eastern trade of the company.

THE SLANY FAMILY, EXPLORATION AND SHIPBUILDING

long survive Mary's birth and, several months later, John married again.

His second wife was Elizabeth Harby (also Hardy, Harvi, Harvy, Harbye), widow of Erasmus who had died in 1593. She was a daughter of Mary and Thomas Browne, a Citizen and Merchant Taylor of London who had died in 1579. The year after her father's death, Elizabeth had married Erasmus Harvy at the London church of St Mildred, Poultry with St Mary Colechurch and they had three children: a daughter, Elizabeth, and two sons, Thomas (born 1581) and John (born 1587).

Figs.55 and 56: Church of St Mildred, Poultry (left) and plaque marking the site of St Mary Colechurch (right). Courtesy of Wikimedia Commons

Elizabeth Browne had a sister, Sara, who, whilst still in her teens, was married on 23 January 1575/6 to Richard Venables of Great Waldingfield, Suffolk. Sara had been born in February 1559/60, her husband some 20 years earlier. Their marriage lasted more than 20 years, until Richard died on 29 July 1598, leaving his widow Sara and no children.

Born in about 1560, Elizabeth Browne/Harby was 12 years older than John Slany, and their marriage of 25 March 1598 appears to have been childless.

In time John Slany became a Warden and, in 1619, Master of the Company of Merchant Taylors. The Company's premises, in the aptly named Threadneedle Street, London, were immediately adjacent to John's city base in St Michael's parish, Cornhill; indeed, part of the Company's building, called the King's Chamber, overhung John Slany's garden there.

John's country seat was at Pansanger in the parish of St Andrews, Hertfordshire where, in 1618, he built two houses, one large and one small, a great barn and various other buildings. Residing there was his housekeeper, Ann Eaton, and her son, Simon.

Besides Pansanger, John Slany owned extensive properties in his native Shropshire, not only agricultural estates but particularly coalmines and ironworks. He also owned Shifnal, a property in Penkridge, Staffordshire; an estate called Parsonage in Rainham, Essex; land in Little Buckenham

Fig.57: Church of St Lawrence, Great Waldingfield, Suffolk

together with a walk of swans; and Hilborough Warren and warren houses and its stock of 'conies' or rabbits, the latter a resource valued predominantly for fur rather than meat at that time.

He obviously moved amongst the elite of London society, for he counted amongst his acquaintances such notable figures as Sir George Manners, 7th Earl of Rutland, Sir George's stepson, Sir Edward Baesh, Chamberlain of His Majesty's Exchequer, and Edward Barrett, Lord Newburgh, Chancellor of the Duchy of Lancaster.

In 1600, the East India Company was established to trade in cotton and silk goods, indigo, saltpetre and spices, and John was soon an investor.

John Slany's financial provenance was such that he was able to offer support and mortgages to friends and acquaintances such as Sir Percival Willoughby, a member of the Kentish branch of that family, who was indebted to John Slany for his estate at Bore Place near Winkhurst Green, Horsham.

With his younger brother, Humphrey, John Slany established a lucrative shipbuilding enterprise and fleet of ships, commissioned for trading and fishing. He and Humphrey were the chief or part-owners of at least 18 vessels. In October 1612 John Slany was awarded a royal grant to build six ships, varying in size from 210 to 300 tonnes burden,[1] a huge project. A Tudor merchant ship of 300 tonnes would have been about 80ft long and taken around 250 Oak trees or 15 acres of woodland to build.

Fig.58: "Azure, three ships with three masts, rigged and under full sail, the sails pennants and ensigns Argent, each charged with a cross Gules; on a chief of the second a pale quarterly Azure and Gules, on the 1st and 4th a fleur-de-lis Or, on the 2nd and 3rd a leopard Or, between two roses Gules seeded Or barbed Vert." The crest on the shield is described, "A sphere without a frame, bounded with the Zodiac in bend Or, between two pennants flottant Argent, each charged with a cross Gules, over the sphere the words *'Deus indicat'* (God indicates). The supporters are two sea lions (lions with fishes' tails) and the motto was *Deo ducente nil nocet* (Where God Leads, Nothing Harms)."
Source: wikipedia.org/wiki/East_India_Company

Fig.59: 17th-century ship. Frances Armytage, *A Planter in the New World*, 1966, p.2

---

1. Cargo capacity.

THE SLANY FAMILY, EXPLORATION AND SHIPBUILDING

For protection from pirates, it would have carried several cannon. At this time, all merchant vessels sailed armed for self-defence, so they were already well equipped to undertake military operations.

To the English government, the merchant fleet and fishing vessels (which numbered some 200 ships) were of vital importance for they were a source of ships and trained seamen. In times of war, these vessels sailed with Letters of Marque, which were permissions granted by the Admiralty Court allowing authorised merchant vessels to cross international borders, seize goods and sell them, thereby adding to their owners' profits. Without the Letters, the ships and crew were deemed pirates.

The Slany brothers combined importing and ship-owning on a large scale, most notably as pioneers of the Guinea trade, gold and ivory being its primary objectives at that time. But they also diversified their overseas business into the markets of the Levant, Spain, the Atlantic islands, Barbary and West Africa and, in addition to the East India Company, they adventured into the Virginia and Somers Islands Companies.

Fig.60: Early settlement at Cuper's Cove, source unknown

From as early as 1574, the Slany family had taken an interest in the colonisation of new territory in America so, true to form, we find John, with his brother Humphrey, as two of 48 patentees of the Newfoundland Company who financed the Cuper's Cove colony on the Avalon Peninsula (now known as Cupids), established by John Guy in 1610. For 18 years John Slany was Treasurer of the Newfoundland Company and later became its Governor.

With the promise of a lucrative trade in cured fish from the

Newfoundland seas, in 1611 John Slany sent his ship *The Vineyard* to fish the shoals of Cod there.

In 1611, a Wampanoag Indian called Tisquantum, or Squanto, was kidnapped from his home in the area of Patuxet, Massachusetts, and taken to Spain where he was sold as a slave. He was freed by some monks of Malaga and later made his way to London, where he arrived in 1614. He was found by John Slany with whom he worked at Cornhill as a free man for a couple of years, learning English. He was taken to Cuper's Cove in 1616 to act as interpreter and share his knowledge of growing food and catching fish. Three years later, he went back to his home to find that his people had been wiped out by smallpox. He imparted valuable survival knowledge to the Mayflower pilgrims in Plymouth Bay, but died of a fever in November 1622.

In 2007, Disney Pictures made a film portraying Squanto, called *Squanto: A Warrior's Tale*, available on DVD and video.

As a local benefactor in Shropshire, in 1618 John Slany financed the building of almshouses and a school on Barrow Hill in Willey near the village of Barrow, endowing them with a supply of coal for their fires. His nephew, John, son of his brother, Richard Slany I, was instructed to maintain the buildings and make any necessary repairs. Two hundred years later, the school building and almshouses were demolished and rebuilt nearer to Barrow church, but today the Barrow 1618 Church of England Free School still honours John's gift.

In 1620, as Master of the Company of Merchant Taylors, John Slany was present at St Paul's Cathedral when King James I visited to inspect its restoration work.

Whilst still in good health, John Slany made his will, bearing the date 17 August 1631, in which he asked to be buried near his late wife and

Fig.61: Map of Newfoundland showing the location of Cupids, on Conception Bay

Fig.62: Cupids, Conception Bay, Newfoundland

Fig.63: Squanto

All images on this page courtesy of Wikimedia Commons

Fig.64: St Giles Church, Barrow, Shropshire

Fig.65: The 12th-century font

Fig.66: St Paul's Cathedral, *c.* 1658, image courtesy of Wikimedia Commons

sons; he died on 7 April the following year. His burial will have been a splendid affair, with his coffin draped in the elaborately embroidered rich purple and gold Merchant Taylors' hearse-cloth with its piece of cloth of gold velvet in the centre. At a magnificent dinner following his interment, for which he left a bequest in his will, his friends and colleagues of the Company will have listened solemnly to the lengthy grace which preceded it and, from their silver goblets, affectionately toasted his memory.

Since his wife, Elizabeth, and his children had already died, John's will defines how various properties were to be distributed amongst his extended Slany family. Though not mentioned specifically, Tickeridge Farm passed to his great nephew, Richard Slany III, born about 1616, and grandson of John's elder brother, Richard Slany I. Detailed bequests include, to "my loving sister Elizabeth Eaton... my housekeeper Ann Eaton and her sonne Symon... and... my godson John Banckes, sonne of Symon Bankes, Rector of South Stoke in Sussex."

Chapter 12
Robert Mills and John Chisman, Tenant Farmers

On 28 November 1628, Robert Mills, a Yeoman of West Hoathly, had been installed as John Slany's new tenant at Tickeridge with a tenancy of 21 years, at an annual rent of £70. By this agreement, Robert was to farm Tickeridge "with all houses, edifices, buildings, barns, stables, orchards, gardens, yards, backsides and lands, meadows, pastures, fields, feedings, woods and underwoods, commons, profits, easements, commodities and appurtenances" belonging to the farm. He could also mine for iron and stone but, although there are mine pits in the area, there are none on the farm's current land. The Oak and Ash trees remained the property of John Slany and he reserved the right of access to remove them.

Members of the Mills family were numerous in West Hoathly at this time, so I am unable to verify Robert's lineage or his immediate family, but

Fig.67: Remains of an old stone quarry in Holmes Wood, anciently part of Tickeridge. Photographed in 2017

I suggest that he may have been the son or grandson of Robert Mills who purchased the Manor of Chiddinglye, West Hoathly in 1577, and was buried in the churchyard there in 1614, leaving two adult children: Mary, who married John Browne of Rectory Farm, West Hoathly in 1594, and Robert, who inherited Chiddinglye and married Elizabeth Fawkenor in April 1604. In 1622, this Robert conveyed Chiddinglye to Edward Payne, and died in West Hoathly in 1641, leaving a will naming his wife Elizabeth and three sons, William, Allan and Robert, who was baptised in West Hoathly on 10 July 1608.

On 25 January 1636/7, the tenancy of the farm was reassigned from Robert Mills to John Chisman/Cheseman, a 30-year-old Yeoman Farmer from Chart Sutton, near Maidstone in Kent. John was baptised in Rotherfield, Sussex, on 30 November 1606, a son of Allexander Cheseman. At Ockley in Surrey, on 2 November 1642, he married Sara Milles. The early years of their marriage coincided with the Civil War in England, the turbulent effects of which were felt locally when a riot broke out at West Hoathly fair between opposing supporters.

In 1639, Richard Slany III decided to sell Tickeridge Farm. With woodland, productive arable land and an annual rental income of £70 a year, it was an attractive proposition. We cannot know where John Chisman's sympathies lay, but he would have had to tread carefully as his new landlord, Simon Eaton, was a committed Parliamentarian.

Chapter 13

The Hamlin Family, Part I

When John Chisman made his will on 22 January 1651/2,[1] he was still "Yeoman of Tickeridge in the parish of West Hoadly". With failing health, he survived only a few months, his will being proved on 14 September 1653; his lands and property in Chart Sutton passed to his widow Sara. Overseers to John's will included Henry Falconer of Gravetye and John Mills of Selsfield, who were also two of the witnesses. His death left a young widow and a vacant tenancy at Tickeridge Farm, both of which were hastily taken up by John Hamlin II, son of Francis Hamlin I of Bolney Farm, Ardingly, a wealthy farmer and landowner.

In the document detailing the arrangements for the marriage between Sara Chisman and John Hamlin in about 1652, the name of John Mills occurs again, which makes me suspect that John Mills, Yeoman of West

Fig.68: Bolney farmhouse, Ardingly, photographed in 2023, with kind permission of James Allen.
To the left is the mid-16th-century house, with the Solar and three bays; on the right, the crosswing, which was built nearly a century later. Wealden Buildings Study Group report

1. National Archives PROB 11/228/544

Fig.69: All Saints Church, Lindfield, with the kind permission of Ashley Fabian

Hoathly, was Sara Mills' brother. The local surname Mills has again prevented me from ascertaining this with any certainty.

John Hamlin II's grandfather, John Hamlin I, and his ancestors, had accumulated land and property in Maresfield during the previous century. John I's marriage in All Saints Church, Lindfield on 1 February 1584/5 to Margaret, widow of Richard Willard, and a daughter of Henry and Dorothy Infield of Gravetye, extended his family's interests westwards, where he and his successors subsequently acquired farms and land in Ardingly, Lindfield and West Hoathly.

John I and Margaret's son, Francis Hamlin I, was born in about 1587 and grew up in Maresfield where he was styled a Husbandman.[2] His status had been raised to Yeoman by the time he married Elizabeth Newnham in Maresfield on 24 November 1612, after which they moved to Ardingly, where their first son, John Hamlin II, was baptised in the parish church of St Peter's on 16 January 1613/14. In 1616, the family moved to West Hoathly where it is likely that John Slany had granted them a tenancy at Tickeridge, though I have no documentary evidence for this; here, more children were born and were baptised at St Margaret's. For 12 years, they lived in West Hoathly, eventually leaving the village in 1628 to move to their new home in the 16th-century timber-framed house at Bolney Farm, Ardingly. Their departure from West Hoathly in 1628 coincided with the appointment of Robert Mills as John Slany's tenant at Tickeridge.

In Ardingly, Elizabeth gave birth to her tenth and last child, for she died shortly afterwards and was buried in Ardingly on 17 April 1630. Several months later, Francis I married another Elizabeth and had six more children, the last of them born in 1644 in Ardingly.

Besides John Hamlin II, three of Francis and Elizabeth's other children will feature in this story of Tickeridge, namely their son, Francis II, baptised in West Hoathly on 17 October 1616, their daughter, Elizabeth, baptised there on 11 March 1619/20, and later married to John Tully, and their daughter, Mary, who became the wife of John Haselden.

---

2. An archaic term for a farmer.

Chapter 14

Simon Eaton – The First Civil War, the Irish Problem and the Rise of Puritanism

WITH CASH TO SPARE and a family network to make him aware of such opportunities, Simon Eaton (son of Ann), now styled "gentleman of Croydon" in Surrey, heard about the estate in Sussex which was for sale. By an indenture dated 25 November 1639, he became the new owner of Tickeridge Farm and its adjoining parcel of land, Meadows and Shelves.

Simon Eaton's mother, Ann Eaton, was baptised on 20 June 1568, a daughter of Bartholomew Tassell of Balsham in Cambridgeshire. She had several siblings, including a brother called William Tassell, a Mercer of London, whose will dated 20 October 1626 mentions his "sister Ann Eaton" to whom he left £5, together with 20s. for her son (unnamed). Ann is also mentioned in her father's will dated 24 February 1576/7 and that of her grandfather, William Tassell, an astrologer and fortune teller of Balsham, who lived to the great age of 100 and made his will on 11 July 1574, the year before he died.

The village of Balsham was home to the religious sect of the Family of Love, or Familists (of a similar persuasion to Quakers) of which Bartholomew Tassell was a staunch adherent. This was a time when more and more people were adopting the Puritan ethos, and the unorthodox practices of the Familists may account for the absence of any record of Ann's marriage to Eaton, bearing in mind that some nuptials were held "in the fields", and that they did not always baptise babies, which could explain why I have found no reference to the subsequent birth or baptism of Simon who was born around 1604.

I have found no evidence to establish the identity of Simon Eaton's father, but perhaps he had siblings, one of whom may have been John Eton, who created a link with the Slany family when, on 9 September 1582, in the parish church of Kinver, Staffordshire, he married Elizabeth, a daughter of Henry Slany (mentioned earlier), and sister of John and

Fig.70: Parish church of St Peter, Kinver, Staffordshire

Humphrey. A family of eight children followed, all born in Kinver, namely William, Isobel, Agnes, Elizabeth, Marie, Alice, Humfrey and John.

This union forged a relationship which I believe was subsequently relevant to the purchase of Tickeridge by Simon Eaton from Richard Slany in 1639.

In 1603 John and Elizabeth Eton's daughter, Isobel, had married Thomas Warner. Their life together began in Canterbury, Kent, where Isobel gave birth to their only son, Henry Warner, in 1606. Shortly afterwards, Isobel must have died, for in 1609 Thomas was married to his

Fig.71: Church of the Holy Trinity, Balsham, Cambridgeshire

second wife, Ann Nicholson. They made their home in Balsham where Thomas Warner, now Doctor of Theology, was instigated Rector in 1611, and a large family followed, including their daughter, Susanna Warner, born in 1617.

Crucial evidence is lacking, but the family trees set out my proposed family connections for Simon Eaton (see Appendices 4, 5 and 6).

When John Slany made his will in 1631, Ann Eaton was his Housekeeper at his two homes: Pansanger, in the parish of St Andrews, in Hertfordshire, and his London base in Threadneedle Street, St Michael's parish, Cornhill.

With no mention of Ann Eaton's husband, it seems he was already dead by 1631 and, according to a document nearly 50 years later, had left to his son, Simon, "one house with the copyhold lands and ffreehold land thereunto belonging situate lying and being in the town of Balsome in Cambridge Shire in the kingdom of England aforesaid (and) the two houses in Laddon Lane in the cittie of London..."

Fig.72: The Swan with Two Necks, Laddon, or Lad Lane, London. An old postcard

This document goes on to state that Simon also inherited Tickeridge from his father, but this is incorrect,[1] as proved by two documents of 1639.

The first of these documents,[2] an Indenture or contract dated 21 September 1639 regarding the sale of Tickeridge from Richard Slany to Simon Eaton, contains a curious statement; "This indenture... between Richard Slany of London Gentleman nephew and heire of John

---

1. Document dated 5 June 1678, ESBHRO SAS D/276
2. ESBHRO SAS D-184

Slany of London merchantaylor deceased of one part and Symon Eaton *als Tassall* of Croydon in the county of Surrey Gentleman of the other part... sells Tickeredge and Shelves situate lying and being in the parishes of East Grinstead and West Hoathly..." Simon's mother was Ann Tassell, but why would he use that surname? The final Bargain and Sale, dated 25 November 1639[3] omits the alias. It's a mystery which I have been unable to solve.

As a widow in need of a safe home, at a time when family connections were of the utmost relevance in all sorts of ways, it would not be unreasonable for a relation to offer Ann a suitable position in his household, and I believe this was the case with John Slany.

During the following two decades, Simon Eaton espoused the cause of his contemporary, Oliver Cromwell. Oliver became MP for Cambridge in 1640 and his passionate opposition during the Long Parliament contributed to the outbreak of the First Civil War in August 1642.

Simon's friend and distant cousin, Henry Warner, from Balsham, shared his allegiance to the Parliamentary forces and joined them as a Lieutenant Colonel under Major General Lawrence Crawford, with whom he would have fought the Royalist army at Marston Moor in July 1644. Perhaps injured in the battle, or having fallen ill shortly afterwards, Henry made his will whilst recuperating in Sheffield. The closeness of their friendship led Henry to appoint Simon Eaton as one of his executors, and to entrust him with an active role in the future well-being of his

Fig.73: Oliver Cromwell's house in Ely

3. ESBHRO SAS D-183

young daughter, Dorothie Warner. By the following summer Henry had died and Simon Eaton was in London to attend the proving of his will.

Unlike his friend, Simon Eaton appears not immediately to have adopted a military role in the conflict, but by the winter of 1648 he was stationed at Warwick Gaol. It may have been the developing Irish problem which had finally spurred him to take up arms as Lieutenant Colonel Simon Eaton.

In 1649 Oliver Cromwell landed at Dublin with his troops to seize control of Ireland from the Irish Catholics who had rebelled in 1641. Simon fought with Cromwell in Ireland and he may have participated in the bloody Siege of Limerick in the summer of 1650. Within a few months he was assigned to serve with Col. Richard Le Hunt's regiment, where he and other officers were tasked with finding new recruits, and each paid a portion of £20.6s., being four weeks' pay for their efforts. In the spring of 1652, he managed to attract 360 to the regiment. Later that year he was organising the transport of 45 tons of Cheshire cheese to Limerick, essential provisions for the troops still stationed there.

With the Irish situation stabilised, and the Protectorate declared in England, Le Hunt's regiment was disbanded in 1653 and Simon's military career appears to have come to an end.

As a punishment for their rebellion, almost all the lands belonging to Irish Catholics were confiscated and given to British settlers or 'adventurers' who had supported Cromwell – amongst these was Simon Eaton. For his services in this Irish war, contributing to the Cromwellian Settlement of Ireland, Simon was granted around 3,500 acres of land and property in counties Limerick, Kerry, Clare and Cork.

In the distribution of land in Co. Clare, he transplanted the overlords of Clondrinagh and Coolmeen in the parish of Kilfiddane, part of the Clonderlaw Barony (1,000 acres). In Kerry he was granted 489 acres in Ballinruddery and Illanamin, in the Barony of Clanmaurice. In Co. Limerick he acquired Dunmoylan, Ballyclogh (400 acres) and other lands extending to 1,500 acres, together with a house in Limerick. He also received a house in Newtown, Co. Cork together with lands in the Barony of Orrery and Kilmore.

Mindful of the need to protect his new estates, Simon settled his household in the castle stronghold at Dunmoylan, about four miles to the south-west of Limerick, near Shanagolden. This great castle comprised a large enclosure surrounded by a defensive stone wall. There were various adjacent buildings, gardens and closes, and a water mill and water course, though the latter were already in decay when Simon arrived. Today, nothing remains of the castle and its exact location is uncertain.

Whilst all this conflict was taking place in Ireland, John and Sara Chisman lived at Tickeridge until John's death in 1652. Sara's subsequent marriage to John Hamlin II was, perhaps, the catalyst which prompted a visit to Sussex by Simon Eaton in the winter of 1654. With John and Sara Hamlin now ensconced at Tickeridge and funds available in the Hamlin family, it may be that they had approached Simon with a view to purchasing the farm.

In November that year, Lt. Col. Simon Eaton arrived in Sussex from Limerick, and temporarily rented a property not far from Ardingly and Bolney Farm, the home of Francis Hamlin I. His rent was paid for by a loan of £35 from Francis' son, John, of Tickeridge. The receipt for the loan was signed by William Abbott, Simon's Factor and kinsman.[4]

On 23 December 1654, Simon Eaton signed and sealed an Indenture, or agreement, to sell the 40 acres of Meadows and Shelves to Francis Hamlin I.[5] For his part, Francis paid a deposit of £100 in cash. However, the agreement was such that, if Simon Eaton paid Francis Hamlin the purchase price plus 12% over the next two years, the sale would be void, and Simon agreed a bond of £200 to Francis Hamlin for performance of covenants in the sale deed, which was witnessed by his son, John Hamlin II, and Henry Faulkner of Gravetye.[6] On the same date, another document confirmed the bond.[7]

For now, Simon retained the ownership of Tickeridge Farm and, once his business was completed, returned to Ireland.

With wealth, status and property, all Simon needed now was a wife, and before long the perfect candidate presented herself.

In 1638, Susanna Warner, half-sister of Henry (Simon's late friend and distant cousin), had married Chichester Phillips and their son, also Chichester, was born in Balsham in 1648. Chichester senior did not live many years after the birth of his son so that in October 1656 his widow Susanna, then aged 39, found herself at the altar in Derry Cathedral, Templemore, Londonderry, plighting her troth to her second husband and long-time family friend, Simon Eaton.

Six months later, in the spring of 1657, the death occurred of Susanna's father, Thomas Warner, minister of the church in Balsham. Shortly beforehand he had made a will dated 25 March, from which we learn that Simon Eaton had sold to Thomas some freehold land in Balsham, had loaned money to Thomas' son, Edward Warner, and had furnished a loan

---

4. ESBHRO SAS-WG/451, dated 5 November 1654.
5. ESBHRO, SAS D232
6. ESBHRO SAS DD/504
7. ESBHRO, SAS D/233

of £208 to his friend, Henry Warner, Thomas' other son. Mentioned in his will are "Lt. Col. Symon Eaton" and "Mr. Simon Eaton"; perhaps Mr. Simon Eaton was the father, or was this just a scribe's error?

Simon and his new wife at first settled on his Irish estates in Ballinaclough, Co. Tipperary, though their son, Simon junior, was born in County Cork in 1660, the same year in which the English monarchy was restored and Charles II finally occupied the throne. Within a few months, many Parliamentarian supporters, including Simon, were officially pardoned for their part in the Civil War.

A period of comparative stability ensued. The family moved to Castletown in Co. Limerick where, in 1661, Simon took on new roles as High Sheriff of that County and local Tax Collector and established a lucrative business selling cattle and large quantities of Irish wool to English buyers.[8] In 1676 he became Sheriff of Co. Kerry. Six years later, his contribution to his adopted country was recognised by King Charles II, who conferred on him the honour of 1st Baronet Eaton of Castletown, Co. Limerick, thereby granting him the right to bear arms emblazoned *Or, a fret vert* which was differenced (distinguished) by the Hand of Ulster.

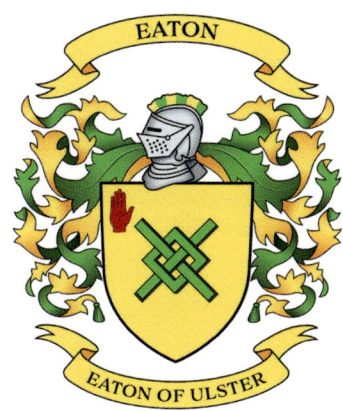

Fig.74: Coat of arms of Sir Simon Eaton of Ulster

During this time, Simon junior was being educated at the Endowed School run by Mr. Wilson, who prepared his pupils for entrance to university and, on 8 October 1676, at the age of 16, he was duly admitted as a Fellow Commoner to Trinity College, Dublin to complete his education.

When still only 12 years old, young Simon Eaton had been betrothed to be married to his equally young bride-to-be Mary Aldworth, a daughter of Sir Richard, a prominent Protestant of Newmarket, Co. Cork. It is inconceivable that love played any part in this arrangement, but politics and finance most certainly did, for here was the potential to unite two great estates and two very wealthy families, with the dignity of title and religious compatibility. The document which records the details of the marriage agreement was dated 6 March 1672[9] and deals with around 3,000 acres of Simon Eaton's Irish land, his properties in Balsham and London, "the Towne lands tenements and hereditaments of Tickeridge situate lying and being in the parish of Greenstead and Hodly in the county of Sussex and Kingdom of England", and hundreds of pounds sterling, all of which were to be endowed on the couple at the time of their marriage. Importantly, though, it contained a clause which would later enable the agreement to be revoked.

---

8. Documents N/A C7/587/118.001 and 002
9. ESBHRO SAS D458

In 1678, when the two young people were old enough to marry, a second agreement was drawn up between the parties whereby Mary's parents agreed to pay to young Simon's parents several thousand pounds, and £1,000 per annum to Mary herself. In return, Simon's parents agreed to provide financial support for Mary should she be widowed. The marriage of Simon Eaton junior and Mary Aldworth finally took place in Cork on 6 June 1678.

Simon junior and Mary Eaton went on to have two children, Aldworth and Martha. Aldworth died very young, soon followed to the grave by his father, Simon, who died on 19 November 1684 and was buried the next day in St Patrick's Cathedral, Limerick.

With the accession to the English throne of James II in February 1685, and the re-emergence of rebellion in Ireland, Sir Simon and Lady Susanna Eaton left Ireland and settled their household in Westminster, London. By now, Sir Simon was around 80 years of age, "weak and infirm", and depending heavily on his wife, and stepson, Chichester Phillips. Now, at Sir Simon's request, and with promises of recompense for his efforts, Captain Chichester Phillips quit his military career in England and regularly travelled to Ireland to take care of the Eaton estates there.[10]

On 16 October 1686, Mary Eaton (née Aldworth), Simon junior's widow, married George Mathew, a union much to the distaste of Mary's father-in-law, Sir Simon Eaton, since George Mathew and his family were Roman Catholics.

George and Mary Mathew had a son, George junior, and Sir Simon Eaton feared that this young Catholic lad would be married off to his granddaughter, Martha Eaton, who was actually young George's half-sister, since they shared the same mother. Under the terms of the marriage agreement of 1672, and following Simon junior's death, Martha would ultimately inherit Sir Simon Eaton's estate, including Tickeridge, much of which he had acquired after fighting against the Irish Catholics so, in April 1688, he started the process of revoking the agreement. (For the family tree showing descent through Mathew, see Appendix 6.)

Uppermost on Sir Simon's mind was still the question of his granddaughter and the future of his property in Ireland. Eventually, in 1692, he took action to avoid his hard-won Irish estates passing into Catholic hands by initiating a final Deed of Revocation of the marriage agreement, effectively preventing Martha from inheriting his estates, divesting him of the obligations of the agreement, and enabling him to sell

---

10. *Reports of Cases, upon Appeals and Writs of Error in the High Court of Parliament, 1697–1713*, by Richard Colles, Esq., Dublin, 1789, p.348.

the 200 acres of Tickeridge Farm. The Deed was executed in June 1695. A decade later, Martha and George Mathew appealed against the Deed, but without success.

Sir Simon Eaton made his will on 1 March 1696/7,[11] naming his stepson, Chichester Phillips, as heir to his estate at Dunmoylan in Ireland and his property in Balsham. He left his widow Susanna well provided for and to Chichester's daughter, Margaret, he bequeathed up to £150 per year, but his granddaughter, Martha, was to receive just £5.

At the great age of 93, Sir Simon Eaton died and on 10 December 1697 was buried in the body of the parish church of St James', Westminster, his grave marked by a simple flat stone bearing the inscription, "Simon Eaton Bar. 1697". In the end, Simon had been right to be concerned for, just two weeks after his death, Martha Eaton and George Mathew junior were married. Sir Simon's widow Susanna died four years later in Limerick.

---

11. Details of the will of Simon Eaton in bibliography.

Chapter 15

The Hamlin Family, Part II – The House and Farm Refurbished

THE PURCHASE OF THE EAST GRINSTEAD PART of Tickeridge by Francis Hamlin I in 1654 and the installation of his son, John Hamlin II, as the farm's tenant, marked a sea change. For many years, its pastoral role had been subordinate to its importance as an investment for its valuable timber. The absentee landlords simply enjoyed the income it generated; it was the tenants who worked the land and made their living from farming, subsidising the landlord's income with their annual rental payments.

But now, the local iron industry was in a period of decline and, with less demand for timber and charcoal, Tickeridge became the subject of new investment so that its potential as a productive farm could be fully exploited, and the process was begun to enhance its agricultural identity.

The history of the great barn at Tickeridge begins with the Hamlin family. Converted into two dwellings in 2006, Tickeridge Barn was originally built in two stages. The oldest portion of five bays (now converted to house number 1) has been dated to around 1650 so was surely built soon after the purchase by Francis Hamlin in 1654. It reflects an injection of new funds into the farm to replace existing, dilapidated farm buildings erected many decades before, and points to the new wealth generated by a flourishing agricultural business.

Raised on the sandstone outcrop opposite the farmhouse, the barn extended to some 60ft in length and was 22ft wide, with five bays. A large threshing bay with opposing double doors is witness to the importance of arable production; the barn also provided storage for crops and accommodation for livestock. It was constructed with a massive Oak timber frame resting on a plinth of fine sandstone blocks which were probably quarried in Holmes Wood, opposite Tickeridge, and part of the farm at that time. Some of its timbers show signs of being recycled from another building and the roof would have been at a much steeper pitch than it is now, and thatched.

To hold the sandstone blocks in place, a kiln was built on-site to produce the lime for the mortar, with the chalk brought from the North or South Downs by pack mules or ox cart. Its location is not known but it is likely to have been in the field formerly known as Jenkins Mead, but later known as Chalk Croft, a name which dates back at least to 1700, through which the footpath runs down to the Medway stream. The output from the kiln would also have helped to improve the heavy clay soils and make them more amenable to arable crops.

The refurbished sandstone plinth of the conversion comprises the original blocks, and the lintels in the fireplaces of both converted properties originally formed a single horizontal support in the 17th-century barn.

Within a year of their marriage, John II and Sarah's first of four children, John Hamlin III, was born at Tickeridge, and baptised in West Hoathly on 2 April 1653, but Sarah did not survive the birth of her fourth child and died in January 1657/8. Not long afterwards, John Hamlin II was married to Elizabeth Smith of Maresfield, widow of William who had died in November the previous year. Tickeridge farmhouse remained John's home, which, at the time, was recorded as having two hearths and 11 windows.

In 1663, John's health was failing and he wrote his will, leaving "household stuff" to his wife, and bequests of money and gold to his sons, John III, Francis and Thomas, whom he left to be guided and protected by his brothers and father. His will was witnessed by his friend and neighbour, Henry Falconer of Gravetye, and John Haselden, his brother-in-law, married to his sister Mary. He was buried in West Hoathly on 13 December that year, survived by his father, Francis Hamlin I.

Three years later, Francis I wrote his will, which was dated 2 May 1666, leaving the benefit of the mortgage on Meadows and Shelves to his sons, Francis II and James, though it was later agreed between them that Francis II would be the sole beneficiary and inherit this land. Aged nearly 80, Francis Hamlin I died at Bolney Farm and was buried at West Hoathly on 27 February 1667/8. His will, proved on 1 April, disposed of the rest of his properties, namely Mascalls and Freelands in Buxted, Robins and Strudgate in Balcombe, and Hapstead Green in Ardingly.

Francis Hamlin II did not live at Tickeridge. In about 1645 he had married Anne Pierce of Ditchling and they had four children: Francis III, baptised in Ardingly on 11 April 1647, John, Anne and Thomas, also baptised in the village but, by the time of his father's death, Francis II and his family were ensconced on his estate at Avins in Ardingly.

It is not clear who was in charge of the day-to-day running of the farm after John Hamlin II's death at Tickeridge in 1663. At that time, his sister,

Elizabeth, and her husband, John Tully, were living at Bolney Farm with her father, Francis I, so it is possible that John Tully supervised Tickeridge.

By his father's death in December 1675, Francis Hamlin III now became the owner of the East Grinstead portion, Meadows and Shelves, and soon appointed his cousin, John Tully's son, Francis, as its tenant. At the same time, Francis Tully became Sir Simon Eaton's tenant of the West Hoathly portion, thereby farming the whole of Tickeridge, where the accommodation included a Brewhouse, Bakehouse and Cellar.

Chapter 16

Francis Tully, Tenant Farmer – His Life and Times

Baptised in Ardingly on 15 April 1652, Francis Tully was the second child of John and Elizabeth Tully. His father, John, was born in Ardingly in 1624 and married Elizabeth Hamlin in about 1647. She was baptised in West Hoathly on 11 March 1619/20, a daughter of Francis Hamlin I and Elizabeth who lived at Bolney Farm, Ardingly. Elizabeth's sister, Mary, married John Haselden in 1657, and her brother, John Hamlin II married Sarah Chisman in about 1652, so Francis Tully was well connected locally.

His siblings, all baptised in Ardingly, were Elizabeth (20 September 1650), John (born *c.* 1653), Thomas (1 May 1654), William (25 May 1656) and James (2 May 1661).

In the parish church of Teston, near Maidstone in Kent, on 18 July 1681, Francis was married to Anne, a daughter of William Seale, sometime of Horsted Keynes and Fletching. Francis and Anne Tully had three children, namely William, baptised in Fletching on 11 June 1682, Frances, their only daughter, baptised 30 July 1684 in West Hoathly, and Benjamin, baptised on 14 July 1685, also in West Hoathly.

On 22 August 1686, in poor health, Francis Tully made his will. To his widow, Ann, he left a piece of gold worth 22s., to his son, William, five silver spoons, to his daughter, Frances, a silver tumbler and a silver taster, and to his son, Benjamin, two of his biggest silver spoons. The bulk of his estate he left in trust to his executors, his father, John, and brother, James of Ardingly, who were to divide it between Ann and her children. He died at Tickeridge a few days later, aged 34, and, wrapped in a woollen shroud, was buried in Ardingly on 29 August. His will was proved on 15 March 1686/7.

Ann was probably still a young woman at the time of Francis' death, and in January or February 1687/8, married her second husband, Richard Page, a Yeoman from Fletching. This union prompted Francis'

Burial in Woollen: By an Act of 1678, in an effort to increase the demand for wool, it was required that the dead were to be wrapped in a woollen shroud for burial.

Fig.75: Woman spinning flax using a spindle, courtesy of the Metropolitan Museum of Art

Flax: Latin name linum, *is an annual plant growing nearly 3ft high. It is harvested by pulling the stems from the ground; these are then soaked in water for several days to break down the pectin that binds the fibres. After drying, the stems are broken down using a wooden paddle to separate the outer core, the boon, from the inner core, the line, which contains the long, high-quality fibres. A metal hackling comb is used, through which the line fibres are pulled to remove any short fibres and align and straighten the long ones. Once the fibres are prepared, they are ready for spinning using either a spindle or a spinning wheel to produce the linen thread, which is then woven into linen cloth, making a hard-wearing material used to make clothing.*

father, John Tully, to initiate a Bill of Complaint against Richard Page.[1] Comprising a set of 11 documents, dated 1686–8, the Bill includes inventories which give detailed information on what had been happening on the farm during Francis' tenure (see Appendix 9).

From one of the documents, it appears that Ann's father, William Seale, may have manipulated her marriage to Richard Page and, with him, vigorously pursued her claim to most of Francis' personal estate, from which, of course, Richard, as her husband, would benefit.

The rest of the documents provide a vivid picture of life on the farm at that time and reveal in great detail the produce harvested, the names of its farm workers and some local farmers, and lists various items relevant to everyday life. Several of the documents are damaged and torn, but from them we learn that Francis employed six regular workers on the farm, plus additional staff at harvest time. Also mentioned are the local craftsmen, including the Blacksmith, Thatcher, Weavers, Candlemaker and Tanner.

On the land grew Grass for grazing and cutting for Hay. Francis sold his harvested crops such as Barley at an average of £1.16s.11d. a ton, Malt Barley at £6.2s.3d. a ton, Wheat at £4.11s.1¼d a ton, Oats at £2.0s.11d a ton, Peas at £8.6s.2½d a ton, Apples at £1 at ton, Beans at £5.12s.0d. a ton and Hops at £14 a ton, by far the most lucrative crop; the straw from his grain crops was also sold. From the woodland he sold faggots. His livestock included working oxen, cows, sheep, pigs, horses (working and for riding), rabbits, ducks, poultry, geese, and bees, which provided not only honey, but also wax for candles. He visited Buxted, Cuckfield, East Grinstead and Rotherfield Fairs to sell oxen and cows. Another crop was Flax which his wife and servants spun into thread that was then sent to weavers to make linen cloth.

Milk from the cows was made into butter and cheese which were sold, as were fattened oxen and steers, heifers, sheep, horses, rabbits, and feathers from the fowl. Hides and skins from dead livestock were treated and sold.

He paid to have his sheep washed and sheared and, to combat the mites which would cause scab in his sheep, he purchased dried tobacco stalks; incorporated into a salve, the crushed stalks, together with wood tar, goose-grease and brimstone, were smeared onto the sheep's skin by parting its fleece. The dry, crushed stalks could also be used in the dovecot to protect the pigeons from mites. With well-known medicinal properties, wood tar – today we call it Stockholm Tar – mixed with fat to make a salve, was applied to any cuts caused during shearing, and a shepherd would

---

1. NA C10/276/60

always have a tar box with him to deal with any injuries to his flock.

In 1686, Francis' flock would have been numbered amongst the estimated 11 million sheep then in England and Wales.

On the farm, threshing the grain was carried out in the threshing bay of the barn. At harvest time, when more labour was needed, workers' wives and a young lad were recruited. Francis' bees provided beeswax and honey, from which he probably made mead. Malted Barley was used to make beer, and Francis kept a hoard of bottles in which to sell it. He paid his rent to Mr. Abbott, Simon Eaton's Factor.

Wood or Pine Tar: Produced by the dry distillation of pine wood by applying heat and pressure in a closed environment. The resulting products are charcoal and pine tar. Large-scale production began in Sweden in the early 17th century. The tar was used to preserve wood and rope, and as a veterinary antiseptic, particularly for treating skin conditions.

Malted Barley was made by soaking the grains in water to encourage them to germinate. The germinated grains were then drained, dried and heated, a process whereby enzymes in the Malted Barley convert its starches into fermentable sugars which serve as food for yeast. For Barley bread, the dried grains were ground into flour; for beer they were crushed into a coarse powder called 'grist' which was mixed with hot water to start the fermenting process. The ale barm, or froth on top of the fermenting beer, was used as a raising agent for manchet or wheaten bread.

Chapter 17

Edward Paine and John Browning – Agriculture Dominates

Following Francis Tully's death in August 1686, a new lease for Tickeridge Farm was drawn up by Sir Simon Eaton on 26 August 1687, and sold for £80 to Edward, a Carpenter, of the ubiquitous Paine/Payne family of East Grinstead, and John Browning who, as its tenants from 29 September for a period of 17 years, would pay an annual rent of £50. The farm comprised "a good estate of inheritance with lands, meadows, pastures, feedings, woods, underwoods[1] and appurtenances." The lease stipulated that 20 acres of meadow, or "mowing ground", must be properly maintained and all the "fences, pales, hedges and ditches" repaired as necessary. Attached to the document was a single seal, believed to be that of Edward Paine.

John Browning had been baptised in East Grinstead on 23 February 1653/4, the second son of William and Anne (née Tugwell). His siblings were also baptised in East Grinstead, viz William (1652), Edward (1656), Thomas (1657), Elizabeth (1660), James (1665) and Stephen (1668). He was married in West Hoathly on 5 October 1686 to Anne, a daughter of Edward Paine who had made his will on 2 April 1668, naming his wife, Jone, and Anne and her two sisters as its beneficiaries. His will was proved 20 years later, on 4 May 1688, when John Browning became Sir Simon Eaton's sole tenant of Tickeridge Farm.

Francis Hamlyn I had purchased Meadows and Shelves from Simon Eaton in 1654. On 16 July 1692, by way of an additional mortgage, his grandson, Francis III, now living at Avins Farm, agreed to pay Simon Eaton 10 guineas in gold "in hand", plus a further £1,050 for the full title of Tickeridge Farm. Acting on his uncle's behalf as a signatory to the Agreement was John Hamlyn III, formerly of Lindfield, but now of Upper Fords Farm, Warbleton, which he had purchased in 1674. The

Fig.76: Sketch of seal.
Source: attached to Document SAS D/431, dated 26 August 1687, East Sussex and Brighton and Hove Record Office at The Keep.

---

1. Coppice.

other signatories were Sir Simon Eaton, John Browning and Edward Harberfield, whose signatures are shown above.

On 10 August 1692, Francis Hamlin of Ardingly paid 5s. for an Indenture for the purchase of Tickeridge and Shelves from Sir Simon Eaton; the following day, the intended purchase was confirmed by the Conveyance by Sir Simon Eaton and his wife Susanna of the capital messuage, tenement and farmhouse known as Tickeridge and Shelves, plus all those lands called Meadows and Shelves. Sketches of the seals on this document are shown below.

Fig.77: Signatures. *Source:* Document SAS D/456, dated 16 July 1692, with kind permission of the East Sussex and Brighton and Hove Record Office at The Keep.

 Sir Simon EATON

 Susan EATON

 John HAMLIN

 No signature but possibly James HAMLIN

 Ffrancis HAMLIN

Fig.78: Sketches of the seals on document. *Source:* SAS D/460, dated 11 August 1692, at East Sussex and Brighton and Hove Record Office at The Keep.

Fig.79: Letter from Simon Eaton, with his signature.
Source: Document DM193, dated 11 April 1693, by kind permission of the East Sussex and Brighton and Hove Record Office at The Keep.

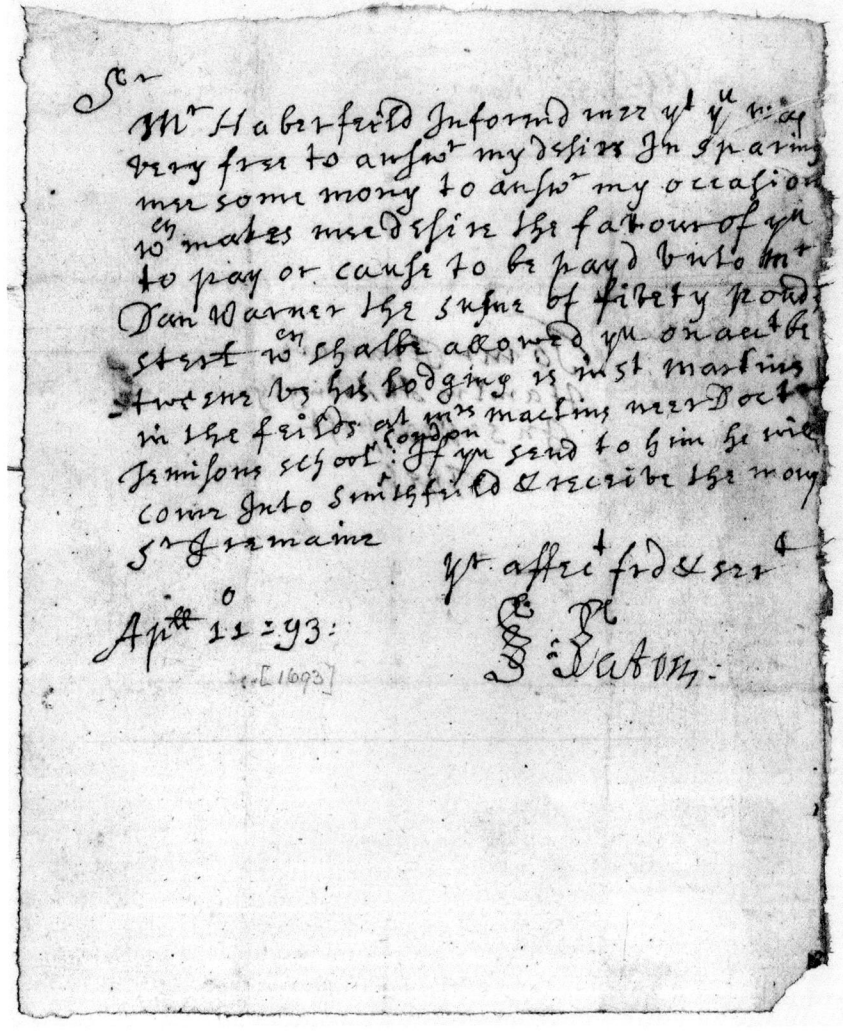

On 11 April 1693, Sir Simon Eaton sent this letter to Francis Hamlin III of Avins.

On 5 September 1693, Francis Hamlin III paid £4.10s. for a post fine for "certain lands lying and being within the several parishes of West Hoathly and East Grinstead in the county of Sussex commonly called or known by the name of Tickridg farme". This payment marked the completion of his purchase of Tickeridge from Simon Eaton. The receipt was signed by Anthony Burnup and witnessed by John Wood and Francis' brother, Thomas, of Sunte.

John Browning's tenure continued, and in March 1700 was reaffirmed by a new lease of Tickeridge Farm by Francis Hamlin III, which specified that John Browning shall, "repair maintain uphold and keep the said

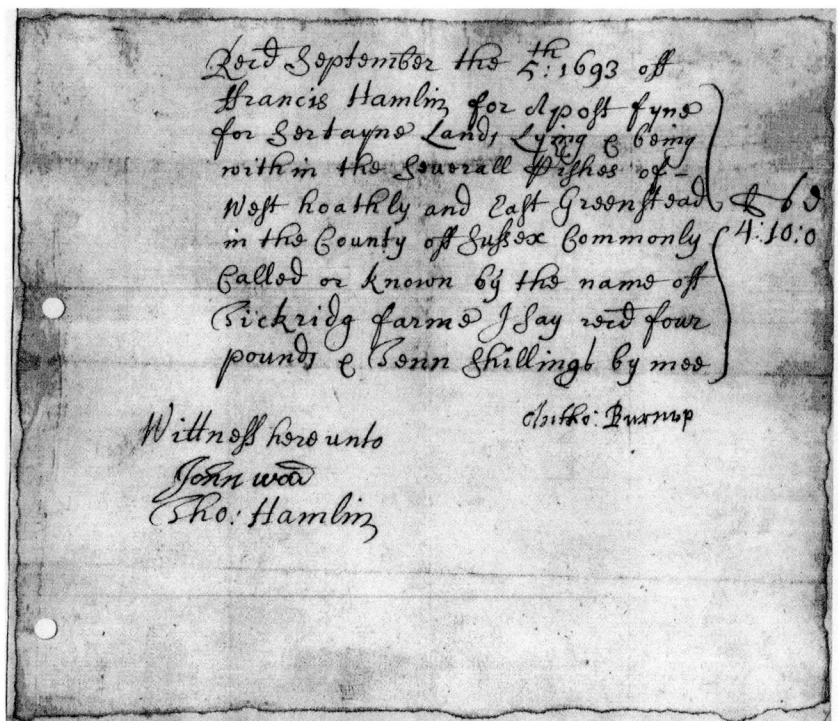

Fig.80: Post Fine for purchase of Tickeridge, dated 5 September 1693.
Source: Document SAS/DM 191, dated 5 September 1693, by kind permission of the East Sussex and Brighton and Hove Record Office at The Keep.

messuage or tenement barns buildings and all the gates barrs posts pailes railes hedges ditches fences inclosures of and belonging to the demised premises ... sufficiently repaired maintained upheld and kept ... and the said John Browning shall ... demise and spend all the hay straw and fodder yearly growing and arising upon the premises hereby demised and upon the same premises and the dung soil and compost thereof yearly lay spread and bestow in and upon the premises or some part thereof in husbandlike manner for the bettering and improvement thereof ... and in case the said John Browning shall att any time or times hereafter during the term ... plow break up dig or eare [sow a grain crop like Wheat or Barley] or cause and procure to be plowed broken up digged or eared all or any part of this the three meadows called the Barns Meade the Chalke Croft and the Nineacre Meade part of the premises then (he) shall pay unto the said ffrancis Hamlin the sum of five pounds for every acre thereof ... John Browning shall have liberty to fodder out the hay and straw growing the last year of this term hereby demised."[2]

John Browning lived at Tickeridge until his death in January 1730/1. He was buried in West Hoathly, leaving a will dated 27 March 1729/30, in which he mentions his wife (Anne), daughter (Susanna), who was married

---

2. Indenture dated 28 March 1700, ESBHRO Add Mss 320.

Fig.81: Sunte House, oldest part built 1700 with later additions. Photo of Sunte, taken in 2010

to Nineon Creasy, his son, John, and his daughter-in-law, Sarah Browning, to whom he leaves all his "goods and chattels at Teckridge within doors and without".

Francis Hamlin III enjoyed considerable wealth and influence, such that on 11 December 1712, he was appointed Sheriff of Sussex. He lived at Avins, Ardingly, and died there in December 1732 to be succeeded by his son, the fourth Francis Hamlin.

Fig.82: Avins, first mentioned in 1568; oldest part of present house built early in the 17th century. Photo of Avins taken in 2004

This Francis IV had his initials carved on an Oak board in Tickeridge farmhouse, together with the date 1748, when he may have carried out a refurbishment.

He will also have instigated the construction of the three-bay extension to the barn which now forms most of house number 2 of the conversion.

Francis chose to live in Lindfield and seems never to have married.

The Rating Assessment Book of West Hoathly records Thomas Bevin as occupier of Tickeridge in 1743, and William Bevin as occupier in 1745. Apart from these two entries, there appears to be no other evidence of their existence.

Of Francis Hamlin's next tenant for Tickeridge Farm there is more; this was William Mason, who took part in beating the bounds of West Hoathly in May 1749. For the purposes of the East Grinstead Land Tax, 1750 to 1757, William was listed as the occupier of the holding of Medway and Shelves, together with Dallingridge Mead, then owned by the Rt Hon. George Lord Abergavenny. He was also confirmed as the occupier of Tickeridge in 1752, when he was responsible for the maintenance of 24ft of the church wall in West Hoathly. On 4 June 1750, William Mason, Yeoman of West Hoathly, made his will, leaving his "goods, chattels, messuages, lands, tenements and hereditaments" to his wife Sarah; no-one else is mentioned in his will. William died in 1758 and was buried in West Hoathly. The inscription on his gravestone reads, "In memory of William Mason who departed this life October the 29th 1758 aged 63 years. Beneath this stone doth he in dust a husband once one of the just a neighbour good industrious." Sarah died in 1768.

After Sarah's death, the tenancy at Tickeridge was soon filled by John Hounsome, whose family connections have so far eluded me. Like William Mason before him, he was also tenant of Medway and Shelves and Dallingridge Mead, but he appears to have resided at Tickeridge until at least 1776.

Fig.83: Photo of Oak board with initials F H and the date 1748

Fig.84: Bar socket on the western threshing bay door frame of the 3-bay extension, measuring 34cm x 14cm

Fig.85: Gravestones of William and Sarah Mason in St Margaret's churchyard, West Hoathly

Fig.86: Tomb of John Hamlin (d. 1774) and his wife, Ann (d. 1771) in Lindfield churchyard

Under the terms of his father's will, Francis Hamlin IV was merely a custodian of Tickeridge Farm, since his lack of any children meant that the estates inherited from his father passed, after his death in 1788, to the heirs of his uncle, Thomas Hamlin III who had died in November 1732. These were the two daughters (Ann and Mary) of Thomas' son, John Hamlin IV of Sunte, who had died in 1774.

Ann Hamlin, the older of the two girls, was born in 1764; her sister, Mary, three years later. Already wealthy, following the deaths of both their parents, these two young women now owned between them some 2,000 acres of land and around 20 farms. In 1785, Ann had become the wife of John Borrer, but Mary's marriage, to William Franklin Hick, did not take place until 22 August 1796 when she was nearly 30. An arrangement was made whereby the inheritance was divided, and the portion containing Tickeridge Farm then formed part of the estates of Mary Hamlin.

By 1780, the farm tenancy had been granted to John Sturt who, on 10 April 1781, a week before his marriage to Jane Gibb, prepared a valuation of the stock on the farm,[3] which included 4 working horses and their harness, 4 colts, 1 riding pony, 3 pigs, 1 bull, 5 cows with calves, 4 oxen, 1 steer and 2 heifers, 4 two-year-old heifers and steers, 4 yearlings, 8 ewes, 7 lambs, 22 tegs (sheep), 10 quarters of Oats, 5 loads of Wheat, and 5,000 Hop poles, used in the five-acre garden opposite the barn on the other side of Vowels Lane. The most valuable item was the Wheat, at £36. John's tenure lasted until June 1794, when he was declared bankrupt and sent to Horsham Goal. The new (joint) tenants that year were James Woodman and Joseph Fairhall, the latter having married Jane Edwards in East Grinstead on 11 April.

James and Joseph were still tenants at the time of Mary Hamlin's marriage in 1796. After this date her husband, William Hick, took over the administration of around 700 acres of her estate, which included the 260 acres of Tickeridge.

William was a corn and seed merchant and a prominent citizen of Lewes. From 1803 to 1815, he captained the town-based voluntary infantrymen when Napoleon threatened our shores, and traded in Dieppe, where he had a residence for a while. He took a keen interest in politics and the management of his wife's estate and lived a comfortable life in their home at 199 High Street, Lewes with his wife and only daughter, Mary Ann. Timber extraction was still an important part of the farm's output, particularly from Holstein and Minepit woods, whose total crop from 50 acres was valued at £112.00 in 1811.

---

3. *Sussex Archaelogical Collections*, vol.48, p.159.

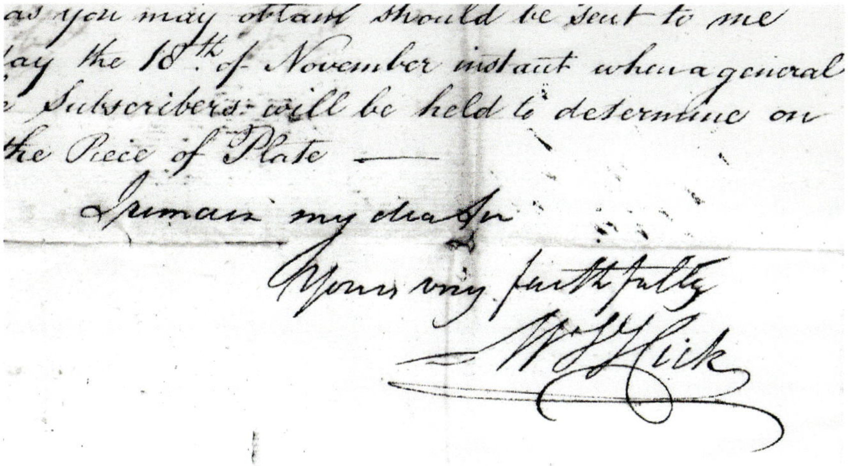

as you may obtain should be sent to me
ay the 18th of November instant when a general
Subscribers will be held to determine on
the Piece of Plate —
I remain my dear Sir
Yours very faithfully
Wm F Hick

Fig.87: Signature of William Franklin Hick.
Source: On document SAS DD/822, dated 4 November 1809, with kind permission of the East Sussex and Brighton and Hove Record Office at The Keep.

In the house, a new piece of equipment was installed over the inglenook fireplace; this was a clockwork roasting jack which would make the roasting of joints far less labour intensive. With a meat joint on the roasting spit, a spring in the jack was wound up to drive and turn the spit in front of the fire. The clockwork jack survives *in situ*.

William Franklin Hick died in 1844, survived by his widow Mary who lived another three years. Their daughter Mary Ann inherited all her mother's estates, including Tickeridge. Soon after the loss of her father, Mary Ann Hick was married to Dr. Thomas Haire, but the marriage failed and the couple were soon separated. By the time her will was proved in 1854, a few months after her death from scarlet fever, Mary Ann had denied her husband any legacy and, without any children, instead left her estate to be divided amongst various relations, friends and tenants – amongst these was William Woodman, to whom she left Tickeridge Farm.

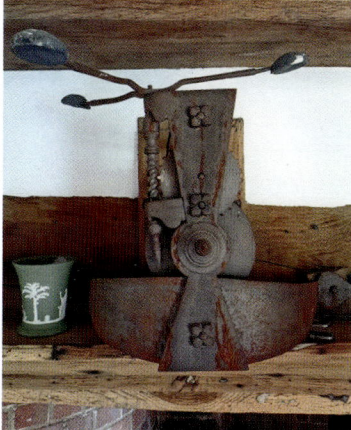

Fig.88: Clockwork roasting jack at Tickeridge, dating from *c.* 18th century. Photo taken in 2024

Chapter 18

The Woodman Family – Tenants to Owners

Fig.89: A Sussex farmer of the mid-19th century. Image courtesy of Wikimedia Commons

The Woodman family was to have an association with Tickeridge extending over three generations. In 1812, James' son William Woodman became the tenant. William lived at Tickeridge with his wife, Sarah, a daughter of John Fuller of Turners Hill. They had seven children, born between 1816 and 1833, being John, James, Anna, Sarah Ann, Caroline, William and Amelia. A few weeks after Amelia's birth, William signed a Boarding Agreement under the West Sussex Poor Law, to accommodate Elizabeth Going who, presumably, would help in the household whilst Sarah nurtured baby Amelia.

In 1846, their daughter, Caroline Woodman, aged 19, was married to Robert Reynolds, a 28-year-old widower of Selsfield House and Farm, whose first wife, Jane Townsend, had died in 1842. In 1848, Caroline's brother, John, was married to Elizabeth Tester and they made their home at Fenland Farm.

With the help of eight men, William farmed 252 acres, 85 acres of which were tithed with the parish of East Grinstead, and 167 with West Hoathly, comprising 100 acres of arable, 45 of pasture, 69 of woodland and 33 of meadow. There was also a 1-acre orchard and a 5-acre Hop garden, for which the Hop poles were harvested from Chestnut coppices.

With his extensive arable land, and a landlord who was a corn and seed merchant, William erected a weatherboarded granary in which to store his harvest of grain. Built opposite the barn and overlooked by the farm house, it rested on eight staddle stones and had a clay tile roof. It survived at the farm until 4 June 1994 when, in a deteriorating state, it was removed to High Salvington and restored to service the working windmill there.

Living with William and Sarah in the farmhouse were five of the farm workers, namely John Backshell and William Fur, both aged 15, William Clarke and William Divall, both aged 20, and Thomas Holder, aged 35. Richard and John Hunt, aged 75+ and 27 respectively, lived in Tickeridge

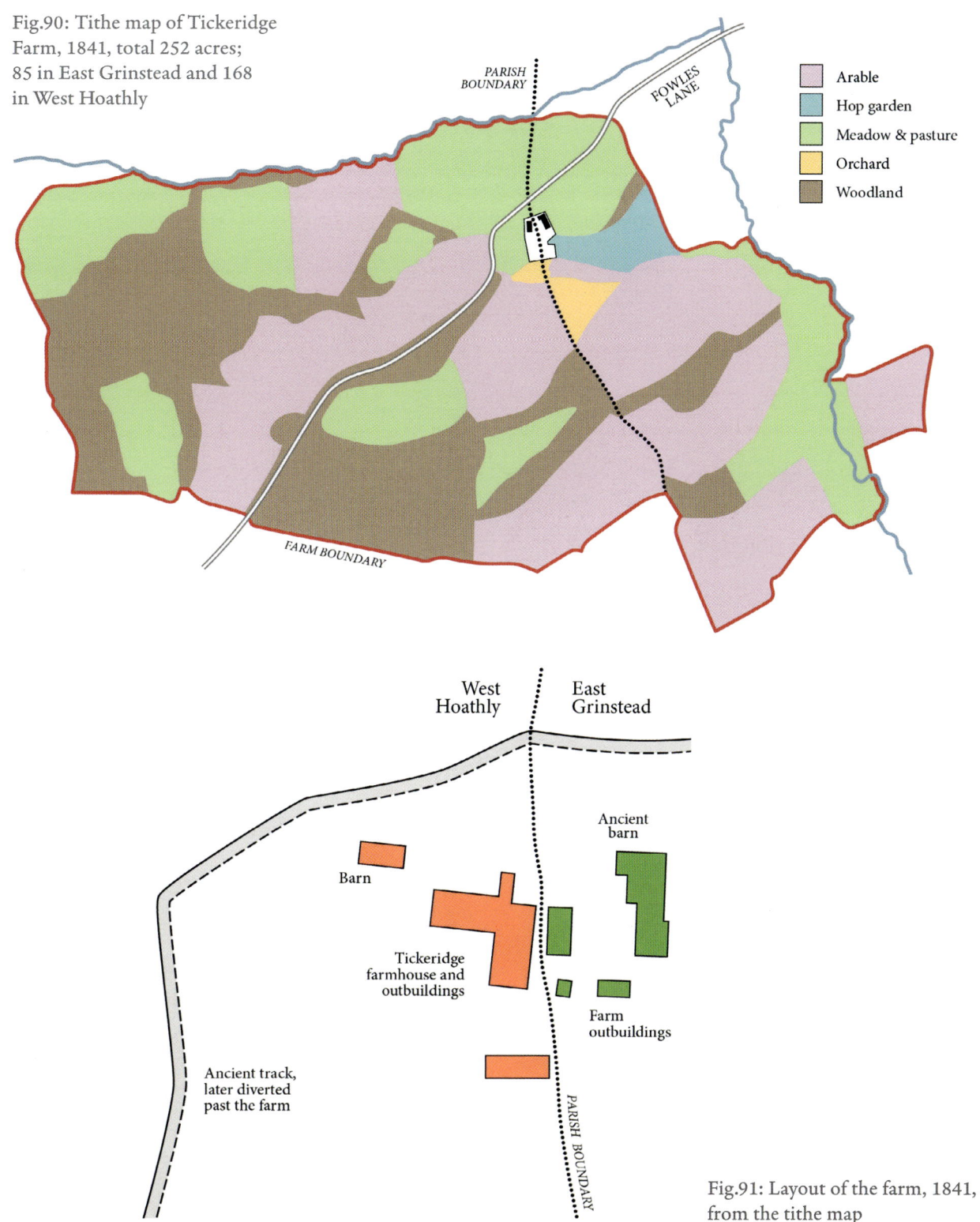

Fig.90: Tithe map of Tickeridge Farm, 1841, total 252 acres; 85 in East Grinstead and 168 in West Hoathly

Fig.91: Layout of the farm, 1841, from the tithe map

THE WOODMAN FAMILY - TENANTS TO OWNERS

Fig.92: Charles E. Graves, *Hop Garden in Alexandra Park, East Sussex*, 1872

Cottage. Two house servants were employed: Ann Langridge, aged 15, and Martha Dench, aged 20. Ann Podmore, with her baby daughter, Harriett, appear to have been visitors.

By 1846, Fowles Lane (i.e. Vowels Lane) from Selsfield to Tickeridge was badly cut up and in a poor state, so William decided to erect a gate to limit access from Selsfield and potentially to create a private road. This did not go down well with "Mr. Turner, proprietor of land in the parish, who broke down the gate in the presence of Mr. Woodman."

West Hoathly parish council became involved and was accused of not maintaining the road at least as a horse and bridleway. But 25 witnesses stated that it had been used as a carriageway for the last 50 years and should be repaired to that standard.

At this time the Sussex landscape, with few wire fences and obstacles, provided excellent territory for the huntsmen of the East Surrey Staghounds, based near Croydon. It was not wild deer that were pursued, but half a dozen stags and hinds which were kept for the purpose of being hunted. On hunting day, one of the deer was chosen to be the quarry; it was put into a horse-drawn cart from their enclosure at the kennels in Epsom to the prearranged release point, and given a 20-minute start before the hounds were set on for the pursuit, often by more than 100 horses and riders.

The hunt might last all day and often covered some 30 miles from the uncarting site to capture. On one such occasion in early 1855, after a particularly good chase, the stag arrived at Tickeridge, where it was cornered and loaded back into the cart to be taken home. From thenceforth, this particular stag was called 'Tickeridge' and was hunted

Fig.93: Basil Bradley, *Laying on the Hounds*, 1874

Granary barn is the latest addition

THE RESTORATION of an early 19th Century granary barn is the latest labour of love of the Friends of High Salvington Windmill.

The 150-year-old building was transported in its entirety last week to Worthing from the hamlet of Kingscote in East Sussex in a delicate operation requiring cranes, low-loader vehicles and a police escort.

The intricate restoration, which will involve replacement of the barn's worm-eaten and rotten joints, boards and roof beams and the fixing of 2,000 traditional clay peg tiles, is expected to take two years and cost about £10,000.

This, however, is small fry to the Friends who have spent £80,000 on the major and as-yet unfinished restoration of the 300-year-old mill itself since they began 18 years ago in 1976!

"The last granary for the mill is now the RAFA Club in Selden," said membership secretary Roger Ashton.

"It stopped being used in 1897 when the mill itself closed down because it was unable to compete with the big steam power roller mills that were taking over on a mass production basis."

The new granary, which will stand out of reach of vermin, being three feet above the ground on traditional mushroom-shaped steddle stones, will be used to store grain for the mill.

High Salvington Mill now produces about half a ton of flour a year on its working days, which take place on the first and third Sundays of each month, April to September, when the mill is open to the public.

"The flour is sold to the public and we can't make enough of it," said Mr Ashton. "The wind is our problem. In the past, the windmill would have stood on a bald hilltop and been blasted from each quarter.

"These days it is surrounded by trees and houses and we have to wait for winds from the Isle of Wight in the south-west or Cissbury Ring in the north-east for an unobstructed breeze."

Fig.94: Old granary *in situ* at Tickeridge, 30 April 1994
Fig.95: Old granary leaves the farm on 4 June 1994
Fig.96: Old granary on its way to High Salvington

Fig.97: *West Sussex Gazette*, 16 June 1994
Fig.98: Restored Tickeridge granary at High Salvington, 25 March 1995

THE WOODMAN FAMILY – TENANTS TO OWNERS

Fig.99: Derelict remains of the bull pen

Fig.100: Cart shed and piggeries, demolished around 1975. Notice the lean-to extension on the barn in the background

Fig.101: Site of demolished bull pen, with a brick floor, photographed in May 2005

again in April that year. In 1859, the hunt again arrived at Tickeridge, passing through and pursuing its quarry to Selsfield.

As the owner of the farm, William updated his buildings, adding more accommodation for his livestock. A bull pen, cart shed and piggeries were located near the entrance to the farm and more stabling and a lean-to may have been added to the barn around this time.

Other projects which may have been tackled during this period were the pumped and soft water systems which supplied the farm. From a pump house over a borehole in Upper Vennels, or Pump Field, a network of pipes brought spring water down to the farm troughs and into tanks in the farm house, a system which was still in use well into the 20th century.

A well near the house provided drinking water.

At the farm itself stood a small wooden building – later called 'the washhouse' – which housed a hand pump over a freshwater reservoir.

The piston creates suction in the pump and draws water through a check valve into the pump cylinder. Its action forces the water to flow out of the water spout at the top of the pump. The mechanism is approximately 13.5cm long.

Figs.102 and 103: Photos of the washhouse/pump shed in 2005

Fig.104: Photo of the hand pump in the pump shed, February 2005

Figs.105 and 106: Two lamps and three sconces found in the pump shed

Fig.107: Sketch of the stroke rod and piston mechanism (not to scale)

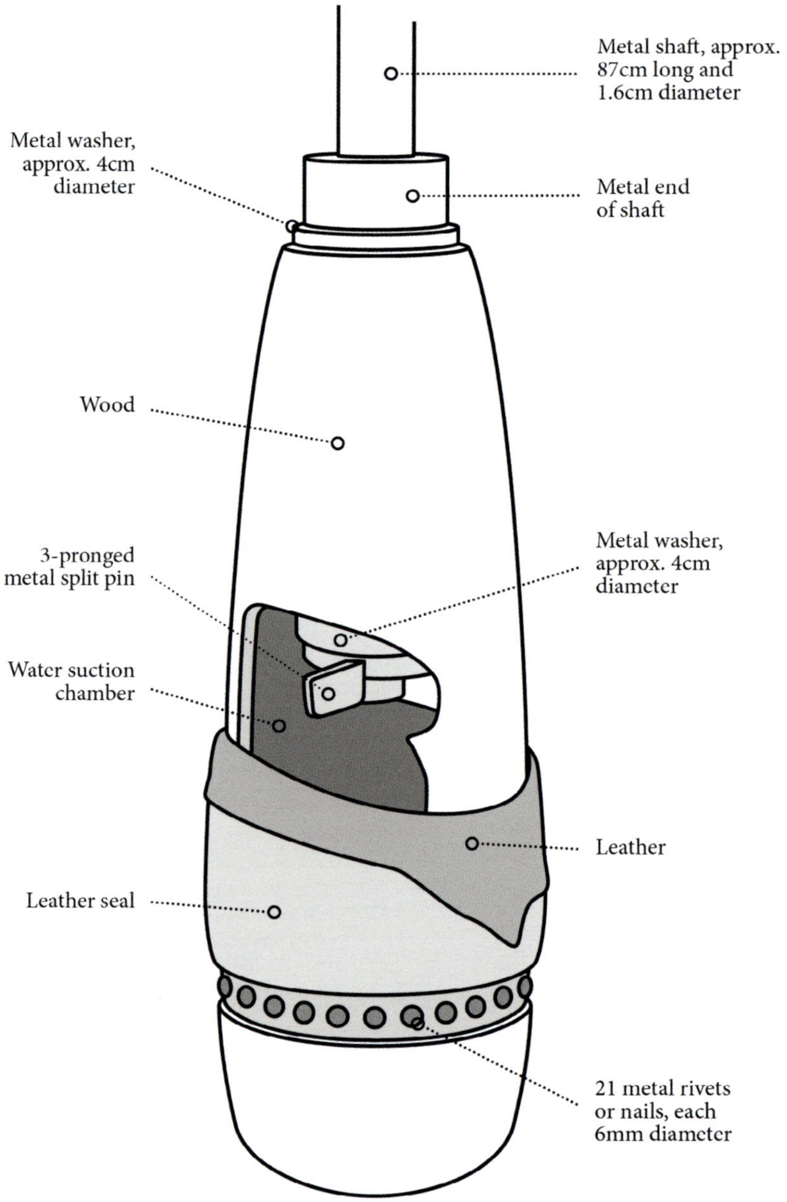

- Metal shaft, approx. 87cm long and 1.6cm diameter
- Metal washer, approx. 4cm diameter
- Metal end of shaft
- Wood
- 3-pronged metal split pin
- Metal washer, approx. 4cm diameter
- Water suction chamber
- Leather
- Leather seal
- 21 metal rivets or nails, each 6mm diameter

Fig.108: Photo of stroke rod from inside the hand pump

Beneath this was a chamber, about 5m deep and 2.5m in diameter, constructed of rendered brick, into which was channelled rainwater from gutters and downpipes on the barn. Attached to the bottom of the pump was a lead pipe some 4m long with a filter on the end.

The pump shed was demolished in 2006 and a concrete slab now covers the chamber.

Timber extraction continued to be a lucrative farm enterprise. On 31 March 1856, two loads from Tickeridge were carted up Vowels

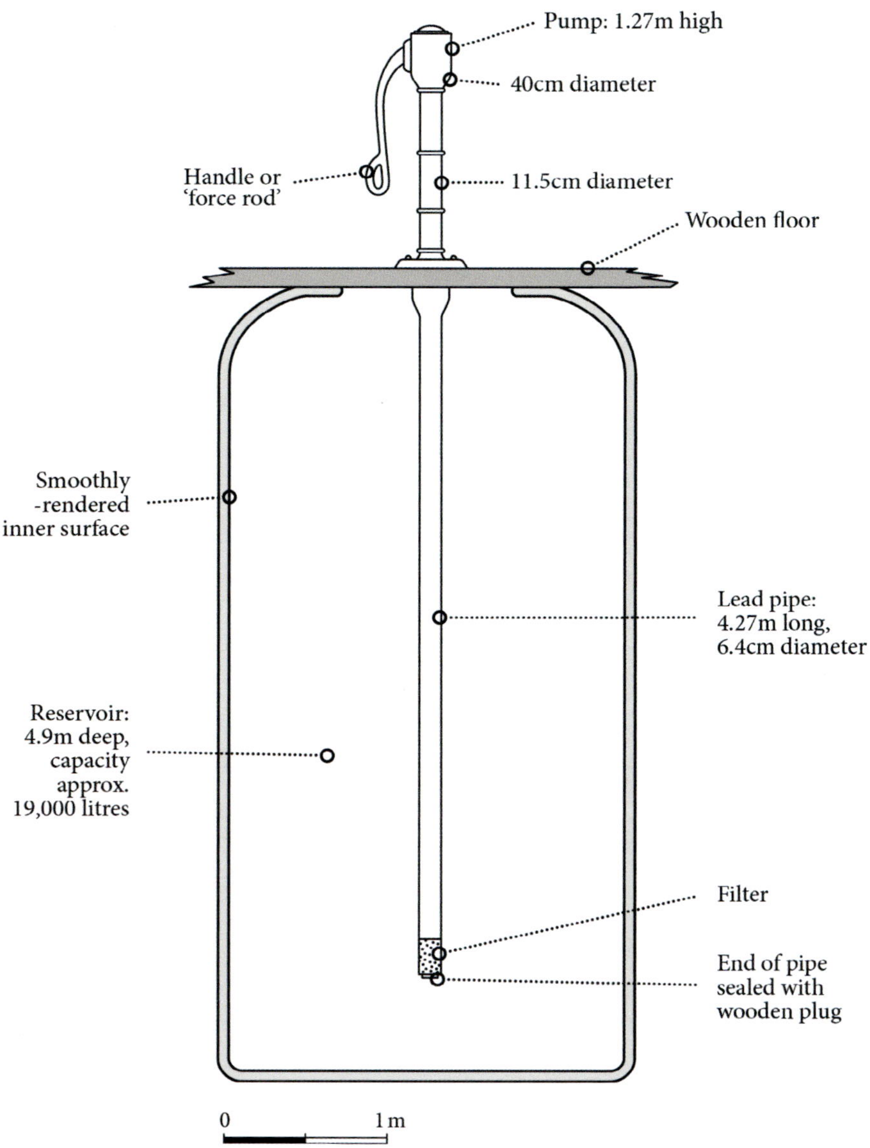

Fig.109: Diagram of the freshwater reservoir

- Pump: 1.27m high
- 40cm diameter
- Handle or 'force rod'
- 11.5cm diameter
- Wooden floor
- Smoothly-rendered inner surface
- Lead pipe: 4.27m long, 6.4cm diameter
- Reservoir: 4.9m deep, capacity approx. 19,000 litres
- Filter
- End of pipe sealed with wooden plug

Lane and onto the Selsfield Road; the first wagon, owned by William Woodman, was driven by Edmund Simmons, the second, owned by William's son-in-law, Robert Reynolds, of Selsfield House, was driven by William Packham. Almost immediately they encountered a flock of 780 sheep being driven towards West Hoathly. Both wagons stopped, but as they cleared the flock and moved on, one sheep ran under the second wagon and was killed. No blame was attached to either carter for the incident since the sheep was deemed to have contributed to its own death!

Fig.110: Photo of the lead pipe and filter

THE WOODMAN FAMILY - TENANTS TO OWNERS

There is no mention of the destination of this timber; it may have been heading for Haywards Heath, where Henry Longley of Upper Selsfield Lodge, and his brother, James, of Rashes Farm, Kingscote, were timber merchants, or perhaps it was heading for Shoreham where there was an important ship-building industry. The Ouse Navigation Canal was established in 1790 and, since 1812, the river had been navigable via Lewes to Newhaven from Pimms Lock in Lindfield and Upper Rylands Bridge in Balcombe, where there were basins large enough for 50ft barges to turn, so it is possible that timber from Tickeridge was taken by road to one of these wharfs, loaded onto barges and carried down to Newhaven before being shipped along the coast to Shoreham.

Robert Reynolds, mentioned above, was born in December 1817 in West Hoathly. He was married to Jane Townsend in 1840 and they lived at Selsfield House, where their son, John, was born. Jane died in 1842 and on 17 December 1845, in Battersea, Caroline Woodman, daughter of William, became Robert's second wife. They went on to have a family of nine children, including their daughter, Caroline Ida, born in 1848 in West Hoathly.

Robert died on 3 November 1862 and was buried in West Hoathly on 7 November. For several years, his widow, Caroline, continued to live at Selsfield House, but by 1901 she was living in the High Street, Cuckfield, aged 74, and head of the household which included her sons, Horace, William and Robert (who was a gamekeeper), plus a servant. Caroline died on 4 November 1908 and was also buried in West Hoathly.

On 30 August 1876, Caroline and Robert's daughter, Caroline Ida Reynolds, was married at St Peter's Church in Brighton to Charles Longley, who was born on 29 May 1840, of More House, Wivelsfield, a timber merchant and farmer of 360 acres, with a workforce of 12 men and 4 boys. Charles was the brother of Henry Longley II who became the owner of Tickeridge later that year.

In the 1861 Census, William Woodman stated that he farmed 300 acres, but his farm workforce had been reduced to six men and three boys. Living with the family in the main accommodation were George Pain, aged 18, born in East Grinstead and employed as a Carter, and three 16-year-old servants: Mary Peckham and William Styles, both born in West Hoathly, and Thomas Bilton, born in East Grinstead.

In the southern portion of the house lived Agricultural Worker, John Francis, aged 68, born in Horsted Keynes, his wife, Ann, aged 62, born in Maresfield, and John's mother, 90-year-old Elizabeth, born in East Grinstead.

William Woodman and his wife, Sarah, lived at Tickeridge almost until William's death in 1863, when his son, John Woodman, inherited both Tickeridge and Fenland Farms.

From his home at Fenland on the Turners Hill Road, John moved into Tickeridge farmhouse with his wife, Elizabeth. In 1871 he employed only four Agricultural Labourers, three of them accommodated with him in the house, namely Isaac Day, aged 18, born in West Hoathly, Henry Langridge, aged 41, and George Tester, aged 57, the latter two born in Cuckfield. There were also three live-in domestic servants: Elizabeth Draper, aged 18 and born in East Grinstead, Emma Kennett, aged 24, born in Charlton, and Sarah Ann Pett, the Cook, aged 31 and born in Heathfield. Francis M. Coley, aged 62, was a lodger. A non-resident boy was also employed on the farm.

The Return of Owners of Land, taken in 1873, records that Tickeridge and Fenland Farms extended to a total of 291 acres, 240 of them comprising Tickeridge.

Chapter 19

The Longley Family

Fig.111: Charles Longley (1840–1905) Image courtesy of Michael Longley

Fig.112: Tomb of Charles and Caroline Longley, West Hoathly

Fig.113: Hauling timber out of woodland near More Crichel, Dorset. Though taken in about 1921, this photo vividly shows the conditions encountered when carting timber across muddy land from woodland to the timber yard.
By kind permission of The Priest's House Museum, Wimbourne, Dorset

JOHN AND ELIZABETH WOODMAN had no offspring, so in July 1876 they put Tickeridge and Fenland Farms up for sale and retired, at first to Cemetery Road, and then to 44 Queens Road, East Grinstead, where Elizabeth died in September 1890, aged 72, and John died in July 1894, aged 78. Both were buried in the Queens Road Cemetery, plot 2.

Described as "Situate in a first-rate Sporting District", and "possessing extensive and magnificent views over the surrounding country", Tickeridge came to the attention of Henry Longley. Born in West Hoathly on 7 November 1837, Henry was a son of Henry and Elizabeth of Withypitts, Turners Hill. Henry senior and his brother, James of Rashes Farm, were timber merchants based in Haywards Heath. Henry Longley senior died on 10 July 1875 and was buried in West Hoathly churchyard. His death will have financially benefitted his

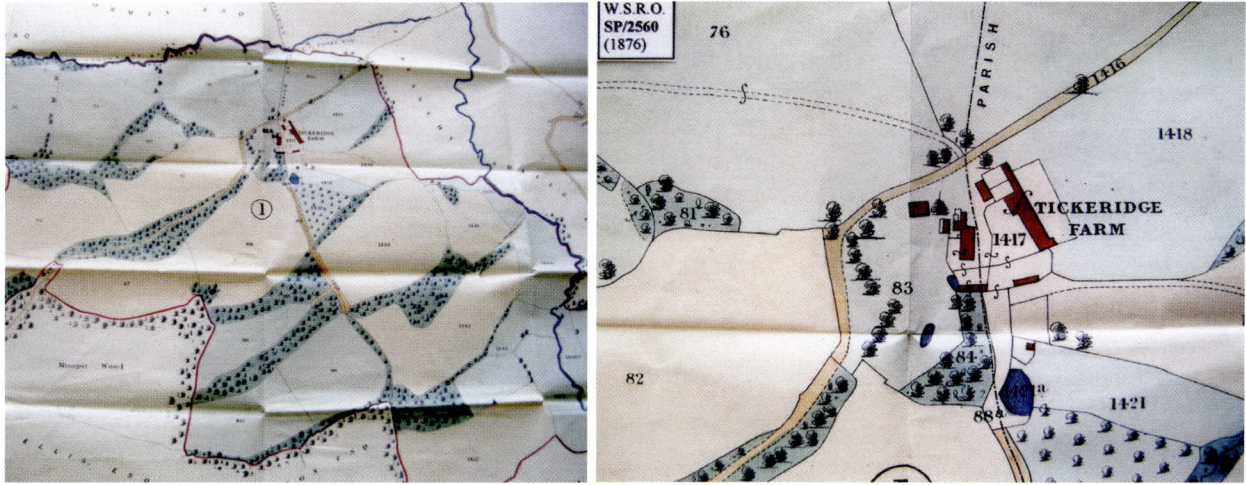

Fig.114: Map dated 1876
Source: Ref. SP/2560, courtesy of the County Archivist, West Sussex Record Office, Chichester.

Fig.115: Close-up of 1876 map, showing Tickeridge Farm.
Field numbers:
82 = Lower Vennels Field
83 = Hog Green
84 = Garden etc.
1417 = Farmhouse and Buildings
1418 = Barn Mead
1421 = Slipley Orchard

son, Henry, who, on 25 October 1876, for the sum of £6,000, officially became the owner of Tickeridge Farm, then extending to 227 acres (92 in East Grinstead and 135 in West Hoathly).

Henry was a local landowner, and worked in partnership, as timber merchants, with his younger brother, Charles, of Moor House Farm, Wivelsfield, who a few months earlier had married Caroline Ida Reynolds, the widow of Robert of Selsfield House, who had died in 1862.

On 12 April 1864, Henry Longley had married Ann Knight of Ditchling, and they lived at Old Selsfield on Selsfield Common with their eight children, all baptised in West Hoathly, namely Henry (1865–1948), Mary (1867–1951), Elizabeth (1868–?), Annie (1870–1945), Flora (1872–1945), Flora's twin, Rosa (1872–1937), Kate (1875–1968) and Frank (1878–1955). Later, for his eldest son Henry, born in 1865, he contracted with his brother, James Longley, a builder, to build Selsfield Place. Two of his maiden daughters lived in the farmhouse nearby.

Besides their local clients, Henry and Charles Longley sold considerable quantities of timber to John and Robert Lee, who lived in Adur Terrace, Southwick. A father and son partnership, they were Carpenters and Shipbuilders with a shipbuilding yard at Kingston by Sea, Shoreham, where they specialised in building high-quality sailing ships. This town had a long history of shipbuilding – in the 16th century, more ships for Henry VIII's navy were built here than anywhere else. The 19th century, however, saw the development of steam-powered vessels which were soon replacing sailing ships, but the Lees could not adapt to this new regime and by 1877 the demand for their vessels was in decline and their business was failing. Robert Lee soon filed for its

Fig.116: Frederick Nash, *Shoreham Harbour, West Sussex*, 1835. Image public domain, original source unknown.

liquidation but in March 1878 a sum of £419.9s.8d due to the Longley brothers for timber supplied, remained unpaid.

Henry's first tenants, after his purchase in 1876, were soon living at Tickeridge Farm; they were brothers John and Joseph Turner, born in Balcombe in 1819 and 1826 respectively, sons of William and Elizabeth. In 1851, Joseph was a Farm Labourer working for Thomas Turner at Naylands Farm, Balcombe, while John was employed as Farm Bailiff to Alexander Cockburn at Wakehurst Place, Ardingly. In 1859, John Turner was married to Amelia Burberry. At first, they lived in Ardingly, where their daughter, Amelia, was baptised on 29 May 1862, one of six children. For many years, John and Amelia shared their accommodation with John's unmarried brothers, Joseph and Richard.

Perhaps at the instigation of the Turner brothers, an additional timber-clad granary was built near the road, in which to store the quantities of grain being grown on the arable land, and a borehole was drilled to enhance the water supply to the farm.

The drilling operation encountered problems when the water flooded the site and its pressure was so great that it proved difficult to cap the supply. Eventually, a Duke and Ockenden pump with an 18in wheel was installed to send the water to tanks in the house. Over the borehole was built a timber-clad pump house, measuring 10ft 6in x 17ft of which only the concrete foundations remain, but see my sketch and plan opposite.

A refurbishment in 1938 confirmed the borehole's depth of 106ft, penetrating the Lower Tunbridge Wells Sands; it was lined with 5in tubes and the water was at 86½ft; a 2½hp Petter engine and other necessary

Fig.117: 19th-century borehole drilling by Dando Pumps

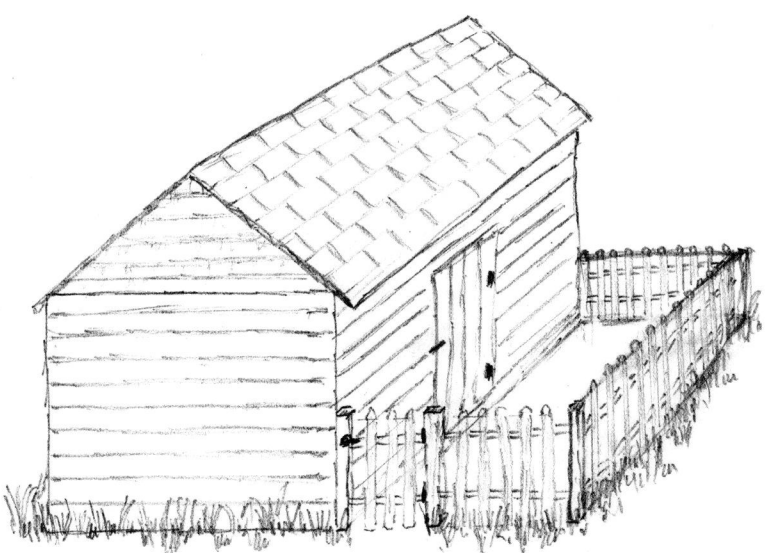

Fig.118: Sketch of pump house over borehole, with wooden tiles on the roof.

Fig.119: Plan of pump house

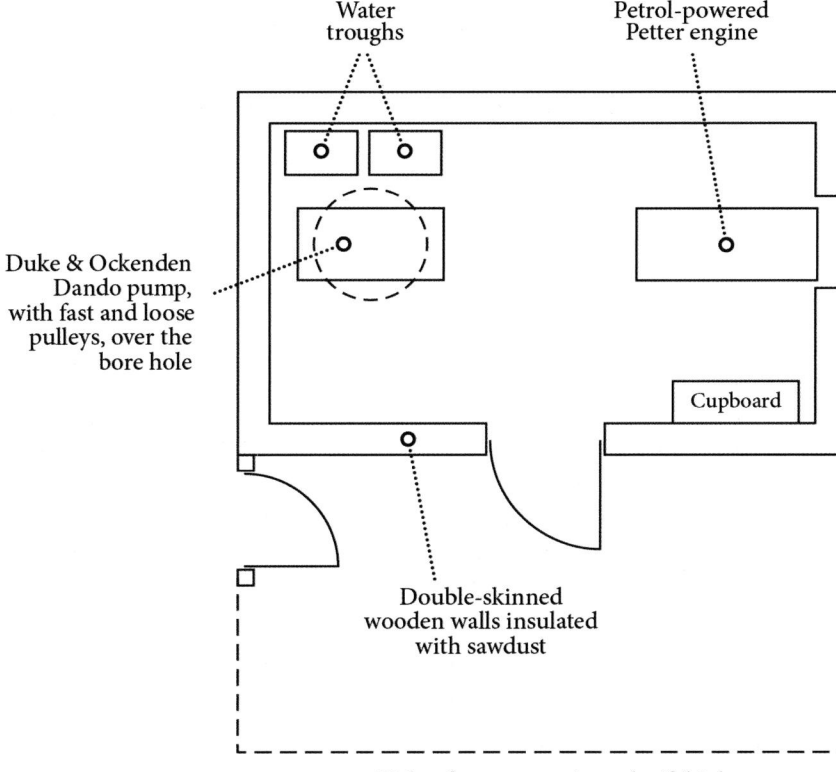

Fig.120: Record of borehole refurbishment, 1938

Fig.121: Remains of Duke and Ockenden deep well pump, April 2005

Fig.122: Site of the borehole and pump house, 2022

equipment was ordered through James Waters & Sons and had been delivered to the farm on 28 July.

The Turner brothers were nothing if not enterprising; when plans for the route of the Lewes and East Grinstead Railway became public in 1878, showing that one of its stations would be located close by, it did not take them long to realise that local travellers may welcome a bevvy or two, so in September 1879, John applied for a license to sell beer at the farm, but his application was refused.

Work on the railway began that year and teams of Navvies arrived; they had a poor reputation for purloining anything on two legs which was edible, but their particular taste was for mutton!

Chapter 20

The Impact of the Railway

For Henry Longley, the railway presented a new business opportunity. Since its route was destined to pass through Tickeridge land, he was able to sell some of it; in June 1880, the railway purchased just over 10 acres from him over which to lay their track and build Kingscote Station.

By September 1880, the section between East Grinstead and Kingscote was almost complete, and the railway was finally opened for public traffic on 1 August 1882. One of its first passengers was Henry's daughter, Kate Longley, born in 1875.

Henry sold off much of the rest of his land on the other side of Vowels Lane but, in 1881, he took the opportunity to buy Holstein (30 acres)

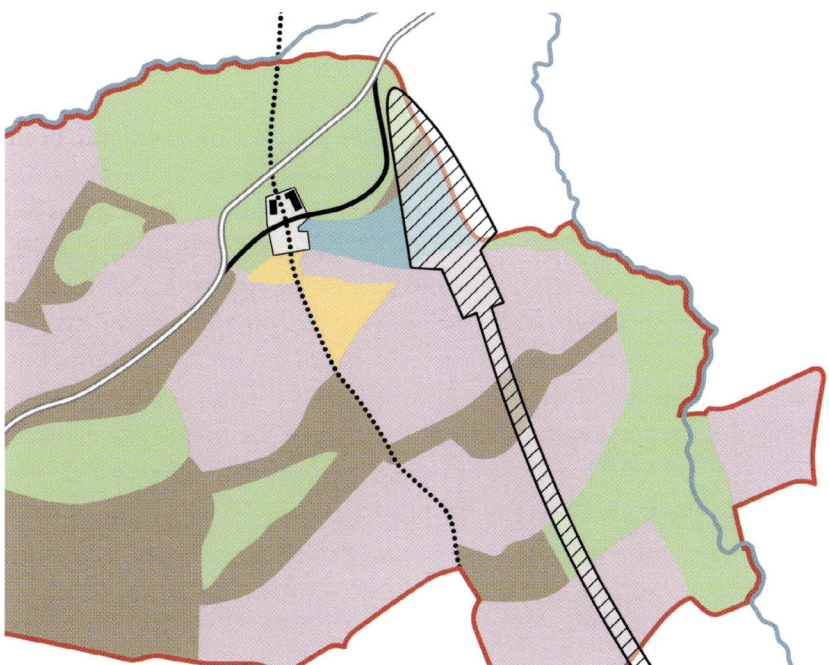

Fig.123: Map of land sold to railway, 1880. Based on West Sussex Record Office document ref. 47,774.

Overlaid on the 1840 tithe map, the land sold to the railway is shown hatched in black. The re-routed Vowels Lane is shown in black.

THE IMPACT OF THE RAILWAY

Fig.124: Longleys Timberyard, photo from Paul Gould

Fig.125: Qwerty keyboard

and Mine Pit (20 acres) Woods for a sum just short of £86, providing a valuable local source of timber for his timberyard which he established beside the railway at Kingscote.

To facilitate access to the railway, Vowels Lane was improved and rerouted past Tickeridge Farm to give direct access to the station. Originally called 'Fowles Lane', recorded in 1846, and 'Bowles Lane' and 'Vowles Lane' in 1898, it may be a coincidence that the typewriter had become standard office equipment in 1874, after which the original name changed. A glance at the Qwerty keyboard may reveal how this happened.

As can be clearly seen, the letters F, V and B are in close proximity to each other and, by a typist, all would be depressed using the left index finger. It is not uncommon for typing errors to be made involving these three letters. I suggest this may be how Fowles Lane morphed, via Bowles Lane, into Vowles Lane in 1899 and eventually into Vowels Lane by 1902, the spelling perhaps 'corrected' by an enthusiastic typist. Of course, once it was on an official document, it became the accepted spelling.

In 1881, George Mason, a young Railway Inspector, was lodging in the other half of Tickeridge farmhouse. He was born on 27 June 1855 in Cobham, Kent, a son of Thomas and Jane Elizabeth Mason (née Ryde) who had married in London in 1846. George obviously had the opportunity to get to know his Turner neighbours well for, on 3 August 1881, in West Hoathly, he was married to John Turner's daughter, Amelia. George's work took him all over the country, but in 1901 he and his family were living in Bushwood Road, Kew and he was Inspector of Works on the new Kew Bridge.

Employed on the farm in the summer of 1891 was William Kemp, aged 15 and living locally with his parents, John and Maryon. Working with the livestock, one of William's tasks was using the chaff cutter to cut up hay and straw to mix with their feed. On 4 July, whilst carrying out some maintenance work on the machine, he slipped and caught his foot in it. William went on to become the Carter at Tickeridge and was married to Mabel Mighall on 7 July 1900. They had several children and lived in West Hoathly, but by 1911 William had changed his job, and was working as a Fish Hawker.

William will have worked with Thomas Rapley who, with his wife, Elizabeth, lived in the house and worked on the farm for nearly ten years. Thomas and Elizabeth had a lodger, William Gibb, who, aged 65 and widowed, worked as a Wood Cleaver, presumably at the timber yard. Born in East Grinstead in 1825, William was a son of Rachel and Richard Gibb; he was still living at Tickeridge in 1901, but died in 1909, aged 84.

Fig.126: Formerly attached to a horse harness, this metal badge was found on the farm. Measuring approximately 2½in x 1¼in, it bears the name "T Rapley"

Thomas Rapley was born on 26 September 1836 in Guy's Cottage, Balcombe, a son of Martha and John, a Farm Labourer. His mother, Martha, was buried in Balcombe on 1 July 1849. John's wages were inadequate to support his family so he moved with his children to live in Cuckfield Workhouse. In 1861, Thomas and his brother, Henry were lodging in the Worth Union Workhouse, in Pound Hill Road, and working as Agricultural Labourers. His marriage in 1864 to Elizabeth Wimhurst of Sevenoaks heralded better times for Thomas Rapley and in the years to come he and Elizabeth moved to Selsfield Common where in 1881 he was employed as a Hoop Maker. He was now local to Tickeridge Farm and had soon moved there to live and work for the next few years, before going to live at Withypitts Farm near Turners Hill, where he and Elizabeth are recorded in the 1901 Census. Elizabeth died in 1907 and Thomas died in 1922.

THE IMPACT OF THE RAILWAY

On 4 January 1899, Henry Longley was granted permission to build Tickeridge Farm Cottages on Vowels Lane opposite his timberyard. In 1900, having harvested its mature timber, he sold Mine Pit Wood to William Robinson of Gravetye.

By the time the Census was taken in March 1901, Henry and Harriet Billings were the tenants at Tickeridge. Henry was born in East Grinstead in 1847, a son of George and Elizabeth. In 1872, he was married to Harriet Stiles, a local girl, born in 1851. They had five sons: Ernest and Harry, born in West Hoathly, Frederick born in Maresfield, and Edwin and Frank, born in Arlington. Having gained his experience as a Farm Labourer, the *Kellys Directory of Sussex*, 1905, records Henry Billings, then aged nearly 60, as Farm Bailiff to Henry Longley at Tickeridge Farm. When he retired, Henry worked as a Gardener, and he and Harriet moved to 155 West Street, East Grinstead, where Harriet died in August 1918 and was buried in Queens Road Cemetery. Their son, Edwin Harold Billings, "Carter of Kingscote", died in June 1913, aged only 25, and was buried at Queens Road Cemetery, so perhaps he too had worked at the farm.

Henry Simmons is recorded as Farm Bailiff at Tickeridge Farm in 1909, and resident there in 1911 as 'Harry' Simmons, demoted to Stockman, born in Kingscote, aged 54, and widowed. Despite an extensive search, I have been unable to find out more about Henry/Harry.

Taking over from him as Farm Bailiff in 1910 was Frederick Buckman. Frederick's grandparents, Edward Buckman and Elizabeth Greenfield, had married in Horsham on 1 June 1817. They made their home in Rudgwick and their son, Thomas, was born there in about 1832. On 7 October 1854, at Itchingfield, near Horsham, Thomas was married to Mary Aylward and a family of four daughters and seven sons followed, including Frederick, who was baptised in Itchingfield on 7 November 1858.

Frederick's father, Thomas Buckman, started his working life as a Farm Labourer but by 1881 had been appointed Farm Bailiff at Bouges Farm, Emms Lane, Brooks Green, Horsham, where he was farming 180 acres, employed by Hugh Penfold, Barrister, Farmer and JP, who lived in Rustington House, Rustington and by whom, later, Thomas' daughter, Alice (b.1873), was employed as Parlourmaid. Thomas and Mary survived into their eighties and ended their days in Norway Cottage, Rustington where they are recorded in the 1911 Census.

In March 1881, Thomas' son, Frederick, then aged 22, was lodging at 1 Peels Street, Brighton in the household of Richard Spyer, Grocer, and working as a Carman, driving a horse-drawn vehicle collecting and delivering goods. Later that year he was married to Margaret Parker, another Brighton resident, working as a Parlourmaid in the household of Hermann Loog, the famous German hatmaker and sewing machine inventor. Margaret was baptised at Southwater on 24 October 1858, a daughter of Allen and Eliza.

By the end of 1882, she and Frederick had married and moved to West Hoathly, where their three daughters were baptised, namely Lilian (baptised 28 January 1883), Rose (baptised 27 December 1885) and Daisy (born 1 June 1888). In 1895, their only son, Allan Thomas, was born in West Chiltington; he served with the Royal Engineers in World War I, survived the war and was married to Elizabeth Bond in 1946. He died in 1953.

In 1891, Frederick Buckman was already working at Tickeridge as a Groom and Domestic Servant. In January that year, he, with William Leppard, a Sawyer, and Frank Longley, Henry's son, went rabbiting in Holstein Wood, bagged nine of them and hung them on a stick between two yew trees but, when Frederick went to fetch them, they had disappeared, which generated a report of the theft in the *Mid Sussex Times*

Fig.127: Tickeridge farmhouse, photographed by Arthur Harding in about 1904. Image reproduced courtesy of East Grinstead Museum

Note: there are outbuildings attached to the 16th-century crosswing, there are no trees hiding the railway in the distance, there are no dormer windows in the roof, and the farm dog has its own private accommodation!

Fig.128: Another metal harness badge found on the farm, measuring approximately 2in x 1½in, and bearing the initials "F B"

Fig.129: Grave of Selina and Frank Longley, photographed in April 2008

of 13 January. There was not enough evidence to convict the suspected thieves, however, and they were discharged. Rabbits were a perennial problem, eating the grass grown for the livestock, but their fur and meat were valued.

William Leppard, mentioned above, had a son, Frank, baptised in West Hoathly on 28 August 1881. It may be a coincidence, but one "Frank Leppard, a young man", pleaded guilty to trespassing on Henry Longley's land at Selsfield in November 1900, in search of rabbits!

The Census for 1901 gives details of Frederick and Margaret Buckman and two of their daughters, Rose and Daisy, and son, Allan Thomas, living at Flaxlands, Liddiard Tregooze, Cricklade, Wootton Bassett near Swindon in Wiltshire where Frederick was employed as the Farm and Timber Yard Foreman.

Why Frederick moved his family to Wiltshire I cannot say, but the experience he gained stood him in good stead for, by the time the Electoral Register for East Grinstead was compiled in 1910, he and his family were back in Sussex and living in the farmhouse at Tickeridge; Frederick had become the Farm Bailiff and was working for Henry Longley as Timber Yard Foreman at Kingscote.

By this time, Frank Longley was living in Oak Lodge with his wife, Selina, whom he had married in 1905. The house had been built in 1904 by his father, Henry, on a plot of Tickeridge land. Selina Longley died in 1941; Frank died in 1955 and was buried at Mount Noddy Cemetery, East Grinstead, in the same grave as his wife.

Chapter 21

Tenant Farmers and Two World Wars

Frederick Buckman's daughter, Daisy, born in 1888, had been courting John Pelling, a local lad, born in Wivelsfield in 1889, who with his father William, worked for Henry Longley at the timber yard. He married Daisy on 28 June 1913. Daisy died in 1976.

On Thursday 11 December 1913, Frederick probably visited the Christmas Fair and livestock auction being held in East Grinstead, with around 50 cattle and some cart horses up for sale.

The poet Edward Thomas was a frequent visitor to the area, and vividly describes that day in his Note Book 67 in which he records his walk into East Grinstead from his lodgings at Selsfield House, the home of his good friend, Vivian Locke Ellis, who was also a poet. He comments on

Fig.130: East Grinstead Fair, photographed in 1900. Image reproduced courtesy of East Grinstead Museum

Fig.131: From the deeds: Map, 1910, showing Tickeridge farmhouse, with its associated paddocks, and Oak Lodge

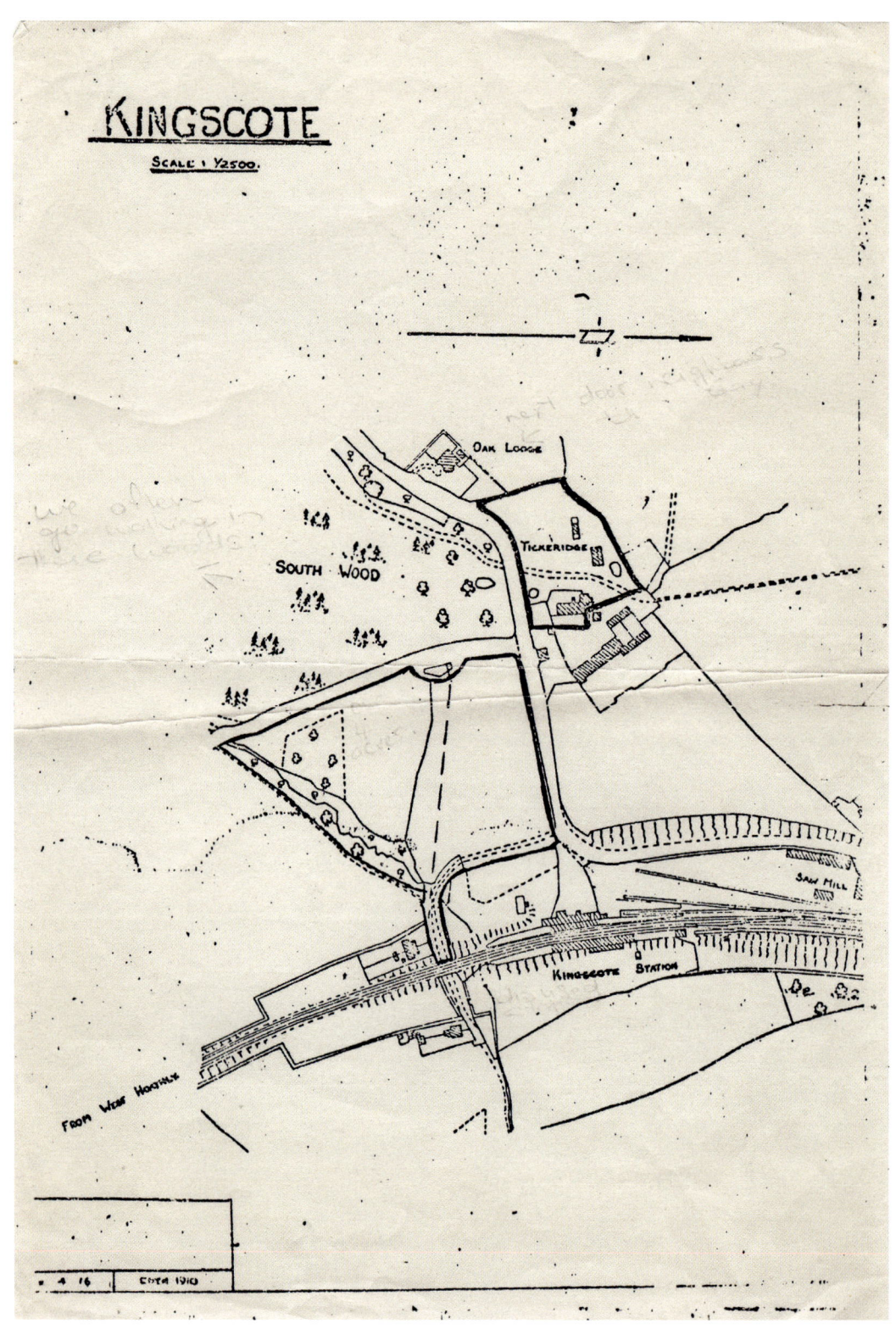

Fig.132: Edward Thomas. Image courtesy of WIkimedia Commons

Fig.133: Sir Alfred James Munnings, *Gypsy Caravan at Ringland Hills*, 1909

the multitude of gypsy caravans on his route, and mentions in particular several parked by Tickeridge, where starlings whistled in the trees. His poem *The Gypsy* records his recollections of the day.[1]

The gypsies brought with them various items for sale, such as aprons and overalls, which local farmers' wives would purchase.

Edward Thomas did not live many years after this visit, for he fought in World War I and was killed in action during the Battle of Arras on 9 April 1917, aged only 39, and was buried in the Military Cemetery at Agny in France. He left his widow, Helen, and three children.

Frederick's neighbour in 1916 was Harold Theodore Elwes, who may have been employed to work on the farm. In February that year, he was fined 15s. for failing to obscure lights on the premises, which were so bright they could be seen from Haywards Heath! Born in Eastbourne on 6 March 1884, Harold was a son of William James Elwes and Henrietta Esther Fletcher, who married in 1873. He died in Herefordshire, "a retired farmer", aged 88.

By 1921, Frederick and Margaret Buckman had moved to Oak Villa, Hamsey Road, West Hoathly, but he appears to have worked for Henry Longley until his death in 1924; he was buried on 31 May in Mount Noddy Cemetery, East Grinstead, in grave 209. Margaret survived him

Fig.134: Grave of Frederick and Margaret Buckman, Mount Noddy Cemetery

---

1. Please see Appendix 10 for Edward Thomas' poem, *The Gypsy*.

TENANT FARMERS AND TWO WORLD WARS

until 1940, when she was buried in the same grave. The inscription on their gravestone reads, "In loving memory of Frederick Buckman. At rest May 27th 1924 Aged 65 years. Also of Margaret his wife who died Sept. 19th 1940 Aged 81 years. Loved by all."

In 1906, Horace and Mary Boakes became the Buckmans' new neighbours at Tickeridge, and Horace worked as a Sawyer at the timberyard. He was a son of Thomas and Frances Boakes of Cowden. Thomas Boakes was born in 1832 and became an Agricultural Worker. In the spring of 1857, he was married to Frances Combes of East Grinstead, and they made their home in Penshurst, Kent, before moving to Kent Water Cottage, Cowden with their daughter and four sons, all four of whom became Agricultural Labourers.

On 16 April 1906, in Cowden, Horace Boakes married Harriette Mary Still (or Mary, as she preferred to be called) who worked as a Domestic Servant. Below are their signatures from their marriage certificate.

Before her marriage to Horace, Mary had given birth to a daughter, Edith Mabel Annie Still, born in the Old Kent Road, Deptford on 2 February 1892. In 1915, in East Grinstead, Edith was married to Horace Gilbert and they had a son, Robin, born in 1916, who later passed on some childhood recollections written by his mother, Edith, in her old age, which included those of her time living at Tickeridge with her mother and stepfather, soon after their marriage. On the following pages are some extracts from her memoir, which give a delightful picture of her life on the farm. (The superscript numbers correspond to notes at the end of the quote which provide further information.)

Fig.135: The marriage certificate of Horace Boakes and Harriette Mary Still

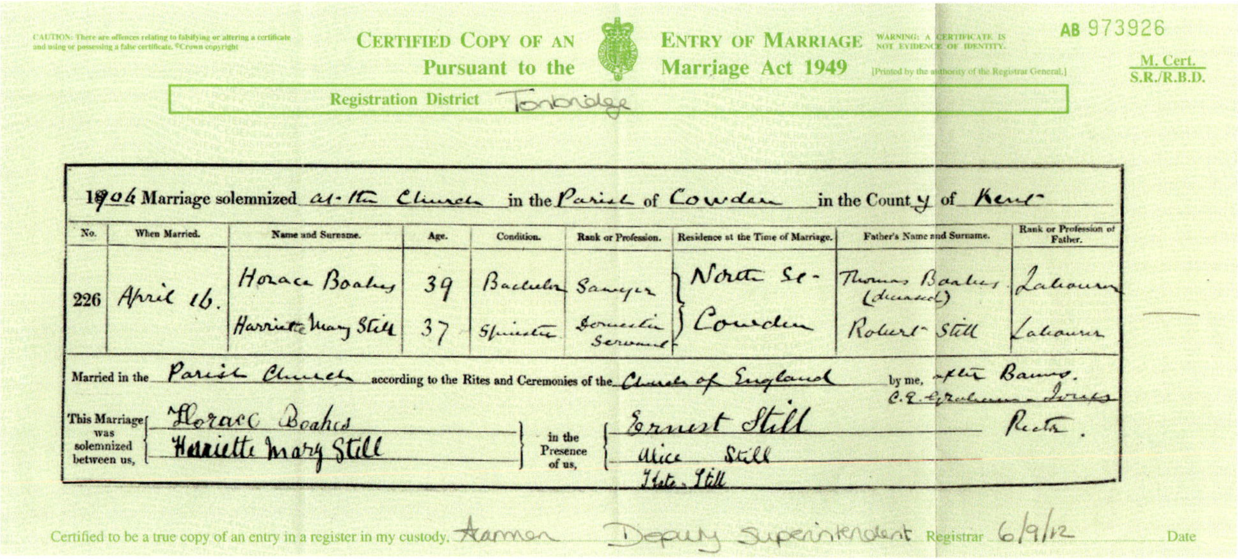

CAUTION: There are offences relating to falsifying or altering a certificate and using or possessing a false certificate. ©Crown copyright

CERTIFIED COPY OF AN ENTRY OF MARRIAGE
Pursuant to the Marriage Act 1949

WARNING: A CERTIFICATE IS NOT EVIDENCE OF IDENTITY.
[Printed by the authority of the Registrar General.]

AB 973926

M. Cert.
S.R./R.B.D.

Registration District Tonbridge

1906 Marriage solemnized at the Church in the Parish of Cowden in the County of Kent

No.	When Married.	Name and Surname.	Age.	Condition.	Rank or Profession.	Residence at the Time of Marriage.	Father's Name and Surname.	Rank or Profession of Father.
226	April 16.	Horace Boakes	39	Bachelor	Sawyer	North St. Cowden	Thomas Boakes (deceased)	Labourer
		Harriette Mary Still	37	Spinster	Domestic Servant	North St. Cowden	Robert Still	Labourer

Married in the Parish Church according to the Rites and Ceremonies of the Church of England by me, after Banns. C. E. Graham Jones Rector.

This Marriage was solemnized between us, Horace Boakes, Harriette Mary Still

in the Presence of us, Ernest Still, Alice Still, Kate Still

Certified to be a true copy of an entry in a register in my custody. Aarmen Deputy Superintendent Registrar 6/9/12 Date

"Kingscote was not even a village. There was the big timberyard, the little station almost joining it; the goods train right into it for the timber to be loaded into the trucks. Straight from the station up the hill was the big farmhouse which belonged to the owner of the timberyard, and where we lived. The big living room had a red brick floor that my mother took great pleasure in polishing, and a long refectory table,[2] with two long forms, one each side; this table, was so polished and shining that it reflected anything that was standing on it.

"But best of all was the enormous fireplace or hearth. The iron fireback was very valuable, although to me it looked just blackened iron. Two benches stood each side.[3] On one my mother would sit and sew, and her sewing basket was always there, except at Christmas time when we had a party, and huge six-foot logs were brought in. We all moved farther and farther back from the blaze.

"Songs and carols were sung, and strange stories were told in the light of the fire. Home-made wine and Christmas fare kept the party going, until the big logs had burned to glowing red embers, when everyone said good-night and went home.

"Mr. Selden and his family always came to our parties; he had the large nursery at the bottom of the hill.

"Then farther along the road was the little tin church run by the Church Army. I went with my mother on Sunday evening, and always enjoyed the singing. A Church Army captain used to take the services, and his sermons were full of 'but yet nevertheless'. I counted twenty, one Sunday night.

---

2. When R.T. Mason visited Tickeridge in 1940, there was a table which he described as "an old table with reversible board". Ursula Ridley visited at about the same time and described the same table as, "a reversible board, at least 4ft. wide, and so large that it must clearly have been made in the room", ascribing it to the Elizabethan period. *The Victoria County History of Sussex,* Volume 7, published in 1940, contains a description of Tickeridge farmhouse and its table, being "an ancient table, 12ft.3in. long by 2ft.9in. wide".

3. Memories of an elderly gentleman visitor to Tickeridge in the 1950s, relayed to me by Heather Chapman: "I can remember coming courting here as a lad. The fireplace brings back memories. When it was really cold in the winter, it used to have benches across each end of the inglenook and we used to take ourselves in there, build up the fire and there were doors you could close to shut it off, to shut yourself in that inglenook; doors you could pull across to keep us really warm." I believe this gentleman may have been John Pelling, who had married Daisy Buckman in 1913.

"I loved the long greenhouses at the nursery, and in the evenings would go down and sometimes help prick out the tiny seedlings. Charlie,[4] Mr. Selden's son who worked for him, one evening gave me a ride on their pony, which was a great thrill, but I had a stern lecture from Sandy[5] when I got home. 'The very idea,' said he, 'a girl riding astride!' He was very strict, so I daren't ride again.

"They were happy days full of little adventures, like going across the field, over the little running brook and another field to fetch the milk,[6] learning to sew. Then my mother had a piano, and after our evening service in the little tin church we would gather round the piano which she would play, and with a friend or two, we would sing. Over the road opposite the farmhouse, was the entrance to Gravetye, William Robinson's famous gardens, and how I enjoyed walking through his flower-starred woods."

---

4. Edith's recollection here is incorrect, since "Mr. Selden" did not have a son called Charles. However, in 1906, when she went to live at Tickeridge, George Head was the Nurseryman at Kingscote, where he grew crops such as cucumbers and tomatoes in the glasshouses, which extended to around 12,500 sq ft. George had been living there since at least 1891 with his wife, Elizabeth, whom he had married in 1876. Born in Lockerley, Hampshire in 1842, George worked as a Gardener at Courtlands, West Hoathly, before taking over the nursery at Kingscote. He and Elizabeth had three children: George, Elizabeth and Charles, who was born in 1889. George Head died on 22 April 1918, aged 76, and the family moved away, though Charles Head had already left the UK in 1912 to live in the USA. It therefore seems that Charles Head was Edith's friend in those early days. After George Head's death, the Selden family moved into the nursery. Born in Hastings in 1867, George Philip Selden had married 23-year-old Maria French in 1890 and their daughter, Lily, was born in Hastings in 1891. In October 1931, their home at Kingscote Nursery was burnt to the ground, the flow from the adjacent river being inadequate to quench the flames. The old house was replaced with a modern bungalow, where they lived until 1938, when the nursery, with its two acres of land and eight glasshouses, was put up for sale and they retired to the New Forest, where George died in 1945 aged 77 and Maria died in 1956, aged 90.

5. I believe "Sandy" was Sir Alexander Rose Stenning, Architect and Surveyor, and JP for East Grinstead, who lived in Hoathly Hill, West Hoathly and was acquainted with Henry Longley. Baptised in Godstone on 16 September 1846, Alexander was a son of William Stenning, a Timber Merchant of Town Farm, Godstone Village, Surrey, and his wife, Elizabeth. In Lewisham, on 30 December 1869, Alexander was married to Theresa Maria Maberly. Created a Knight Batchelor in 1910, Alexander died in Kensington on 22 April 1928 and is buried in the graveyard at St Margaret's, West Hoathly, together with his first wife, Theresa, who died in 1913.

6. From the dairy at Fenland Farm.

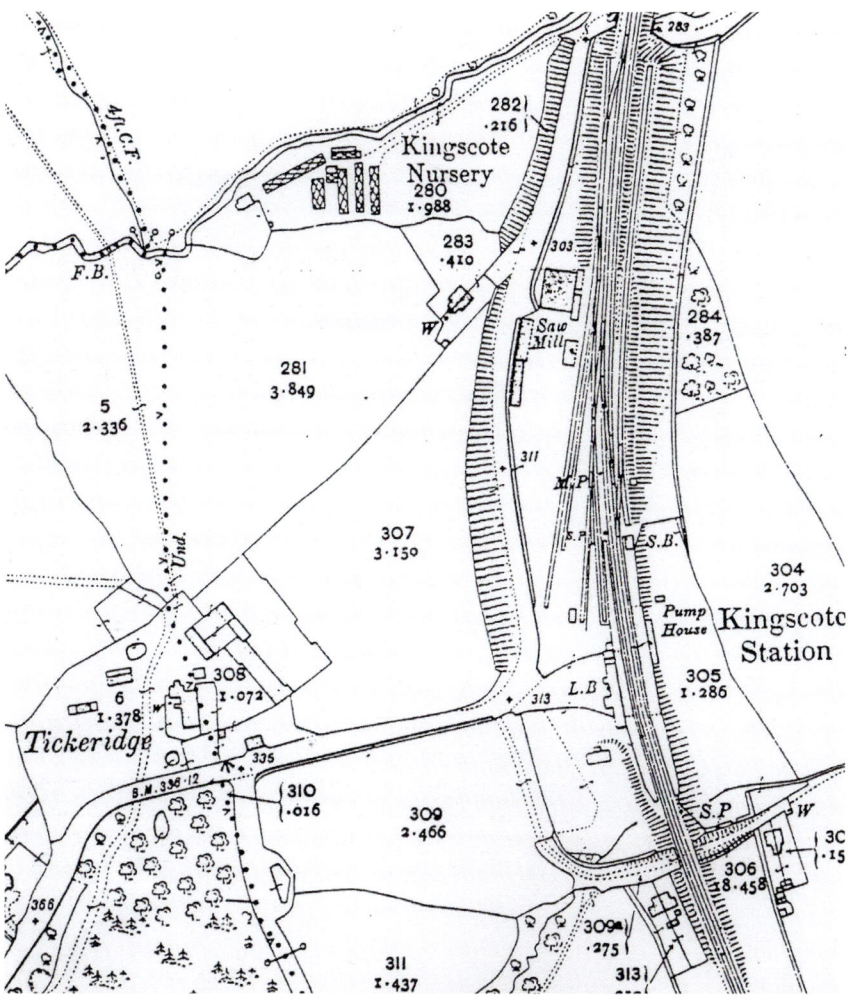

Fig.136: Extract of 1910 OS map showing Kingscote Nursery

Fig.137: Kingscote Nursery, some years later. Photo from Paul Gould

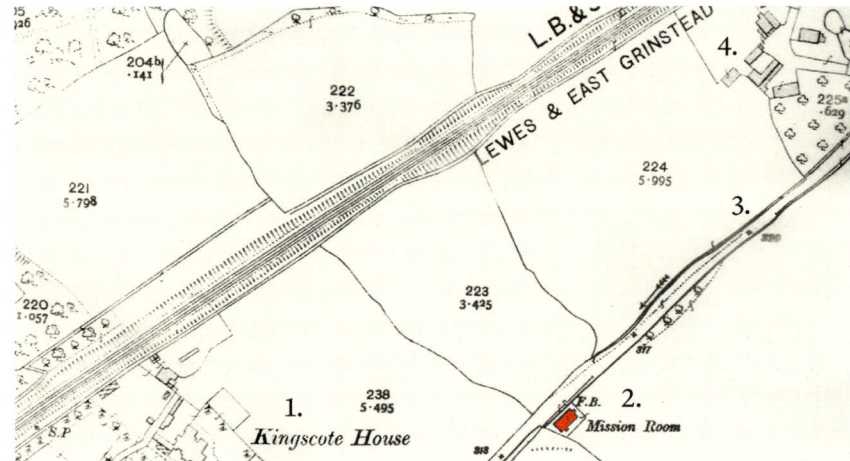

Fig.138: Map showing former location of the Church Army Mission Room on the Turners Hill Road, built in 1902.

1. – Kingscote House
2. – Mission Room
3. – Turners Hill Road, B2110
4. – Hazelden Farm

When he retired, Horace Boakes moved to East Grinstead with his wife Harriette, where she died in 1943, aged 74, and was buried on 18 September that year in Mount Noddy Cemetery, East Grinstead, grave number 434. Horace died nine years later, aged 85, and was buried on 30 December 1952 in the same grave as his wife.

When the Electoral Register was taken in 1935, Ernest Alfred and Daisy Emma Everest were renting accommodation at Tickeridge. Ernest was born in Norwood, Middlesex, in 1884, a son of Robert and Mary, and spent his early working days as a Painter; his father was a Carpenter. As for Daisy, her lineage is a mystery. She was widowed in 1947, when Ernest died aged 63. Daisy died in 1957, aged 63.

In 1910, Thomas and Bertha Simmonds had moved into the other half of the house. Thomas was a son of Edward Simmonds and Amelia Dadswell, both of Crowborough. Edward was baptised in Littlehampton on 8 July 1838, a son of Edward and Eliza Simmonds. Edward and Amelia's banns were read in Crowborough in October 1877, followed by their marriage on 3 November at St John's Church, Withyham, when Edward was an Agricultural Labourer aged 29 and Amelia, daughter of James and Jane, was 21. Edward signed the register, but Amelia made her mark. They went on to have six children: Albert Edward, born in Rotherfield in 1879, Charles, born in Cowden in 1880, Thomas, born in Cowden in 1882, Emily, born in 1884, Harriett, born in Hartfield in 1886, and Arthur James, born in Hartfield in 1888. Charles Simmonds was married to Jane Pocknell in 1912 and they had a son, Sidney Robert, born in 1915, who will feature again later.

Amelia Simmonds died in 1893, aged 37, leaving Edward a widower. He spent his last days in the Union Workhouse, East Grinstead, where he died in 1912.

Thomas Simmonds attended school in Hartfield and by the age of 18 was working as Stockman for Thomas Tester, Farmer, of Smithers Farm, Lingfield, Surrey. In the spring of 1910 he was married to Bertha Jane Coomber who had been born in Lingfield in 1885, a daughter of Harriett and Thomas, he a Sawyer born in Oxted.

Initially, Thomas and Bertha Simmonds made their home on Smithers Farm, where he was already working as a Stockman/Farm Labourer. By 1910, Thomas's brother, Arthur James Simmonds, had taken over as Stockman and Thomas and Bertha were living at Tickeridge, he employed as Working Farm Foreman for H.&F. Longley, Timber Merchants. Their son, Herbert Leslie, was born in 1911. His experience with livestock meant that Thomas worked with the only horse on the farm, which pulled the cart carrying Kale out to the bullocks, as well as looking after the suckler cows and other general work. He is described as being clean-shaven, with very dark curly hair, even in old age; he was very short and thin and walked "from his knees", according to Nobbie Bennett.

In March 1981, I met Nobbie Bennett who knew Henry Longley and worked for him at Tickeridge. By that time, Henry was a large man and used two sticks to aid his walking. Nobbie was born in West Hoathly on 24 January 1903 and registered as William Charles Bennett, a son of Alfred John and Catherine Emma Bennett. He died on 28 August 1987.

Sometime around 1920, an Evans hydraulic ram had been installed in the stream to pump water up to the farm's water troughs.

An inlet pipe, a little further upstream, fed water to the ram.

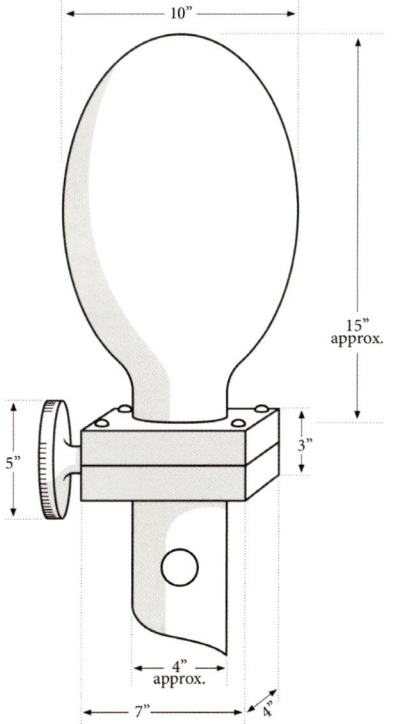

Fig.139: Sketch of Evans ram

Fig.140: Photo of Evans ram, December 2009

Fig.141: Hydraulic ram intake pipe, photographed in 2009

Fig.142: Ox cues
Fig.143: Horn tips

Fig.144: Henry Longley (1837–1922). Image courtesy of Michael Longley

Fig.145: Sussex timber carriage, source unknown

Working oxen had almost disappeared from farms by this time, but evidence of their historical presence at Tickeridge are the two ox shoes or *cues* found on the farm by the SHSS. With cloven hooves, each ox wore two crescent-shaped metal shoes on each hoof. Also found were two ox tips or *knobs*, shown above. These were screwed onto the end of each ox horn to protect the handler from being injured by their sharp points.

By now into his eighties, in 1918 Henry Longley conveyed jointly to his sons Henry and Frank 60 acres of the land which lay in East Grinstead parish, alongside the railway and down to the River Medway, in return for an annuity from them of £100 during his life, which ended on 21 August 1922.

He was buried in Turners Hill. His wife, Ann, died in 1926 and was buried in the same grave.

Their home, Selsfield Place, was put up for sale, with its farm buildings, nine cottages, blacksmiths and wheelwrights' shops and 110 acres.

Working with the horses at Tickeridge was Joseph Henley; he had been born in Petworth, and baptised there on 9 January 1859, a son of John and Eliza. As a young man he was employed as a Carter for Longley & Sons, Timber Merchants, driving a four-wheeled timber tug with six horses. The back wheels of the tug slid on a central pole so that its length could be adjusted to carry two or three tree trunks.

On 11 October 1891, at All Saints, Crawley Down, Joseph was married to Mary Louisa Styles of Turners Hill. Their first home was in Grange Road, Crawley Down, where two daughters and a son were born. Around 1901, the family moved to Kingscote, accommodated in one of the farm cottages, where seven more daughters and two more sons were born. Joseph's health began to fail in 1924 and he died at home in Tickeridge

Fig.146: Grave of Henry and Ann Longley (d. 1922 and 1926), parish church of St Leonards, Turners Hill

Fig.147: An early photo of Selsfield Place, kindly given to me by Michael Longley

Cottage on 8 October 1927, aged 68; he was buried at Mount Noddy Cemetery, East Grinstead. Worn by one of his horses, he treasured this brass, given to me by his grandson, Pat Stone.

The two Longley brothers, Frank and Henry, dissolved their partnership in 1929, and the live and dead stock on the farm was sold off at an auction held on 1 October. The catalogue (see overleaf) featured, amongst other things, a large collection of farm and timber machinery, "3 excellent dairy cows", various other cattle, and "2 strong and active cart horses, Darling, a bay mare and Smiler, a brown mare, which had worked regularly in all gears and on the road." Perhaps one of them wore the large horseshoe found on the farm.

Fig.148: Horse brass, 9cm in diameter

TENANT FARMERS AND TWO WORLD WARS

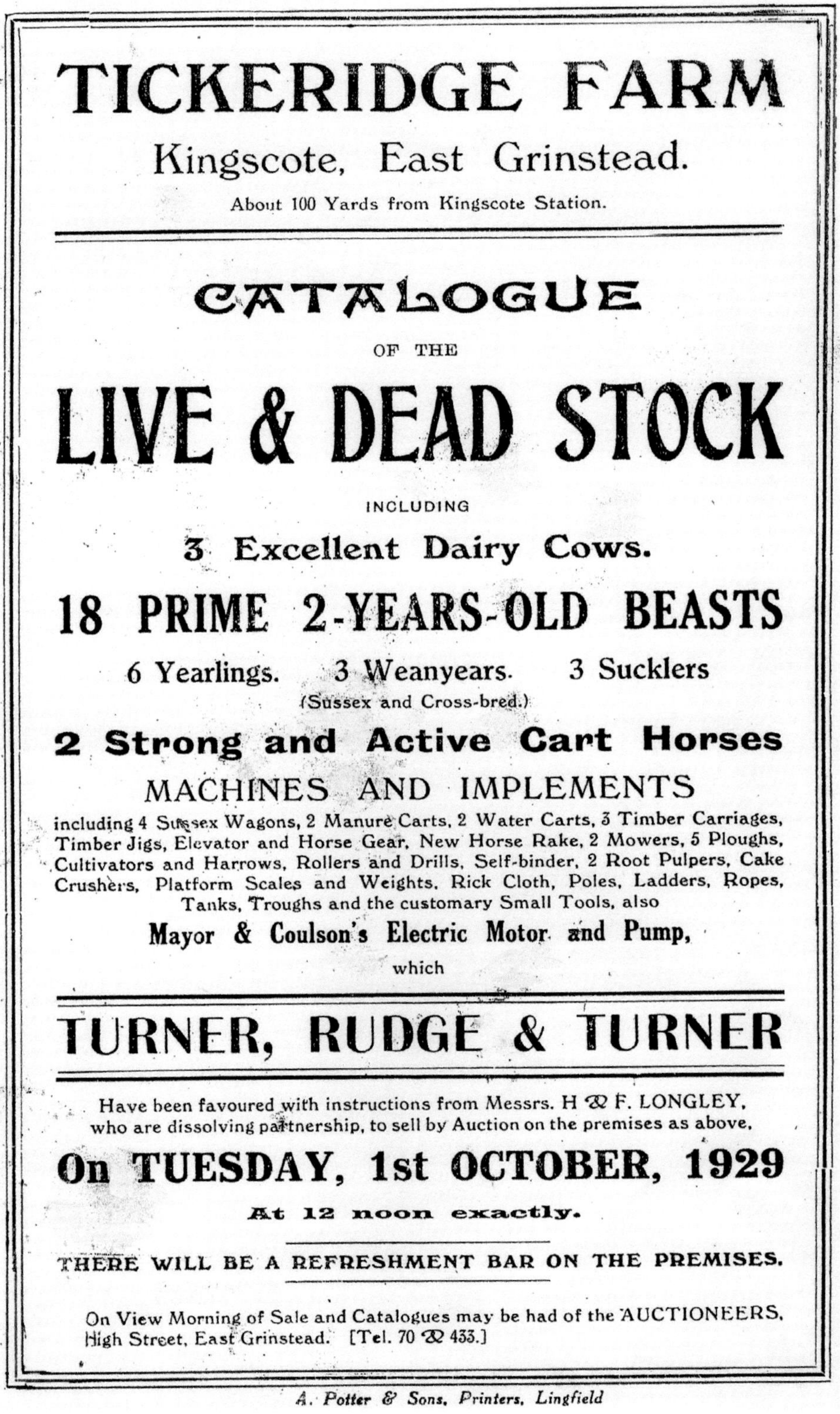

Fig.149: Sale catalogue/poster

TICKERIDGE FARM

Kingscote, East Grinstead.

About 100 Yards from Kingscote Station.

CATALOGUE

OF THE

LIVE & DEAD STOCK

INCLUDING

3 Excellent Dairy Cows.

18 PRIME 2-YEARS-OLD BEASTS

6 Yearlings.   3 Weanyears.   3 Sucklers

(Sussex and Cross-bred.)

2 Strong and Active Cart Horses

MACHINES AND IMPLEMENTS

including 4 Sussex Wagons, 2 Manure Carts, 2 Water Carts, 3 Timber Carriages, Timber Jigs, Elevator and Horse Gear, New Horse Rake, 2 Mowers, 5 Ploughs, Cultivators and Harrows, Rollers and Drills, Self-binder, 2 Root Pulpers, Cake Crushers, Platform Scales and Weights, Rick Cloth, Poles, Ladders, Ropes, Tanks, Troughs and the customary Small Tools, also

Mayor & Coulson's Electric Motor and Pump,

which

TURNER, RUDGE & TURNER

Have been favoured with instructions from Messrs. H & F. LONGLEY, who are dissolving partnership, to sell by Auction on the premises as above.

On TUESDAY, 1st OCTOBER, 1929

At 12 noon exactly.

THERE WILL BE A REFRESHMENT BAR ON THE PREMISES.

On View Morning of Sale and Catalogues may be had of the AUCTIONEERS, High Street, East Grinstead. [Tel. 70 & 433.]

A. Potter & Sons, Printers, Lingfield

At this time, Viscountess Frances Garnet Wolseley was living at Culpepers in Ardingly and enjoying discovering the local villages. On one of her travels, she passed down Vowels Lane and recorded her visit as follows; "Before reaching Kingscote Station, I wish to draw attention to an old timber and plaster house on the left, which in spite of a modern tiled roof shows many signs of antiquity. The narrow terraces of flower beds below it, outlined by rick stools, are attractive features, and to those who enjoy as I do hunting up the early history of old houses, this one, named Tickeridge, will provide plenty of opportunity for research." How right she was!

In 1927, Joseph Simmons had joined the staff at Tickeridge as Farm Bailiff to Frank Longley. Born in 1903, Joe or Joseph Simmons was a son of Joseph and Elizabeth Simmons, Farmers of Charlwood Farm, Forest Row. In 1928 he was married to Daisy Jones and they set up home near the farm, apparently not living in the house. Joe left his job at the farm soon after 1938.

Joe and Daisy will have known Alfred Ansfield who lodged at Tickeridge Farm and was employed as Gamekeeper to Major Higgin of Ridge Hill. Alfred was the fourth son of Edward and Eliza of Slaugham; in 1935 he was engaged to be married, but was suffering from severe mental stress and, aged only 22, shot himself in the chest on Wednesday 13 March. His father, also a Gamekeeper, found his body in woods at Ridge Hill.

For Thomas and Bertha Simmonds too, tragedy was to strike when the conflict of World War II claimed their only son. Herbert had married Hilda Mary Brand on 11 September 1937 at St Johns, Hurst Green and their daughter, Jean, was born two years later. They lived at The Beeches, Holland Lane, Oxted in Surrey.

Herbert was a keen footballer for his local Oxted team and was Captain of the second eleven, but in December 1942 he joined the Royal Artillery 186 Field Regiment as a Gunner; he survived just three months. Aged only 32, Herbert was killed on 13 March 1943, but his remains were never found. For his service to his country, he was awarded two posthumous campaign medals, the 1939–45 Star, and the War or 'Victory' Medal, and his sacrifice is recorded at the Brookwood Memorial to the Missing in Surrey, panel 3, column 3.

Sometime before 1939, Charles Foster was the farm's tenant, living in the northern part of the farmhouse, which was accessed via wooden steps from the farmyard.

Born on 17 August 1879, Charles was a son of Isaac and Jane, sometime of Ridge Hill, Turners Hill, and Hurley and Hazelden Farms, Kingscote,

Fig.150: Herbert Leslie Simmonds on his wedding day, 1937. *Sevenoaks Chronicle & Kentish Advertiser*, Friday 17 September 1937

Fig.151: Brookwood Memorial to the Missing, 1939–1945

Fig.152: Herbert's memorial at Brookwood Cemetery

who had married in 1876. In 1902 he was married to Charlotte Smith from Worcestershire, known as Lottie. Before moving to Tickeridge, Charles and Charlotte lived at Harwoods Farm, East Grinstead, where Charles was Farm Foreman. They had four children: Dorothy Ellen, Gilbert Charles, Harold Goodwin and Roland.

A survey of the farm, taken on 1 October 1942, recorded that Swedes and Oats were being grown and, though on heavy land, its arable land was said to be adequately fertilised and its pasture was treated with lime; both were in good condition. There were 41 head of cattle and two working horses. Its farmhouse, buildings, farm roads, fences and ditches were all well maintained, and rats and mice were under control, but rabbits, moles, rooks and wood pigeons were a problem. In addition to the well, there was a piped water supply to the farmhouse and buildings, but no public electricity supply. The survey concluded that it was a good farm, well managed and rated B+.

At this time, the lean-to shed on the southern end of the barn had a calf pen at one end and stalls for a few dairy cows, which were hand milked; their dung was merely shovelled outside.

When Charles retired, he and Charlotte moved to The Hollies, Turners Hill, where they both died and were buried in the village churchyard. Charles died in 1950, aged 71 and Charlotte died in 1966, aged 85.

The devastating effects of World War II were felt locally when, in April 1940, a bomb fell on Hurley Farm nearby and, in September, Mill Place Farm was hit by a cluster of incendiaries.

Preparations for attack included mined roads and barbed wire entanglements, anti-tank cones of concrete, and sheets of clear plastic stuck over windows to prevent shattered glass causing injury. In 1941, Canadian troops were quartered on Ashdown Forest and their Officers were stationed at Gravetye. In February 1942, the 116 District Ammunition Depot was established in Gravetye woods, with a variety of munitions stored in dozens of small tin huts. The railway played a vital part in bringing the munitions to Kingscote, which were transported from the station by lorry, into the woods near Kingscote Cottage, and unloaded via the ramp which still survives there.

Fig.153: Charles Foster, centre, in October 1948

Fig.154: World War II lorry loading ramp, photographed in 2005

The Pioneer Corps manned a checkpoint with a sentry box, sited near the end of the lane to Mill Place, to restrict access to the Gravetye woods; concrete and brick remnants of a small structure still remain just beyond the southern boundary of fields belonging to Tickeridge.

Perhaps a member of the Corps dropped the tin, from a NAAFI canteen

Fig.155: Tin lid from NAAFI Stores

Figs.156 and 157: Remnants of the small structure by the lane to Mill Place, measuring 12ft x 16ft, photographed in 2025

Fig.158: Concrete blocks from the gun emplacement on the farm

Fig.159: James Edward Moon, c.1915. Photo by kind permission of the West Hoathly Archives Collection

pack, some 3½in x 3in and embossed with the words, "NAAFI STORES FOR H.M. FORCES", found on the farm by a member of the SHSS.

At Kingscote Station, trains loaded with tanks occupied the sidings, an anti-aircraft gun emplacement was located on the farm, and searchlights were located all around the area.

Then suddenly, in early June 1944, the ammunition and the soldiers were gone from Gravetye to play their part on the Normandy beaches. That same month, 'doodlebugs' or flying bombs started to arrive.

During the war, Frank Longley gave up active farming and, having let the farm, he disposed of his own live and dead stock at an auction held on Friday 7 May 1943. His livestock included two cows, twenty-six in-calf and other heifers, a Shorthorn bull, two cart horses, and the usual implements and machinery, including plough rolls, three wagons, two carts, mowers, two hay swoops, an elevator, 650 cleft Chestnut fencing posts and various other items.

Thomas and Bertha Simmonds continued to live at Tickeridge until Thomas retired, when they moved to 4 Westcote Cottages, West Hoathly. They both died in Kent, probably in Cowden, Thomas in 1958, aged 76, and Bertha in 1964, aged 78.

Jo and Lucy Simmonds remained on the farm throughout the war and a local agricultural contractor, James Edward Moon from West Hoathly, and his son, Robin, known as Bob, worked with Jo, as did Eddie Budgen.

Born Edmund James on 5 July 1881, a son of Isaac and Margaret Budgen, Eddie was married in 1908 to Kate Annie Covey and they lived at Withypitts, Turners Hill. Kate died in 1971, and Eddie died in 1976.

Besides his agricultural contracting work, James Edward Moon also transported materials for the large rockery opposite Preston Park in Brighton. He was born on 7 April 1897 in Buxted, a son of Jasper and Elizabeth. In 1915, he joined the Navy in Barrow-in-Furness, Lancashire,

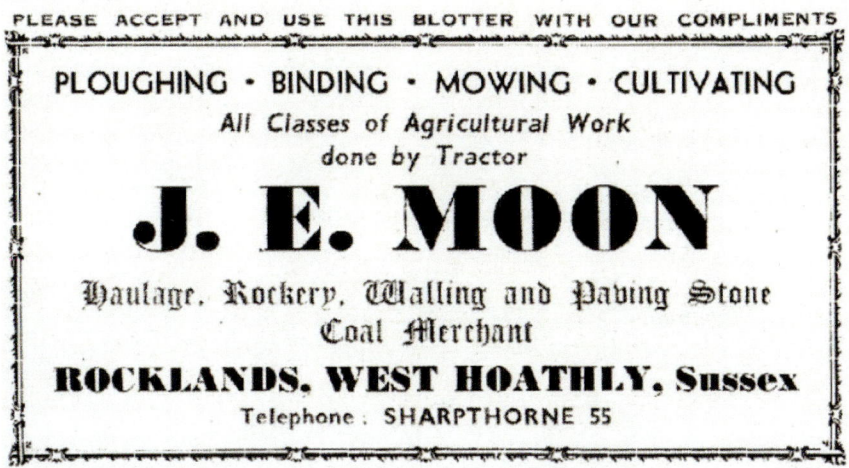

Fig.160: J.E. Moon advertising blotter, from the West Hoathly Archives collection, with their kind permission

where he met Ethel Worrall, whom he married in 1920. Their union produced three sons, all born in West Hoathly, namely Sidney in 1929, Robin Dennis in 1930 and Colin in 1932.

James Edward Moon died in 1950, his son, Bob, in 2007.

In 2005, I met with Arthur Bowers, who told me that his father, Charles Alfred Bowers, the local haulier, employed a driver called James Muggridge. Born in 1899, James was married to Elsie Jenden in 1942, and soon afterwards they rented accommodation in Tickeridge farmhouse, where they lived for about four or five years.

During the 1940s and 50s, Doris Rice and Joan Bingham Aske used the Bothy or 'Wendy House' in the garden at Tickeridge as an art studio, often joined by hens who would casually wander in and out. Built sometime after 1910, of timber-framed construction, clad in asbestos sheeting and with a clay-tiled roof, this small building had previously been used by three shooting syndicates as their lunching room.

Doris, born in 1920, was a daughter of Joseph and Dora Rice, and a granddaughter of Sophia and Joseph Rice, Managing Director of Rice Bros., East Grinstead. She was tall, well-built and fair-haired; she died in 1963 following complications after a minor operation.

Joan was born on 19 March 1918, the daughter of Captain Eric Bingham Ackerley, who bought the 300 acres of Tickeridge Farm from Frank Longley in 1948. Formerly of the Cheshire Regiment, Eric and his wife, Winifred, whom he had married in 1915, lived at Westcote Farm, now called Duckyls, on the Selsfield Road, West Hoathly.

Eric Ackerley was born in Liverpool in 1892, the son of Francis and Emily, and started his working life as a Fire Insurance Clerk, before becoming a partner in an agricultural produce business, until it was

Fig.161: James Edward Moon *c.* 1948, courtesy of James Moon jnr.

Fig.162: Bob (Robin) Moon

TENANT FARMERS AND TWO WORLD WARS

Figs.163 and 164: Tickeridge farmhouse in 1942, west elevation and South elevation. *Source: Sussex Archaelogical Collections*, vol.82, 1942, p.66)

Note the buildings on the 16th-century extension have been removed, but the rick stools are still in position at the south end.

TICKERIDGE: WEST SIDE

TICKERIDGE: SOUTH END

Fig.165: The Bothy or 'Wendy House', 2002

Fig.166: Doris Rice, Painting of the west elevation of Tickeridge farmhouse, 1942

dissolved in 1920. Eric and Winifred lived in Liverpool, before moving to Cobham in Surrey, where their daughter, Joan, was married to Robert Edward Aske in January 1940. Joan and Robert's only son, Robert John Bingham Aske, later became the 3rd Baronet Aske.

I am indebted to Sir Robert for his memories conveyed to me in 2010. As a child, he visited Tickeridge farmhouse and, whilst there, noticed what he thought was mud in the corner of a window but, when poked with a lolly stick, the bat flew away!

At that time, the Lewes and East Grinstead Railway was still operating, and he remembered one day when the train arrived at Kingscote Station, "the box car at the back burst open, and a group of horses clambered out, cart horses, riding ponies, all sorts".

Following his purchase, Captain Ackerley installed a sewage system and cesspit, and an internal WC for the northern end of the house, but tenants who lived in the other half still had the use only of a chamber pot or the privy outside.

To manage Tickeridge Farm, Captain Ackerley employed Duncan Linton from Callander in Scotland, who moved into the northern half of the house with his wife Joey and two sons, John and James.

With their shared Scottish ancestry, they soon became friends with John and Jean Bayne of Old House Farm, Ardingly, and visited each other's homes. Jean recalled how at Tickeridge, from the ground floor, she could see shafts of light from the bedroom above as there was no ceiling and the floorboards were uncovered. She also related the tale of Duncan's narrow escape from injury when, driving his Standard Fordson

Fig.167: Outside WC photographed in 2005. Once the house was further modernised, it was used as a dog kennel!

Fig.168: Duncan and Joey Linton. *Source:* Mid-Sussex Caledonian Society Newsletter

tractor down Vowels Lane, it missed a gear, trundled down the lane, out of control, veered into the station yard and came to a grinding halt.

A long, narrow kitchen garden ran parallel to Vowels Lane, and, in 1949, Captain Ackerley had a rockery created below the south end of the house.

After the war, tenants again briefly occupied the other half of the house – in June 1947, William George and Josefine Gladman were living there. William George Gladman was born in Lewes in 1881, a son of William and Mary Ann who in 1891 were living at Peacelands, Ardingly, where William worked as an Agricultural Labourer. By 1901 they were living in Lindfield, and William was employed as the Farm Carter and then as Cowman. Meanwhile, William George, his son, worked in the local laundry.

Josefine, William George's wife, was a daughter of Stephen and Gertrude Link of Baden in Germany, where she was born on 2 February and baptised on 19 March 1900. She and William George Gladman were married in Uckfield in 1925. William George Gladman died in 1957, aged 76 and Josefine died in 1969, aged 69.

Fig.169, *opposite*: aerial view of Tickeridge Farm, Kingscote Station and the greenhouses of Kingscote Nursery, May 1947, courtesy of Historic England

Chapter 22

The House and Farm Part Company

After Captain Ackerley died in 1951, aged 58, his widow, Winifred, and their daughter, Joan, put Tickeridge Farm and its house on the market, the whole described as "An extensive agricultural and sporting property, charming 16th century farmhouse, pair of cottages, with light, well-watered arable and pasture" with 200 acres of land. It was soon snapped up by John and Elsie Chapman and their daughter, Heather, who jointly purchased Tickeridge Farm, its house, and 1 Tickeridge Cottages, on 24 June 1953, for £21,000. The Lintons vacated the house and moved to Kent.

John Chapman had an import/export business and was a Builder, of the firm Chapman & Sons Builders Merchants, of Tamworth Road, Croydon. It took about a year of work on the house to refurbish its lower portions with brickwork and make repairs and alterations. Amongst these, the inglenook was modified to form a smaller fireplace, and three windows in the roof were created for the first-floor rooms facing west. The large tree growing at the front of the house was removed and a porch built.

Once all the work was completed, John and his family were able to move in from their home at Povey Cross Farm, Reigate Road, Hookwood, near Gatwick Airport.

I am indebted to Heather's daughter, Elizabeth, for sharing her memories of living at Tickeridge with her mother and grandparents. She recalls that an Aga cooker was installed in the kitchen, along with an electric washing machine; there was a central island in the kitchen with a red and white Formica worktop, and lots of drawers. The lounge had a long dining table with sofas, armchairs and a Murphy Console television. From the entrance hall there was a wide flight of stairs up to a balcony around all four sides of the bay. Off this balcony were two bedrooms and a bathroom.

Fig.170: Heather Sargent, photographed on 10 March 2005

The main bedroom was in the middle of the house, spanning its width, with windows on both sides. "My grandparents told me that the cupboard in their bedroom was a priest's hole. A stained-glass window was above the staircase in their bedroom."

Living in the house at Kingscote Station were Ernest and Marjorie Marshall. Ernest William Marshall was born on 27 November 1922; he had married Marjorie M. Robinson in 1946 and they had lived at Kingscote since 1951, where Ernest, or 'Ernie', was employed as Porter-Signalman. In 2005, I enjoyed some time with Heather, who told me that Mrs. Marshall, known as 'Marshie', was employed by her mother, Elsie Chapman, to help with the housework. Mrs. Covey, from Turners Hill, also helped in the house.

Elizabeth recalled that many happy days were spent paddling in the stream and walking in the woods carpeted in Bluebells; as a young child, when there was little traffic on Vowels Lane, she could safely pedal her tricycle down to Kingscote Station to see Mr. and Mrs. Marshall. On one of her visits, she was tasked with collecting some eggs from them

Fig.171: Old door into west-facing bedroom in the south wing. Photographed in 2002

Fig.172: Tickeridge farmhouse, photograph by Alan Duncan. *Sussex County Magazine*, Volume 29, Number 11, November 1955, p.515

but unfortunately, no consideration had been taken as to the poor state of the road surface. Placed in the little carrier on the back of the tricycle, many of the eggs failed to survive the bumpy ride back to the farm!

The Marshalls left Kingscote in 1968.

Heather was a keen horsewoman and kept her own hack, and a pony for Elizabeth. On quiet roads, it was safe for Heather, riding her horse Matilda, and leading the pony, Candy, to fetch Elizabeth from her kindergarten at Fonthill Lodge, from where they both rode home. Dogs and cats were the other family pets.

Electricity for the farmhouse and milking parlour was provided by a generator in the dairy, and water came via a private supply from Barkhamridge Kennels, further up Vowels Lane, where Miss Ethel Dorothy Bass lived in a caravan and operated dog kennels.

Fig.173: East elevation of milking parlour and dairy, 2010, before conversion

Fig.174: One of the stable floor bricks

Fig.175: West elevation of milking parlour, 2005

To accommodate his herd of around 25 dairy cows (initially Jerseys, but by 1957 Shorthorns), John rebuilt an old shed to create a Fullwood abreast milking parlour, with Alfa Laval equipment. Adjacent was the dairy and generator room, and a stable with black quartered bricks on the floor.

The milk was poured into ten-gallon churns which were labelled with details of the quantity and source, sealed, then taken out to the roadside where they were placed on the metal churn stand which had been fabricated at John's builders' yard. The churns were collected by lorry and taken to United Dairies' Curtis & Dumbrill milk depot and bottling plant in Valley Road, Streatham. Clean churns were left by the lorry for use the next day.

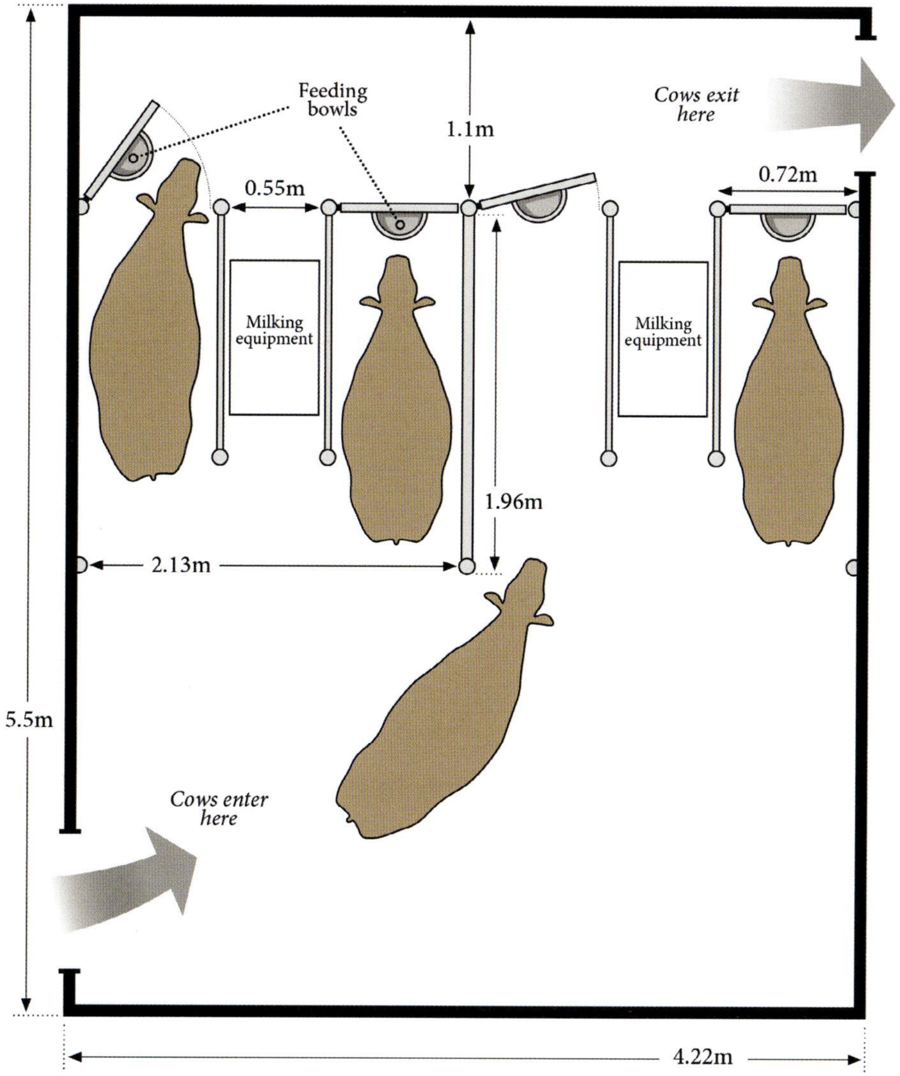

Fig.176: Plan of abreast milking parlour at Tickeridge, now part of the Annexe

Fig.177: Photo of metal churn stand, taken in 2025. Kindly returned to the farm by Alan Reed

Fig.178: Curtis & Dumbrill dairy and milk bottling plant, Valley Road, Streatham, 1926

THE HOUSE AND FARM PART COMPANY

Fig.179: Remains of cattle feed trough outside milking parlour, 2005

Fig.180: The collecting yard, photographed in 2005

Fig.181: After milking, the cows would collect in this yard before going out to graze. Photo taken in spring 1979, when the yard was still in use for beef cattle

Fig.182: Derelict stables in January 1998, with straw bales stored in the yard

Fig.183: Remains of the stables in 2005

Store cattle were reared and transported to Haywards Heath or East Grinstead markets in cattle trucks run by Arthur Bowers, the local haulier. Crops included Wheat, Hay, silage and Kale.

Henry Filtness was the senior worker on the farm; he drove the Fordson Major tractor and milked the cows in the new parlour. Henry William Filtness was a son of Henry and Naomi; born on 11 February 1908 in West Hoathly, he married Kathleen Minnie Hyder in 1935 and they had five sons (Henry K., Donald C., Peter J., Michael J., and Dennis R.) and a daughter (Marigold J.), born between 1936 and 1947. Henry William and his family were accommodated in 2 Tickeridge Cottages. At busy times of the year, he would go to West Hoathly to recruit additional workers. Henry William died in 1974.

Some small stables were built beyond the courtyard wall (demolished in 2005), and a WC for the farm workers who tended the land, which

included growing crops of Mangolds (or Fodder Beet). A large, open-fronted shed was erected north-east of the ancient barn.

The local expert on medieval houses, R.T. Mason, who lived in Balcombe, visited Tickeridge several times, sporting a moustache and wearing a Trilby hat. In 1955, he was approached by John Chapman in regard to some queries he had about Tickeridge. Reg Mason's letter in response is shown below:

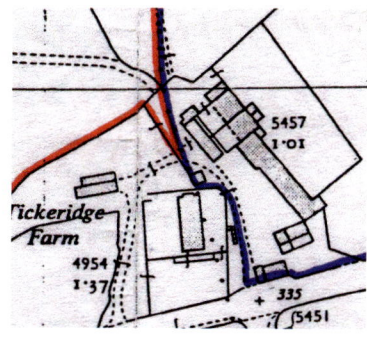

Fig.184: OS map TQ3635 of Tickeridge Farm, 1956

```
R. T. MASON. A.I.A.S.                    OAKFIELD COTTAGE.,
                                         NEWLANDS,
12.7.55.                                 BALCOMBE,
                                         SUSSEX.

                      Telephone. Balcombe 250.


Dear Mr. Chapman,
           Thank you for your letter of 8th June, in which you mention
a number of interesting points connected with Tickeridge. Perhaps
you will bear with me while I comment on them in the same order.

           Firstly, Sussex County Magazine can be got from any local
Newsagent and costs 1/6d monthly. The photographs are alwasy a delight.

           (a). John Beneke, according to my information may have belonged
to either Tickeridge or Pickeridge - both in West Hoathly. I have never
heard that he was an ironmaster but 1500 would be a bit early for the
local ironworks which really got going about 1570. The two nearest
Tickeridge were Gravetye and Mill Place. As you say, Mrs. Ridley may
have some further information.

           (b). I had a good look at the Barn in 1940 and it is indeed
a very fine one. I should think it is certainly the longest barn in
Sussex. I do not believe it is as old as the house.

           (c). I noted that your spit rack and jack was still in position.
When I saw the house in 1940 the old table, with reversable board also
was still there.

           I do not think there could have been many such survivals in
existence then. Still fewer now, of course.

           Thank you again for your kindness.

                           Yours sincerely,

                               R. T. Mason.
```

Fig.185: Letter from R.T. Mason to John Chapman, 12 July 1955

In spite of all his renovation and building works, in April 1957 John Chapman appointed Joint Agents Wm. Wood, Son & Gardner of Crawley, and Knight, Frank & Rutley of London, to put the house and farm on the market. It was described by them as "in beautiful unspoilt country, a first-rate residential T.T. and Attested farm of about

TICKERIDGE FARM

Kingscote, Near East Grinstead — Sussex and Surrey Borders

East Grinstead 2½ miles   London 30 miles

A First-class Residential T.T. Attested Farm of about 230 Acres

A beautiful 15th century house, recently restored and modernised at considerable cost and now in immaculate order.

Three Reception Rooms   Five Bedrooms   Two Bathrooms
Oil-fired Central Heating   Main Water and Electricity

EXCELLENT RANGE OF BUILDINGS WITH MILKING PARLOUR
PAIR OF MODERNISED COTTAGES

The property includes good grass and arable and about 100 acres of woodland and forms a capital small Sporting Estate

JOINT AGENTS & AUCTIONEERS:

WM. WOOD, SON & GARDNER   **KNIGHT, FRANK & RUTLEY**
Crawley, Sussex.   20, Hanover Square, London, W.1
Tel.: No. 1. (three lines) and at Horley, Surrey   *Tel.:* MAYfair 3771 (15 lines)

Fig.186, *opposite*: Estate agent's particulars for the sale of the farm in April 1957

Fig.187: Tickeridge farmhouse, south elevation, April 1957

230 acres... an excellent range of buildings with milking parlour and a pair of modernised cottages... good grass and arable land, about 100 acres of woodland and forms a capital small sporting estate." The "beautiful 15th [sic] century house, carefully restored and modernised at considerable cost and now in immaculate order". It comprised three reception rooms, five bedrooms, two bathrooms, oil-fired central heating and mains water and electricity.

Chapter 23

Progress in the 20th Century

Fig.188: The farm buildings which used to stand by Vowels Lane, 1957
1. – Bull pen
2. – Big granary
3. – Tractor shed
4. – Silage pit
5. – Churn stand
6. – Farm sign
7. – Lean-to-granary

JOHN SOON HAD A CHANGE OF HEART, however, and, in 1958 instructed Powell and Partner, Agents in Forest Row, to place just Tickeridge Farm on the market. At the time, Gilbert William Ernest Reed, living at Grange Farm, Southwater, was looking to buy a farm and was sent its particulars; for £7,250, he purchased its 120 acres with a mortgage and, on 21 November 1958, became its new owner. Since that time, the house and farm have been owned separately.

John Chapman retained the house where he and his family lived until his death in 1977, when his widow sold it and moved to East Grinstead.

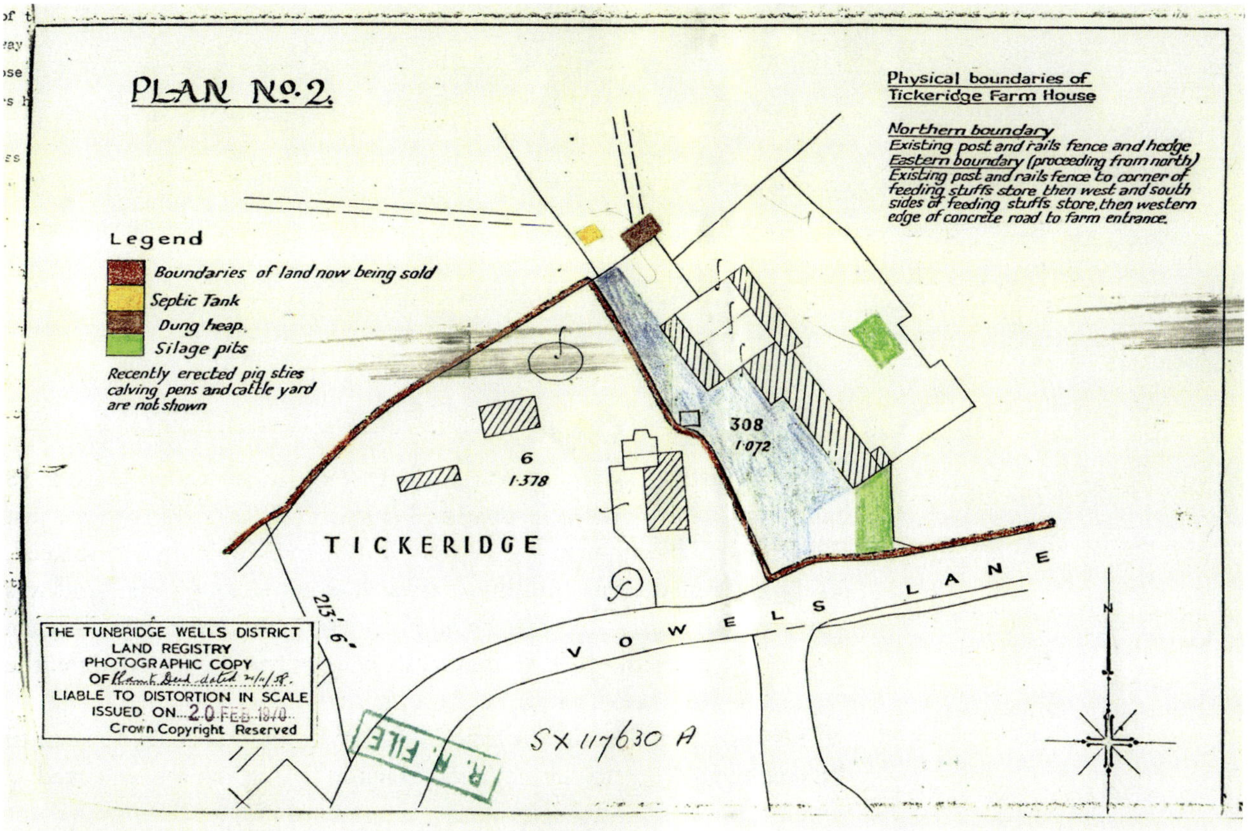

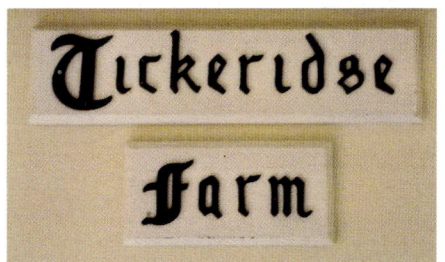

Fig.189: Plan of Tickeridge dated November 1958

Fig.190: Thelma Ullman, Painting of the farm entrance driveway, c. 1958

Fig.191: The farm sign which used to be on the side of the lean-to granary

Gilbert W.E. Reed was born in Surrey on 26 May 1902 and was married in 1929 to Rose Breakspear, who was born in 1908. They had a daughter, Catherine, and three sons, Gilbert G., John, and Alan D., who worked with Gilbert senior on the farm.

Mains water was laid on in 1962 and in June 1963, to provide housing for their dairy cattle, Gilbert was granted planning permission to erect the Sitecast building which stands in Chalk Croft field. With a floor area of 3,750 sq ft it was constructed of 9in thick concrete blocks, with a roof of asbestos concrete sheets. A settlement tank was installed to contain the effluent, which was pumped onto adjoining fields.

The open-fronted shed was enclosed to provide housing for some of their pigs. Around 200 of them were fattened in part of the ancient barn, as well as several additional small buildings which were put up for them and to store their feedstuffs, though these have all since been demolished. Chickens were kept in the lean-to which used to stand at the southern end of the ancient barn until houses for them were erected in the field north of the barn, then called Cottage Field. Hay and straw were stored in the barn.

Gilbert purchased store pigs from Haywards Heath Market and fattened them to about 300lb at seven months old, when they were sold to Walls in Atlas Road, Wilsden, North London, Brazils at Amersham, Harris at Calne, Somerset, or to the Horsham bacon factory, transported by Gilbert in his lorry. He fed them on waste bread from the local bakery, stored in the granary below the house. Fishmeal protein came from Liverpool; from Reigate Council, he received 'Tottenham Puddings', being compressed pig swill. His near neighbour at Bonnors, William Scrage, collected waste bread from the Sunblest bakery in Croydon. Clifford Harbidge of Burleigh Oaks Farm, Turners Hill, also had lorries and brought bread from the Lyons bakery in Crawley, Sugar Puffs from the Quaker Oats factory in Southall, Ealing, West London, and biscuits from the Elkes factory in Uttoxeter. Indeed, any waste food from local factories was included in the pigs' diet.

His herd of around 40 Jersey cows were milked in the abreast parlour. After milking, they were confined in the enclosed yard to the east of the parlour, where there were lean-to, open-fronted buildings in which to house them. The milk was stored in ten-gallon churns which were placed on the churn stand by the side of Vowels Lane, to be collected by a lorry and taken to the dairy in Streatham.

Grass was an important crop for the cows, as were Barley and Wheat, and Potatoes were grown, which Gilbert delivered locally at £1.4s. per cwt.

In 1965, Gilbert senior applied for and was granted permission to build a house on the farm and transferred 10 acres of its land to his son,

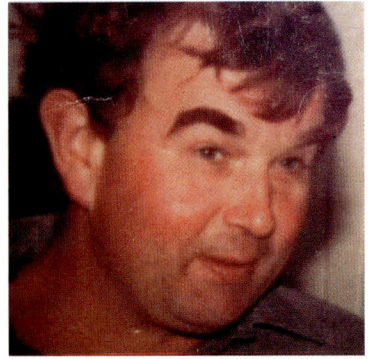

Fig.192: Gilbert Reed (1939–2019)

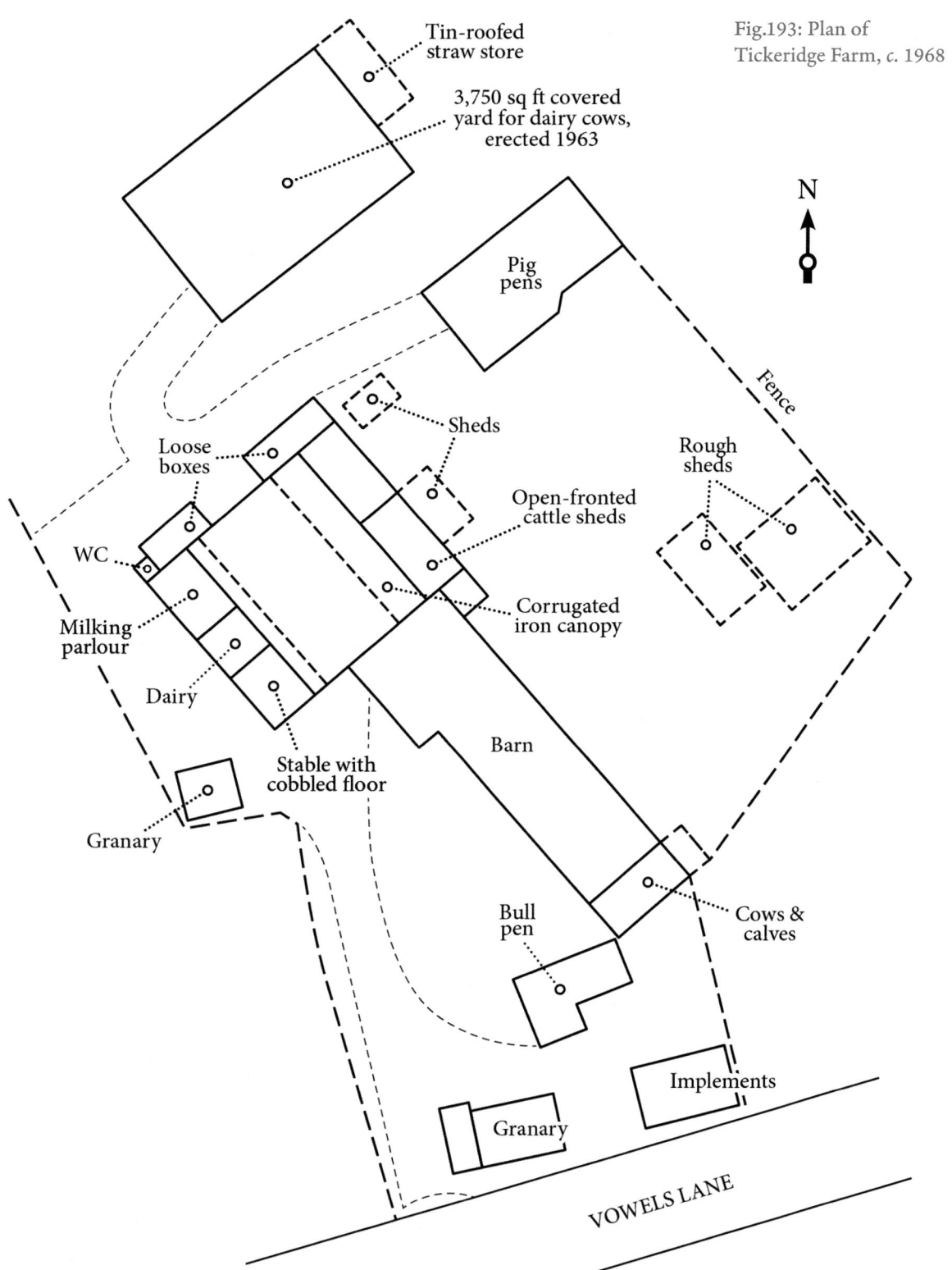

Fig.193: Plan of Tickeridge Farm, *c.* 1968

PROGRESS IN THE 20TH CENTURY

Fig.194: Tickeridge farmhouse, 1969. *Source:* R.T. Mason, *Framed Buildings of the Weald*, 2nd edn., 1969, p.16

Fig.195: Tickeridge farmhouse in 1970, photo from Heather Sargent

Fig.196: Tickeridge farmhouse 1976, photo given to me by Geraldine Warren

Gilbert, on which to build Meadowlands, in the field formerly known as Kennel Field, where Miss Bass had her kennels. Gilbert and his family then moved to live there.

Two years later, the farm comprised 35 acres of arable land, 58½ acres of leys, 12½ acres of shaws and other land, and 3 acres covered by buildings – in all given as 113 acres. The buildings were the covered yard, 50ft x 75ft; piggery for 200; pig yard and feed store; granaries; loose boxes; feed store; two deep litter houses; dairy and milking parlour; engine room; implement shed; three covered pig yards; feed stores; tractor shed; calf boxes; silage pit and pig yard.

On Thursday 30 May 1968, Gilbert Reed junior sold the live and dead farming stock at an auction sale held at Tickeridge and conducted by the auctioneer from T. Bannister & Co. His livestock comprised 11 Ayrshire, Guernsey and Friesian heifers and cows, 14 beef store cattle, 200 pigs and nearly 800 chickens. His vehicles and machinery included three tractors – a 1951 International Farmall, a 1952 Massey Ferguson and a 1955 International Super. He also sold two combine harvesters, two x three-furrow ploughs, a flat roller, a muck spreader, trailers, various baling and handling equipment, and the usual miscellaneous tools and workshop equipment.

Gilbert Reed senior died in 1989. His son, Gilbert, died on 3 February 2019.

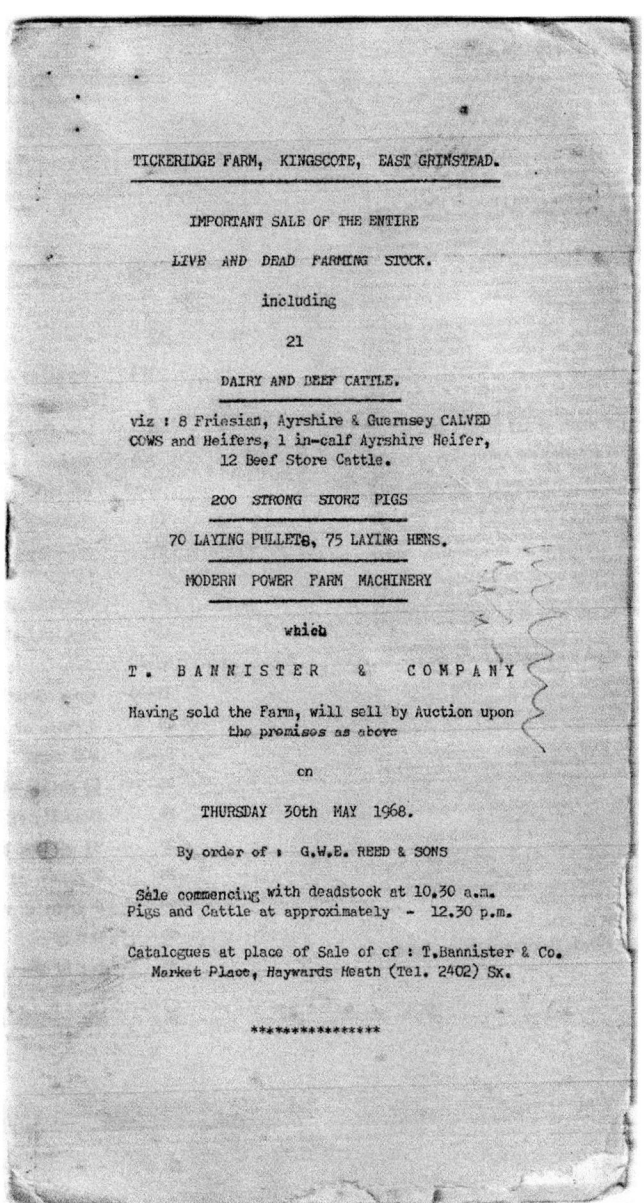

Fig.197: Sale catalogue, 30 May 1968, kindly supplied by Alan Reed

Chapter 24

Design Changes in the 21st Century

For £21,000, the 112.33 acres of Tickeridge Farm were purchased by Veronica Tritton of Parham and the Paddockhurst Estate, by whom, on 23 December 1968, for an annual rent of £588, 104.66 of its acres were let out to one of the Estate's existing tenants, John Bayne. In about 1953, John had moved from Old House Farm, Ardingly, to Monks Farm in Balcombe, where he established a dairy herd of British Friesians.

Fig.198: The farmyard, 1970

An early encounter with his neighbour at Oak Lodge did not go well for John. In June 1971, Charles W.R. Hendry, of that address, decided to empty his above-ground swimming pool. When he pulled out the plug, its water flooded across the adjoining field and damaged the grass – Mr. B. was not amused!

To upgrade cattle accommodation, modifications were made to the portal-framed covered yard which had been erected in 1963. A simple

Fig.199: Alteration work on portal-framed building, 27 October 1984

feed delivery system was created whereby a sloping structure from its adjoining land, into the building, enabled small hay bales to be slid down into a trough which extended across part of the width of the shed. The hay was scattered along the trough which could be accessed by the cattle from both sides.

The additional acres and accommodation at Tickeridge enabled John to keep all the calves from his Friesian dairy herd. The heifer calves were reared to join the herd; the steers and beef crosses were fattened on home-grown Hay and Barley, the main crop at Tickeridge, and finished at 24 to 27 months old. In October 1971, 27 two-year-old beef cattle occupied the newly upgraded cattle yard.

In the early 1970s, Dutch Elm disease arrived in the UK, killing off thousands of trees. Around this time, the ancient barn was in need of re-cladding, so felled Elms from the Parham Estate in West Sussex were brought to the sawmill on the Paddockhurst Estate and sawn up to create new cladding for the barn.

Occasionally, Wheat and Oats were also grown on the farm. To harvest them, Phil Mariner, a Contractor from Strood Farm, Wivelsfield Green, sent his combine, which was driven by Ted Bennett. Later, Vernon Johnson drove his Claas Matador combine to Tickeridge from Picts Lane in Warninglid.

On the farm, the combine sent the grain into a trailer. Via a bagging-off chute on the trailer, John fed the grain into reject plastic fertiliser bags which were then loaded onto another trailer to be taken by tractor to the mill owned by A.H. Rayward & Sons Ltd., Millers and Corn Merchants in Judges Close, East Grinstead. Here, the bags of grain were offloaded by hand and taken into the mill. One by one, each bag was attached to a

Fig.200: Waney Elm on the ancient barn

DESIGN CHANGES IN THE 21ST CENTURY

chain which lifted it up through trap doors to the second floor where the grain was emptied into a hopper. From the hopper, it dropped down into the mill which was below the hopper, on the first floor. Here the grain was rolled into coarse animal feed which dropped down into hessian sacks on the ground floor. Each sack was sealed using a needle and thread and stored on one side until John returned to collect it.

When Rayward's went out of business, in about 1970, John purchased their Hunt corn roller mill and an elevator. To run the mill, he bought a Lister engine from Mr. Mutton of Biddenden, Kent, who delivered it in his lorry. The Massey Ferguson 135 tractor only just managed to unload it!

Initially, the mill was set up in the stable bay at the south end of the milking shed, with the engine located outside. Now, grain off the combine brought to Tickeridge was treated with Propcorn (Proprionic Acid) and augered[1] onto the floor of the old granary which stood on brick piers beside the road, its walls newly lined with plywood sheets in an attempt to make it rat proof. From this granary, as needed, the grain was augered back into a trailer and delivered via the auger into the hopper above the mill in the shed. The rolled grain was then mixed with fishmeal protein and fed through a hole in the wall onto the floor of the adjoining bay, from whence it was shovelled up by hand into bags to be carried to the livestock in the yard outside and the nearby small stables.

For £36,000, on 25 March 1974, Veronica Tritton sold the 112.33 acres of Tickeridge Farm and 1 Tickeridge Cottages into a trust with the Cowdray Trust Ltd. and the Dickinson Trust Ltd. of Millbank Tower, London. In 1978, new trustees were appointed for the farm, and in May 1982, this process was repeated. John Bayne remained as the farm's tenant, paying a yearly rent which, by 1977, had risen to £1,300 and by 1980 to £2,150. Agents for the trust were R.H. and R.W. Clutton of 92 High Street, East Grinstead.

In that same year, 1974, the Estate erected a Knighton-Butler RSJ portal-framed cattle shed, designed by Grubb and Preston of East Grinstead. With a span of 60ft and eight bays each of 20ft, it was built to house young stock from the dairy herd at Balcombe. Of its total cost of £19,697.21, £7,792.72 was covered by a grant, £10,329.07 was paid by Paddockhurst Estate and £1,575.42 was paid by John Bayne who spent another £113.40 to purchase 38 Elm sleepers from Parham to create the cattle pens.

Beside the cattle shed was erected a grain store which measured 40ft x

---

1. An auger is a mechanical transferring device with a screw-like shaft.

30ft (since demolished). Using a 12-volt pump, Propcorn was applied as the grain was augered into the grain store. The mill was now moved onto a concrete plinth inside the western end of the eight-bay cattle shed and the Lister engine was relocated outside this shed. Using a loader bucket on a tractor, grain from the store was transported a short distance to the cattle shed where it was augered into two 10ft x 10ft bins, each with a capacity of 28 tons of grain. As needed, it was milled into coarse meal, shovelled off the floor into bags and then carried via wheelbarrow or a truck to the cattle feed troughs. John recalled that it was "very hard work, dirty and dusty."

In 1980, Alan Hughes, the Agent for Paddockhurst Estate, wrote to John Bayne to confirm that the Estate would take down the lean-to at the south end of the ancient barn, and, in March 1982, John was

Fig.201: Knighton Butler eight-bay cattle shed (on the left), and grain store, 2005

Fig.202: Beef cattle in the eight-bay shed

Fig.203: Roller mill, inside the cattle shed

Fig.204: Roller mill and rolled grain

DESIGN CHANGES IN THE 21ST CENTURY

Fig.205: The farm's workhorse, Massey Ferguson 135 tractor, registration EPX 147C

Fig.206: The 12 hp Lister diesel engine, Type 10/2, built *c*. 1930, which stood outside the cattle shed to run the mill

Fig.207: Silage making outside eight-bay shed, September 1980

given permission to pull down the building beside Vowels Lane, and to create an earth bank in its place. Meanwhile, Jack Dunlop, John's neighbour at Rashes Farm, was granted Sporting Rights over Tickeridge.

By 1983, the state of the roof of the barn was deteriorating and storms that year damaged it and the hay stored within, but the Estate was disinclined to carry out repairs unless John paid for them.

The earlier portal-framed building was updated again in 1984, when a feeding trough was created along the outside of its south-east wall. An external passageway provided access for a tractor with a Lecompte self-loading side-delivery forage box to deliver silage into the trough.

Fig.208: Silage pit at farm entrance, March 1982

Fig.209: Preparation work for the new feeding trough, 19 November 1984

Fig.210: Lecompte forage box gathering silage from the pit at Tickeridge, October 1984

Fig.211: Upgraded cattle accommodation in the portal-framed shed, November 1984, which served the farm well into the next century

DESIGN CHANGES IN THE 21ST CENTURY

Fig.212: Mr. B. junior with his cattle, 2016

Fig.213: Tickeridge farmhouse, west elevation, in 1981

Figs.214 and 215: House repairs, 1981. Photographs from Michael and Maggie Amos

Fig.216: View from across Vowels Lane, 1981

From Elsie Chapman, the farmhouse was purchased by Kenneth and Susan Fleming, who erected the block wall alongside the driveway to the farm.

Having been briefly owned by Herbert and Magdalena Kean, in 1981 it was purchased by Michael and Maggie Amos, who carried out major restoration work on the timbers of the 16th-century crosswing. They also carried out some roof repairs and created a room in the roof.

In 1984, new owners created the pond in the front garden and had the patio area to the back of the house constructed. By this time, the house was wired, partly double-glazed and had oil-fired central heating; its accommodation comprised entrance hall, cloakroom, drawing room, dining room, sitting room, study, breakfast room/kitchen, four

Fig.217: Tickeridge farmhouse, March 1984

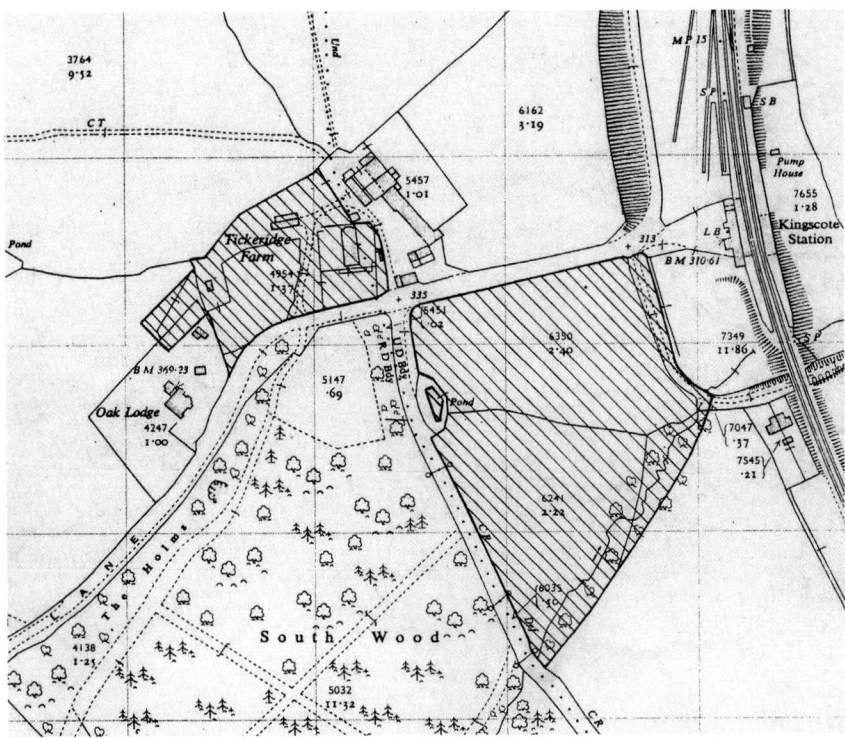

Fig.218: Plan of Tickeridge farmhouse property, March 1984

bedrooms, dressing room/bedroom five and two bathrooms. There was a 'boiler house' accommodated in the cellar and, outside, an 800-gallon oil tank, a garage, wood shed and tool store. Its plot extended to about 1¾ acres, with an additional 4½ acres of rough grazing on the other side of Vowels Lane.

Since that time, the interior of the house has been considerably modernised, the timbers have been sand-blasted and the rooms rearranged, with a single-storey extension added on the eastern end of the 16th-century crosswing to provide more space in the kitchen.

The Wealden Buildings Study Group visited the ancient barn in October 1985 and concluded that the first five bays were built in the mid-17th century and that the three bays, separately framed, were added in the 18th century, "making it almost twice the length of any other barn so far recorded in the area" at 110ft, with a width of 22ft.

In mid-October 1987, the 'Great Storm' hit the UK, felling hundreds of trees in Sussex and damaging numerous buildings, including the ancient barn, part of whose roof on the eastern side was almost torn away. Christopher Schooling was the Agent for Paddockhurst Estate at that time, and he agreed that repairs were necessary in order to protect the building. To this end, builder Alf Poland and his team were given the task of installing tin roofing sheets.

By 2000, the ancient barn was in danger of collapsing and it was decided that conversion was the only viable option which would ensure its continued existence. The County Architectural Adviser reported that its condition was generally poor, with damage by water penetration and decay.

Planning permission was finally obtained in 2005 and, based on the design by Architects George Baxter and Associates, Chalvington Barns carried out the conversion process.

Fig.219: Tickeridge farmhouse, west elevation, September 2000, by kind permission of David Gadsby

Fig.220: Eastern elevation of the house, September 2000, with the stained-glass window clearly visible to the right of the large multi-paned window. By kind permission of David Gadsby

Fig.221: Tickeridge farmhouse, East elevation, December 2005

Fig.222: Aerial view of Tickeridge Farm taken in December 1996

Fig.223: Tickeridge Barn, January 2002

Fig.224: Eastern elevation of the barn, 2002

Fig.225: Massey Ferguson 590 tractor, OYJ 322R, photographed in the barn in 2005

Fig.226: Barn roof before being restored. February 2005

Fig.227: Work in progress, 28 October 2005

Fig.228: New roof timbers being lifted into position, January 2006

Fig.229: Phil and John Shopland, 28 August 2010

Fig.230: Tickeridge Barn, May 2006

Phil and John Shopland were the Carpenters and it was John who created the new roof beams, working at ground level before they were lifted by crane into position.

In July 2006, the barn's conversion into two dwellings was completed.

Later, the old milking parlour and dairy were converted, so that by December 2011, a residential annexe had been created.

Since 2022, members of the Sussex Historical Search Society have been using their metal detectors to scour our fields. Their finds have included several very early coins: besides the Roman coin, a Charles II farthing of 1675, a William III silver shilling of 1696 and a George III Cartwheel penny of 1797, together with numerous more recent coins.

Shown here, right, are some of their other finds, including a 16th-century hammer head measuring 13cm, several lead bag seals dating from the late 19th/early 20th century, each one bearing a number and used to seal seed or fertiliser sacks, a 16th-century lead Pixie Pilgrim badge (a religious souvenir of a visit to a holy shrine) and a pewter spoon bowl of about the same date.

Fig.231: Hammer head, spoon bowl, bag seals and Pixie Pilgrim badge found by the SHSS

Fig.232: Coins found at Tickeridge by members of the SHSS

William III silver shilling, 1696 found at Tickerage

Charles II farthing, 1675 found at Tickerage

William III farthing found at Tickerage

George III Cartwheel penny, 1797 found at Tickerage (weighs nearly an ounce)

DESIGN CHANGES IN THE 21ST CENTURY

Fig.233: BBC film crew and horse boxes parked at Tickeridge, 17 October 2000

Figs.234 and 235: Film crew tents and vehicles parked near the railway, 2023

In October 2000, Tickeridge Farm featured briefly in the film *Station Jim*, made by the BBC and shown on BBC 1 on Sunday 30 December 2001; with scenes at Kingscote Station, where Prunella Scales played the part of Queen Victoria. The horse boxes accommodating the carriage horses were parked at Tickeridge, and one scene shows children running down Vowels Lane, past the farm. The film is available on DVD and video.

A film crew again visited the farm in March 2023, when their tents and service vehicles were parked in one of its fields. The renowned director Steve McQueen was working on his film *Blitz*, using the Bluebell Railway for some of the scenes.

In Conclusion

Today, the fields of Tickeridge Farm are grazed by flocks of sheep and herds of cattle, Fallow deer, the occasional Roe deer and Muntjak, and rabbits, the prey of the local foxes. Beneath the sward, moles excavate their tunnels, dispatching any worms encountered on the way, whilst Buzzards, Kites, Sparrowhawks and Kestrels patrol the sky, hunting for a meatier meal. Swallows nest here in the summer and Tawny and Barn Owls are resident. At dusk, bats emerge from their roost in the roof space of the barn and, under its eaves, House Sparrows snuggle into their nests.

A variety of other birds frequent the farm including Blackbirds, Blue Tits, Chaffinches, Coal Tits, Dunnocks, Goldcrests, Gold Finches, Great Tits, Greenfinches, Grey and Pied Wagtails, Marsh Tits, Nuthatches, Song Thrushes, Wood Pigeons, Stock Doves, Collared Doves, Jackdaws, Crows, Magpies, Great Spotted and Green Woodpeckers, Robins, Starlings and Wrens. Pheasants, migrants from the local shoot, find sanctuary here. Herons, Canada Geese and Little Egrets are occasional visitors and a pair of Parakeets have recently paid a brief visit.

Described as "picturesque" and "beautiful", the valley of Tickeridge Farm has rightly earned its place to lie within the designated Area of Outstanding Natural Beauty on the High Weald of Sussex.

Fig.236: Tickeridge Farm, September 2025

Bibliography and References

Key to abbreviations
BEGS = *Bulletin of the East Grinstead Society*
ESBHRO = East Sussex Brighton and Hove Record Office, the Keep
N/A = National Archives
SAC = *Sussex Archaeological Collections*
SFH = *Sussex Family Historian*
SNQ = *Sussex Notes and Queries*
SRS = *Sussex Record Society*
VCH = *Victoria County History*
WBSG = Wealden Buildings Study Group
WSRO = West Sussex Record Office, Chichester

Acton, Sir William, Will proved 30 May 1650, mentions Dame Frances and Sir John Weld of Arnolds. Shrops. Archives ref.2089/9/2/3-4

Airne, C.W., 1935, *The Story of Saxon and Norman Britain Told in Pictures*, p.54, illustration of ox cart

Andrews, Kenneth R., 1991, *Ships, Money & Politics*, pub.CUP. p.50 and note 56

Appels, Andrew & Laycock, Stuart, 14 June 2007, *Roman Buckles and Military Fittings*, Ed. Greg Payne, Greenlight Publishing

Armytage, Frances, 1966, *A Planter in the New World*, Red History Book Shelf: The Age of the Stuarts, Ginn & Co. Ltd.

Attree, Col.F.W.T., ed.,1912, *SRS* vol.14, 'Post Mortem Inquisitions taken in Sussex', 1485–1649: p.16, No.75, held at Horsham on 12 May 1592: 22 Oct.1587, Thomas Banks/Benckes, Grocer of London, died owning Tickeridge which was held in soccage in chief. p.48, Thomas & Francis Challoner, 16th century; No.692, 10 June 1572 mentions a yardland in West Hoathly

Awty, Brian G., 2019, *Adventure in Iron*, Parts 1 & 2, Wealden Iron Research Group

Backhouse, Janet, 1989, *The Luttrell Psalter*, The British Library

Balsham, 1614–17, 3 maps of Balsham, Cambs., Corporation of London Archive Service, ACC/1876/MP/02/03

Banck, Thomas, Citizen and Grocer of London, Will dated 16 Oct.1587, N/A PROB 11/71/348, (born circa 1553). Will proved November 1587

Bankes, Henry, Rector of Thakeham, Will dated 24 Nov.1678, N/A PROB 11/363/704

Banks, John, Citizen and Merchant Tailor of London, Will dated 2 Jan.1542, N/A PROB 11/29/387

Banks, Simon, Clerk of South Stoke, Will dated 26 Nov.1640, N/A PROB 11/190/398

Barber, Geoffrey, 2017, 'Oral Wills and the Death Bed Transfer in Manorial Records' in *Sussex Family Historian*, vol.22, no.7, pp.295-6

Balsham, Map dated 1617, Cambridgeshire Record Office, ACC/1876/MP/02/03

Bateson, Janet, 2004, 'The East India Company', The RH7 History Group, aka Felbridge & District History Group

Bayne, Kim, 2005, 'Has anyone seen Mr. Hick?', *SFH*, March 2006, Vol.17, No.1: William Franklin Hick

Bayne, Kim, 2022, 'The History of the Kingscote Wine Estate, East Grinstead, Formerly Mill Place Farm, Its Role in the Wealden Iron Industry and Notes on its People'

BBC, 2001, *Station Jim*, DVD and video

BEGS 74, Autumn 2001, p.8: Shellvys aka Shelves

BEGS 85, Spring 2005, p.7: 1538–40, transition from open halls to houses with chimneys

BEGS No.83, Autumn 2004: p.4, map gives location of Mission Room, Kingscote

Bexhill on Sea Chronicle, Friday 10 July 1891, p.2. Accident at Kingscote, William Kemp

Benke, Edmundi, of the parish of West Hothlighe, Will dated 25 Oct.1559, N/A PROB 11/43/350: daughters Jane, Susan, Sara, Roberta and Phebe; wife Jone to whom he left his freehold lands and wood called Shelfys. Will proved 25 May 1560

Berry, William, 1830, *County Genealogies: Pedigrees of The Families in The County of Sussex*: p.136, mid-17th century, Ann Culpeper m. Thomas Wood of Hodley; Katherine Culpeper m. Richard Infield of Hodley, both were daughters of Sir Edward Culpeper of Wakehurst; p.323, John Haselden of EG; p.277, William Hicks of Salehurst

Biscoe, Joseph, of the Inner Temple, Will dated 31 Jan.1749, N/A PROB 11/784/278

Black, James, of Morden, Surrey, 1777, *Observations on the Tillage of the Earth, and on the Theory of Instruments Adapted to this End*, London

Blagrave, Joseph, 1685, *The Epitomie of the Art of Husbandry*, 2 vols.

Blencowe, Robert, 1847, 'Extracts from the Journal and Account Book of the Rev. Giles Moore, Rector of Horsted Keynes, from 1655 to 1679', *SAC* vol.1. p.76, the growing of Flax and Hemp; p.77, Wealden ironworks; pp.84-5, charcoal making; p.96, eating Wheatears; p.104, the state of Sussex roads; p.110, Wassailing; and p.122, travelling by coach

Bluebell Railway Archives and the Preservation Society

Borer, Mary Cathcart, 1977, *The City of London: A History*, Constable, London. Pages 246–7 describe Lad Lane

Bottigheimer, Karl S., 1971, *English Money & Irish Land: The Adventurers in the Cromwellian Settlement of Ireland*, Clarendon Press

Bowden, Peter J., 1962, *The Wool Trade in Tudor and Stuart England*, Macmillan & Co. Ltd., London, p.17

Bradgate, Robert, Merchant Tailor London, Will dated 15 June 1593, N/A PROB 11/82/383, proved 3 September 1593

Brandon, Peter, 1974, *The Sussex Landscape*, Hodder & Stoughton, pp.72 & 78

Brandon, Peter, 28 April 2009, talk at Balcombe, "Settlements in the Weald were not mentioned in Domesday Book because they were temporary/seasonal only, so settlers were counted with the main manor."

Brenner, Robert, 2003, *Merchants and Revolution: Commercial Change, Political Conflict, and London's Overseas Traders, 1550–1653*, Verso Books

Brent, Colin, 1993, *Georgian Lewes, 1714–1830: The Heyday of a County Town*, pp.5, 30-31, 78

Bridgland, David R., 2003, *The Evolution of the River Medway, SE England, in the context of Quarternary palaeoclimate and the Palaeolithic occupation of NW Europe*

Briggs, Howard, 1982, *The River Medway*, pub. Terence Dalton Ltd.

British History online: 'Sussex Subsidy of 1332, Rape of Lewes, p.17, Villat' de Lyndefeld, Rico de Thegheregge, Agn' le Benek'; p.18, Rico le Beneke

Broad, Gwen, 2008, 'Hill Place during the occupancy of the Broad family', Felbridge & District History Society

Brodgate/Bradgate, Richard, Citizen and Skinner of London, Will dated 15 Oct.1589, N/A PROB 11/74/504, proved 3 December 1589

Browne, Andrew, of West Hoathly, Will dated 16 Oct.1595, ESBHRO A10.P140

Browne, Henry, of East Grinstead, Will dated 7 June 1597, ESBHRO A10.P171

Browne, Humphrey, of Bristol, Will dated 27 Jan.1630, (mentions John Slanie), dated 27 Jan.1630; see McGrath, Patrick, pp.53-56

Browne, John, of West Hoathly, Will dated 30 April 1546, ESBHRO A1.P143, mentions dau. Jone/Jane

Browne, John, George and Henry, 20 Sept.1613, Recital of Lease dated 24 Aug.1613, to John Slaney et al, to dig coals in Earnewood, Staffs., Shropshire Archives ref. SRO 1045/88

Browne, John, of West Hoathly, Will dated 7 Aug.1608, ESBHRO A12.312, Witness, Robert Mills the elder

Browne, Richard, of West Hoathly, Will dated 1641, ESBHRO U1/328, m/f XA26/26

Browne, Thomas, Citizen and Merchant Tailor of London, Will dated 1 July 1579, N/A PROB 11/61/391, mentions dau. Sara, wife of Richard Venables, & John Welde

Browne, Thomas, of West Hoathly, Will dated 22 Jan.1581, ESBHRO m/fiche A7. p.256

Browning, John the elder, Yeoman of West Hoathly, Will dated 27 March 1729, N/A PROB 11/647/193, of Teckridge

Budgen, Rev. W., 1946, The acreage of the Sussex Hide of Land, SNQ 11

Burchell, M.J., ed., 1980, 'Hundred of Streat – North, Burrough of West Hoathly', p.28, Sussex Hearth Tax Assessments, 1662, Sussex Genealogical Society

Burtenshaw, Richard, of Lindfield, gent, Probate of will proved at Lewes, 26 April 1773, ESBHRO SAS-WA/129, re Hamlin

Bysshe, Edward, of Smallfield in the parish of Burstow, Will dated 11 Mar.1675, N/A PROB 11/363/56. Codicil dated 6 Dec.1679, names wife Margaret

Caswell, J. William, 2015, *The Eon Staircase*

Cell, G.T., 1965, 'The Newfoundland Company', *William & Mary Quarterly*, vol.22, p.615

Cell, G.T., 1969, English Enterprise in Newfoundland, 1577–1660

Cell, G.T., 1982, 'Newfoundland Discovered', Hakluyt Society

Cheal, Henry, 1921, *The Story of Shoreham*, pub.G.E. & P.P. Bysh (re Dix)

Chisman, John, Yeoman of Tickeridge, West Hoathly, Will dated 22 Jan.1651/2, N/A PROB 11/228/544, mentions wife Sara; brother Thomas and his son John; brothers-in-law Crips and Trice; friends Henry ffalconer of Gravety and John Mills of Celsfield. Proved 15 Sept. 1653

Clode, C.M., 1888, *The Early History of the Guild of Merchant Taylors*, vol.II, London, p.345 (Slany & Benkes); p.322, 1574 policy of colonisation of new settlements in America; pp.195, 350, George Heton

Clode, C.M., Memorials of the Guild of Merchant Taylors: p.575, Appendix C, Slany's property in Cornhill; p.99, MT coat of arms

Coleman, W.H., 1836, *Flora of East Grinstead*, ed.T.C.G. Rich, Sussex Botanical Recording Society, p.14, no.219, Hieracium maculatum

Comber, John, 1932, *Sussex Genealogies*, Ardingly Centre, pub. W.Heffer & Sons Ltd., Cambridge

Cooke, Arthur O., 1920, *A Book of Dovecotes*, pub. T.N.Foulis

Country Life Magazine, 5 October 2000, p.106

Coutin, K., et al, 2005, *Out and about in West Hoathly from Early Days to Modern Times*, pp.46-47, 49; p.35, in 1309 "the land of Simon Thigeregge"

Cowper, John, Yeoman of Leigh, Essex, Will dated 6 December 1552, N/A PROB 11/36/309: wife Ann

Craven, Lydia, *c.* 1948, *Wilmington*, The Book Shop, Wilmington, East Grinstead

Crawley & District Observer, 28 April 1950, p.14, Kingscote Nursery for sale, with about 12,500 ft2 glasshouses

Crossingham Gower, Graham, Dec.1996, 'The origin of the surname Teague', *Sussex Family Historian*, Vol.12, no.4, pp.146-8

Crossley, D.W., 1974, 'Ralph Hogge's Ironworks Accounts 1576–81', *SAC* 112: p.55, "payd to Bankes (for) 20 cordes cuttyn, 8s."

Cuthbert Blaxland, Rev.G., 1900, 'The Story of Squanto', *Sunday at Home*, Religious Tract Society, pp.705-708, 762-768

Daily Mirror, Thursday, 14 March 1935, p.2. 'Suicide of Alfred Ansfield'

Denton, Nicholas J., 2022, notes on Edward Thomas' poem 'The Gypsy'

Drummie, A.C., 1924, *Practical Forestry From a Workman's Point of View*, pub. George Routledge & Sons Ltd.

Du Boulay, F.R.H., 1961, 'Denns, Droving and Danger', in *Archaeologia Cantiana*, Vol.76

Dugdale, Sir William, 1658, *The History of St Paul's Cathedral*, p.136

Dungate, Ann, widow of Worth, Sussex, Will dated 25 Aug.1680, Sussex Online Parish Clerks: sisters Mary Milles and Elizabeth Best, her sons Robert and Nicholas; William Feldwick and his son John; cousin and executor John Milles to whom she leaves her property in Worth; cousins Wicker and Nicholas Underhill; witness Thomas Woodman

Dungate, Stephen, Yeoman of East Grinstead, Will dated 5 Aug.1652, N/A PROB 11/224/508: wife Ann; children Ann, Sara, Elizabeth, Joseph and John; 5 acres of wood Riddens; friend Henry ffaulconer, Yeoman of E. Grinstead

Dunkin, Edwin H.W., 1915, *Sussex Feet of Fines 1509–1833*, SRS vol.20: p.350, John Banckes esq., manor of Pickstones, 1629; p.355, John Browning

East Grinstead and Weald Magazine, No.14, pp.5-6, East Grinstead martyrs

East Grinstead and Weald Magazine, 1987, No.8, p.12, 'An East Grinstead High Street Walk', includes a photo of the cattle market in the High Street

East Grinstead and Weald Magazine, August 1987, No.5, 'Perspectives of Farming in the Weald', pp.7-8 cover the period 1600–1900

East Grinstead and Weald Magazine, June 1988, No.15, cover photo of a Sussex Farmer, of 1845

East Grinstead and Weald Magazine, May 1987, No.2, 'The Barns at Ashdown Forest Centre', p.18, notes on barn construction

East Grinstead Observer, 30 August 1923, re the naming of Kingscote

East Grinstead Observer, 24 September 1965, re: beating the parish bounds, 1808

Eaton, Simon, 21 September 1639, Indenture, purchase of "Tickeridge and Shelves" from Richard Slany, ESBHRO, SAS D/184

Eaton, Simon, 25 November 1639, Indenture, re: purchase of Tickeridge, ESBHRO SAS D/183

Eaton, Simon, c. 1673, Document, Simpson v. Simon Eaton, N/A C7/587/118.001

Eaton, Simon, 11 April 1693, Letter from Sir Simon Eaton to Francis Hamlin requesting an advance of £50 on the mortgage on Tickeridge, ESBHRO SAS DM193

Eaton, Simon, 16 May 1693, Letter from Sir Simon Eaton to Francis Hamlin Jun., again requesting the £50. ESBHRO SAS DM194

Eaton, Sir Simon of Dunmoylen in the county of Lymrick, Will dated 1 Mar.1696, N/A PROB 11/442/54, mentions wife Susannah, late son Simon and his widow Mary, their dau. Martha, Chichester Phillips, and witness Henry Warner

Eaton, Sir Simon of St James Westminster, Sentence dated 24 May 1698 (Sir Simon Eaton died at St James Westminster in 1697)

Eaton, Sir Simon, c. 1673, Document, Simpson v. Sir Simon Eaton, N/A C7/587/118.002

eatongenealogy.com

Edlin, H.L., 1949, *Woodland Crafts in Britain: An Account of the Traditional Uses of Trees and Timbers in the British Countryside*, pub. B.T. Batsford Ltd., p.7, Fell Oak in April; p.49, Hop poles; p.63, Hazel coppices; p.66, trees grown amongst Hazel eg standard timber; p.89, Oak bark used in tanneries; p.120, Poplar used for the floor of oast houses; pp.135-6, the reason for angled brickwork in a timber-framed house; pp.138 & 157, 4ft. logs used in hearths; p.144, keels of ships made from elm; p.148, Ox-yokes; pp.161-2, charcoal making; p.176, the pannage season; p.177, the dangers to pigs eating hard acorns; p.178, the uses of different woods

Ellis, Markman, 2004, *The Coffee-House: A Cultural History*: apprenticeships

Ellis, W.S., 1857, 'Subsidy Roll, Collection within the Rape of Lewes, 1621', *SAC* 9: pp.87-88, West Hoathly

Ellman, Rev. Edward Boys, 1912, *Recollections of a Sussex Parson*, pub. London: p.29 re Miss Hick, and pp.58-59

ESBHRO, SAS A19, 4 July 1555, Conveyance, Carew to Mascall: mentions Edmund Benke with one copyhold yardland called Tekeredge

ESBHRO, Add Mss 6367/3, 1575, Account roll of manor of Plumpton Buskage. Also in SNQ 3, p.175

ESBHRO, SAS D300, 25 June 1636, Assignment of lease, from Robert Mills, Yeoman of West Hoathly, to John Cheesman, Yeoman of Chart Sutton, Kent

ESBHRO, SAS D184, 21 September 1639, Draft of Bargain and Sale re Tickeridge, Richard Slany to Symon Eaton "als Tassall"

ESBHRO, SAS D183, 25 November 1639, Bargain and Sale, Richard Slany of London to Symon Eaton of Croydon, Gent: sells 'Tickeredg and Shelves' to Simon Eaton

ESBHRO, SAS D225, 20 May 1652, Marriage Settlement, John Hamlin to Sarah Chisman

ESBHRO, SAS D232, 23 December 1654, Eaton to Hamlyn, re Meadows and Shelves

ESBHRO, SAS DD504, 23 December 1654, Deed of ffoeffment re Meadows and Shelves. Simon Eaton of Limbriske, Ireland, to ffrancis Hamlyn the elder, Yeoman of Ardingly

ESBHRO, SAS D340, 14 October 1658, Marriage Agreement, John Hamlyn, Yeoman of West Hoathly to Elizabeth Smith of Maresfield

ESBHRO, SAS D458, 6 March 1672, Articles of Agreement re intended marriage of Simon Eaton Junior to Mary Aldworth

ESBHRO, SAS D276, 5 June 1678, Marriage Settlement, Simon Eaton junior to Mary Aldworth

ESBHRO, SAS D431, 26 August 1687, Lease of Tickeridge by Sir Symon Eaton to Edward Paine and John Browning

ESBHRO, SAS D456, 16 July 1692, Agreement re sale of Tickeridge by Sir Simon Eaton to ffrancis Hamlyn. Includes signatures of Sir Simon Eaton, John Hamlyn and John Browning

ESBHRO, SAS D458, 1 August 1692, Deed of Revocation by Sir Simon Eaton re his son's marriage to Mary Aldworth

ESBHRO, SAS D459, 10 August 1692, Indenture re Tickeridge and Shelves, between Sir Simon Eaton of Dunmoylen and John and James Hamlyn, grandsons of Francis Hamlyn who died 1667/8

ESBHRO, SAS D460, 11 August 1692, Indenture re Tickeridge and Shelves, between Sir Simon and Dame Susanna Eaton of Dunmoylen and John Hamlyn, Yeoman of Warbleton and James Hamlyn, Yeoman of Buxted, grandsons of Francis Hamlyn who died 1667/8

ESBHTO, SAS D461, 11 August 1692, Receipt for £950 and 10 gns received by Sir Simon Eaton from ffrancis Hamlyn, grandson of ffrancis who died 1667/8, for purchase of Tickeridge and Shelves

ESBHRO, SAS D462, 11 August 1692, Bond by Sir Simon Eaton for performance of covenants re sale of Tickeridge and Shelves

ESBHRO, SAS D463, 12 August 1692, Mortgage agreement re purchase of Tickeridge and Shelves. £750 received by Sir Simon Eaton from ffrancis Hamlin, Yeoman of Ardingly

ESBHRO, SAS D464, 12 August 1692, Counterpart of D463

ESBHRO, SAS DM191, 1693, Receipt for a post fine of £4.10s. on Tickeridge, paid by Francis Hamlin

ESBHRO, Add MS 320, 28 March 1700, Indenture for a lease of Tickeridge by ffrancis Hamlin, Yeoman of Ardingly, to John Browning, Husbandman of West Hoathly

ESBHRO, SAS D/DD/89, 14 April 1720, Marriage Settlement, Thomas Hamlin to Dorcas Wade. Includes seals

ESBHRO, SAS DD201, 15 June 1763, Marriage Settlement, John Hamlin, Yeoman of Lindfield to Ann Wade, Spinster of Lindfield. Signatures and seals

ESBHRO, AMS 6355/1, 4-5 August 1796, Settlement, Lease and Release, William F. Hick of Lewes, Merchant, and Mary Hamlin of Henfield, Spinster, to Francis Whitfield and Benjamin Comber of Lewes, Bankers, lands in trust for WFH and MH and their heirs, in tail

ESBHRO, AMS 6355/1, 5 August 1796, Marriage Settlement, William Franklin Hick to Mary Hamlin. Mentions capital messuage called Tickeridge and Shelves (40a) and 4 parcels of land known as Dallingridge Meads (7a), occupied by Woodman and Fairhall

ESBHRO, SAS DM254, 1812, Recovery of Land Tax on Tickeridge by William F. Hick. William Woodman, Occupier

ESBHRO, AMS 6354/1, 1818 and 1837, Nutley Court Rolls: Death of Francis Hamlyn

ESBHRO, SAS DM291, 25 February 1819, Valuation of timber at Tickeridge, occupied by William Woodman

ESBHRO, SAS DM292, 8 January 1821, Valuation of timber at Tickeridge, occupied by William Woodman

Essex Architectural Research Society, 1971, letter re visit to house then owned by Chapman who converted Tickeridge House back to one dwelling, from two

Fairhall, John, Farmer, 1791 Directory

Fairhall, John, Farmer, *Universal British Directory*, East Grinstead, 1793–1798

Fairhall, Joseph, Farmer of East Grinstead, Will dated 11 Oct.1813, ESBHRO A71.712, no.15, proved 12 March 1814

Fairhall, William, Inkeeper of Lindfield, Will dated 17 Sept.1795, WSRO SAS-WA/122: wife Mary, children Sarah, Sybil, Thomas, William, Mary, Ann, Charity, Joseph, Emily and Elizabeth

Familysearch.org., baptisms, marriages and burials from the 16thC

Feet of Fines 1308–1509, *SRS* vol.23, no.3051

Felbridge & District History Group, 2019, 'The Manorial Court Records of South Malling Lindfield and Walsted', includes details of the customs of the manor; Tenures Abolition Act in 1660, required all obligations of service and military provision to be replaced by monetary payments

Fitzgerald, Patrick, & M'Gregor, John James, 1827, *The History, Topography and Antiquities of the County and City of Limerick*, Vol.II, Appendix 8, p.xlviii, Simon Eaton, High Sheriff of Limerick in 1661

Foxe, John, 1576, *Book of Martyrs*, 3rd edn., 'The Actes and Monuments of these Latter and Perillous Days, Touching Matters of the Church'. The Unabridged Acts and Monuments Online or TAMO, The Digital Humanities Institute, Sheffield, 2011, available from http//www.dhi.ac.uk/foxe

Fuller, John, Yeoman of Turners Hill, Probate dated 3 Aug.1825, WSRO SAS-B/744: children – John, to whom he leaves his blacksmiths shop in Turners Hill, Ann, Thomas, Mary and Sarah, the wife of William Woodman

Garraway Rice, R., & Godfrey, W.H., 1936, 'Transcripts of Sussex Wills', *SRS* Vol.17

Gaunt, Peter, 1987, *The Cromwellian Gazetteer, An Illustrated Guide to Britain in the Civil War and Commonwealth*, pub. Alan Sutton & The Cromwell Association, includes itinerary of Cromwell's movements, 1642–1651

Gilbert, Mrs. Edith, 1920, notes on her life at Tickeridge from 1906–1920

Gilbert, Richard, 1970, The Rev. Thomas Hamlin, *SNQ* vol.17, pp.132 & 168: see also *SAC* vol.106, p.14

Godfrey, Walter H., 1928, 'The Book of John Rowe, 1622', *SRS* vol.34: pp.238-239, Thomas Benke for a yard land called Tickeridges *best beast*, 12s.6d.; Nicholas Backshill for a tenement and lands called Sharpthorne, Bedelland, and Benkeland, 14s.11d.; Caleb Kempe for halfe a yard of land called Wellers (?Sellers), 6s.5d.

Gould, David, 1995, 'A Railway Built, Opened, Closed and Rebuilt', *Bulletin of the East Grinstead Society*, Spring 1995, No.56, pp.13-16: 300 navvies; Birch Farm embankment; Kingscote Station

Grocers' Company, 1567, Wardens' Accounts for Premium of Admission: Summer 1567, Thomas Banks appointed apprentice of Humphrey Slough for eight years. He became a Freeman of the Grocers' Company in 1576, aged about 21

Haire, Mary Ann, of Lewes, Will dated 13 Dec.1845, N/A PROB 11/2194/277: husband Thomas, Doctor in Medicine

Haire, Mary, 1875, Conveyance re the will of Mary Haire, ESBHRO AddMss 47,770

Hamblyn, John, Yeoman of Warbleton, Will dated 16 Oct.1693, ESBHRO A42.24 no.66: uncle James Hamblyn and his children; the Hamblyns of Ardingly; brother ffrancis

Hamlin, Dorcas, widow of Sunt, Lindfield, Will dated 30 Aug.1742, ESBHRO W/SM/D8, p.157, and Codicil dated 27 July 1744, ESBHRO W/SM/D8, p.160: sons William, Thomas and John; bro-in-law ffrancis Hamlin dec'd

Hamlyn, Francis the elder, Yeoman of Ardingly, Will dated 2 May 1666, N/A PROB 11/326/442: Symon Eaton's lands; sons Thomas, Joshuah, James, daughters Elizabeth, Frances, Ediffe, Mercy, and Mary wife of John Hazelden

Hamlin, Francis the elder of Ardingly, Will dated 4 Dec.1675, N/A PROB 11/350/83, wife Anne, brother William, children Francis, John, Anne and Thomas

Hamlin, Francis of Avens in Ardingly, Will dated 5 June 1732, ESBHRO DD119, A54.86, XA26-59 no.7: late brother Thomas and his dau. Sara; son ffrancis; late dau. Anne. Will proved 1743/3, ref.DD145

Hamlin, Francis of Lindfield, Will dated 6 Oct.1778, N/A PROB 11/1167/151, proved 18 June 1788, ESBHRO SAS-DD/252, WG233

Hamlin, John, 5 November 1654, Receipt from Lt. Col. Simon Eaton, ESBHRO SAS WG451

Hamlyn, John of Tickeridge, West Hoathly, Will dated 1 Dec.1663, N/A PROB 11/313/80: brothers Francis and Thomas, sister Mary married to John Hazelden, sons Francis, Thomas, James, William and John, friend Henry Falconer

Hamlyn, John, Yeoman of Warbleton, Will dated 16 October 1693, ESBHRO A42.24, m/f XA26/50. Proved 12 June 1694

Hamlin, John, Yeoman of Ardingly, Will dated 24 Dec.1716, ESBHRO SAS D73: brothers ffrancis of Ardingly and Thomas; niece Anne Hamlin; Dorcas Wade of Lindfield

Hamlin, John, Gentleman of Sunt, Will dated 25 November 1772, ESBHRO SM D9 149. Proved 1 October 1774

Hamlin, Thomas of Sunt, Lindfield, Will dated 23 Dec.1725, ESBHRO SM/D6, pp.169-171: wife Dorcas; sons John, Thomas and William. Proved 16 June 1733

Hamlin, William of Ardingly, Will dated 24 April 1662, N/A PROB 11/311/443: father Francis; wife Elizabeth; children Elizabeth and William

Harbye, Erasmus, Citizen and Skinner of London, resident in Cornhill, Will dated 20 July 1593, with additions dated 24 July 1593, N/A PROB 11/82/400: wife Elizabeth, children John and Elizabeth, brothers John and Thomas, sister Isabell Atkins and her son Erasmus, sister Sara Venables wife of Richard. Will proved 25 October 1593

Hartley, Barbara, et al, 1994, *West Hoathly Past and Present*, pp.11, 29

Haselden, John, Yeoman of East Grinstead, Will dated 8 July 1607, ESBHRO A12.2291-104: wife Margarett, dau. of John Smith of Clayton; son John and four other children; "to Margarett my wife ...parcel or close of land called Jenkyns Meade "with all the greate woods and trees thereon growing or beinge"; John Byshe, witness. Proved 8 August 1607

Hastings & St Leonards Observer, 23 July 1938, p.23, For sale by Mr. Selden, Kingscote Nursery, with eight glasshouses

Hennessy, Rev. George, 1900, *Chichester Diocese Clergy Lists*, St Peter's Press, London, p.142, Simon Bankes, Rector of St Leonard's church, South Stoke in 1616

Hick, Mary, widow of All Saints, Lewes, Administration dated 25 May 1850, Family Records Centre IR 26/268; Mary Ann Haire, Administratix, of Brighton

Hick, William Franklin, of Lewes, Will dated 25 July 1835, N/A PROB 11/1991/269: wife Mary, daughter Mary Ann

Hick, William Franklin, of Lewes, died in Paris 20 Sept.1843, Probate dated 24 January 1844, Family Records Centre IR 26/1676

Hickinbottom, Des, 2009, Memories of the WW2 ammunition depot at Gravetye, West Hoathly Hub document no.0205. Also, 'The Soldier's Tale', in the Archive at The Priest House

Hidden, Norman, 1995, 'Alias: A case of concealment?' *Family Tree Magazine*, October 1995, pp.23-24

highweald.org, 'Area of Outstanding Natural Beauty, Livestock and Landscape'

highweald.org, 'Area of Outstanding Natural Beauty, The Making of the High Weald'

Hills, W.H., 1906, *The History of East Grinstead*, Farncombe & Co.

Hitchin-Kemp, Frederick, 1902, 'A general history of the Kemp and Kempe families of Great Britain and her Colonies', Leadenhall Press, London

Hodgkinson, Jeremy, 2008, *The Wealden Iron Industry*, The History Press

Holgate, Mary S., 1925, 'The Dedication of West Hoathly Church', *SAC* 66: p.233, dated to around 1257-8, "William de Teggeherugge, carpenter", was one of the witnesses to the deed of dedication

Holgate, Mary S., ed., 1927, Sussex Inquisitions, *SRS* vol.33, p.67, no.235, held at Horsham 12 May 1592: Thomas Bankes, died 22 Oct.29 Eliz. (1587) Messuage or tenement with lands meadows etc., called Tickeridge in WH held in soccage in chief, 40s. Lands etc., called Shelves *alias* Midway *alias* John at the Midwaye in EG held of William Dixe and others, 20s.

Holgate, Mary S., 1929, 'The Canons' Manor of South Malling', *SAC* 70

Holgate, Mary S., 1930, 'The Sussex Manors of Frances Carewe', 1575, *SNQ* Vol.3, pp.174-175, Benkeland and Thomas Benke re Sykridge

Holgate, Mary S., 2001, 'The Place Names of Ardingly (compiled 1926–1934)', Ardingly History Society. Pp.30-31, Bolney Farm; pp.9, 31 and 43, Hamlyn

Horsfield, T.W., 1835, *History of Sussex, Vol.1, Rape of Pevensey*: p.384, Lindfield

Horsfield, T.W., 1835, *History of Sussex, Vol.II*, pub. J. Baxter, Lewes, App.3: p.23, Mr. Durrant Cooper's Parliamentary History of Sussex

House of Lords Journal, Vol.17, 25 January 1703/4, Mathew & Ux. Versus Phillips & al. George and Martha Mathew endeavour to overturn Sir Simon Eaton's revocation

Hudson, Rev. William, ed. 1910, 'The Three Earliest Subsidies for the County of Sussex', 1296, 1327 and 1332, *SRS* vol.10: Hundred of Buttinghill, p.292, in 1332, John atte Theghe, paid 5s.0d.; p.104, in 1296 Simon de Thegheregg, one of the villani of Hugonis Bardulf paid 3s.0d.; p.181, in 1327 Simone de …gg of Hothleigh paid 1s.0d.

Hughes, Dr. Annabelle, 27 Jan. 2010, "The size of a timber-framed house was not so relevant to the wealth of its builder as the size of the timbers used in its construction."

Hughes, Dr. Annabelle, 'An Introduction to Timber-Framed Construction', Barcombe and Hamsey History Society

Huxford, J.F., 1982, *Arms of Sussex Families*, Phillimore: pp.200-201, Bardolf; p.244, Dennett

Infield, Richard of Gravetye, Will dated 11 March 1570/1: (see Coutin, 2005, p.61) "To my servant John Benke, 5s."

Jenkyne, Edmund, of West Hoathly, Will dated 16 April 1559, ESBHRO m/f A4, p.502: son William, brother Thomas and sisters Joyce, Dorotye, Annis and Alyce Chamberlayne who is "to be paid out of the money that Edmund Benke doth owe me."

Jessup, R.F., 1957, *Little Guide to Sussex*, Methuen

Jones, N.L., & Woolf, D.R., eds., 2007, Local Identities in Late Medieval and Early Modern England, Macmillan, pp.190, 197-199, Venables, Slaney, Weld

Kempe, Caleb, Will dated 17 Dec.1638, N/A PROB 11/179/198: wife Rose, sister Mary Megud, brother John, father-in-law John Rippon

Kempe, John, parson of ffreshwater in the Isle of Wight, Will dated 15 July 1579, N/A PROB 11/70/212: wife Annys; sons Tobias, John and Caleb; brothers Richard and Edward; daughter Hannah; Thomas Banks. Will proved 24 April 1587

Kenyon, G.H., 1967, *The Glass Industry of the Weald*, Leicester University Press, pp.101, 140

Kirk, J.C., 2004, *The early-modern carpenter and timber framing in the rural Sussex Weald*, SAC, Vol.142, pp.93-105

Lambarde, W., *A Perambulation of Kent*, 1576

Leppard, M.J., Autumn 1996, 'The naming of Kingscote', *BEGS* No.59, p.12

Leppard, M.J., Autumn 1996, 'High Street Cellars', *BEGS* No.59, p.11

Leppard, M.J., Autumn 1996, 'East Grinstead in Domesday Book', *BEGS* No.59, p.5

Leppard, M.J., Autumn 1997, 'Ironworking in Anglo-Saxon and later Medieval East Grinstead', *BEGS* No.62, p.17

Leppard, M.J., Spring 2001, 'East Grinstead Hundred in 1579', *BEGS* No.73, p.5: 1579 survey of the boundaries of the hundreds in the Duchy of Lancaster within the Rape of Pevensey: Banckes gate and Jenkins Mead to a Brook called Stone Brook; p.6, Birch Farm, Richard Infield of Gravetye; the Shells, alias Shelves; includes a map on p.8. ref. ESBHRO ASH 1171A

Leppard, M.J., 2001, *A History of East Grinstead*, Phillimore

Leppard, M.J., Autumn 2001, *BEGS* No.74, 'What was going on here then?', p.7, concerning London merchants and their investments in EG area; p.8, 'East Grinstead Hundred, 1579 and 1564'

Leppard, M.J., Autumn 2004, *BEGS* No.83, p.3, the benefits of living in East Grinstead and the scent of the hop (see Pepper, 1885); p.10, on the origin of 'Sellers' and Shelves alias Medway; p.11, field called Bankes

Leppard, M.J., Spring 2005, 'The Pre-History of Ridge Hill', *BEGS* No.85, pp.4-5

Loder, Gerald W.E., ed., 1913, 'The Parish Registers of Ardingly,1558–1812', *SRS* vol.17: pp.198-199, 1562, Francis Hamlin, gent; c. 1674, Francis Hamlin jnr. & senr., and John Cheesman for his farme of Sir W. Culpepers; 1667, John Tullye

Long, Pamela O., 2011, *Artisan/Practitioners and the Rise of the New Sciences,1400–1600*, Oregon State University Press; on Medieval Carpenters

Lovell v. Bankes, 1621–1625, N/A C3/365/33_001, Claim by Hannah Lovell for Jointure Rights

Lovell v. Bankes, 1621–1625, N/A C3/365/33_002: re Tickeridge

Lovell, Thomas, minister of the gospel of Great Waldingfield in Suffolk, Will dated 20 May 1610, N/A PROB 11/116/446: wife Hanna, daughter Sara, sons Thomas and Titus; sister Bridgett Hayes; son and daughter-in-law Simon and Eunice Banks

MacDougall, Philip, Autumn 2006, 'Sussex Timber and the Royal Dockyards', West Sussex History, *Journal of West Sussex Archives Society*, No.75: pp.42-43, 48, shipbuilding and conservation of oak woodlands

MAF, 1 October 1942, Farm Survey, N/A ref. MAF 32/1015/25, C578920

Marsh, Christopher W., 1994, *The Family of Love in English Society, 1550–1630*, CUP. pp.70-71

Margary, Ivan D., 1946, 'The Early Development of Tracks and Roads in and near East Grinstead', *SNQ* 11, pp.78-79

Margary, Ivan D., 1948, *Roman Ways in the Weald*, Phoenix House

Margary, Ivan D., 1973 (1st pub.1965), *Roman Roads in Britain*, 3rd edn., John Baker: Route 150, pp.37, 63

Marx, Klaus, 2000, *An Illustrated History of the Lewes and East Grinstead Railway*, Oxford Publishing Co.

Mason, R.T., 1939, 'East Grinstead, Notes on its Architecture, Part I, The High Street', *SAC* vol.80, pp.3-27. Includes detailed notes on the three 14th century houses in East Grinstead. Outlines of moulded beams of Amherst and Wilmington on p.27

Mason, R.T., 1940, 'East Grinstead, Notes on its Architecture, Part II, Medieval Farms', *SAC* vol.81, pp.2-18

Mason, R.T., 1942, 'Tickeridge – a 14th Century Farmhouse', *SAC* vol.82, pp.65-72

Mason, R.T., 12 July 1955, Letter to Mr. Chapman of Tickeridge. Mentions the old table with reversable board, still in the house in 1940

Mason, R.T., Nov & Dec. 1955, 'Medieval Cottages', in *Sussex County Magazine*, Vol.29, No.11, pp.27-31; pp.512-518 & 566-571, includes photo of Tickeridge and its dais beam, and illustrations of King posts

Mason, R.T., 1957, 'Fourteenth Century Halls in Sussex', *SAC* vol.95: pp.72-74, 82-91; includes outline of moulded beam, and photo of Tickeridge house on p.85

Mason, R.T., 1969, *Framed Buildings of the Weald*, 2nd edn.: Tickeridge, pp.16, 22, 24, 52

Mason, R.T., 1975, The Dating of Timber Framed Vernacular Architecture in Sussex, *SAC* vol.113, pp.1-6

Mason, William, Yeoman of West Hoathly, Will dated 4 June 1750, ESBHRO m/f A59-750, leaves everything to wife Sarah

Mawer, A & Stenton, F.M., eds.,1930, *The Place Names of Sussex*, Part 2, Cambridge University Press, p.273: Rape of Lewes, Buttinghill Hundred, Tickeridge

Mayo, Isabella Fyvie, 1899, 'In the Heart of London', *The Sunday at Home*, pub. The Religious Tract Society, p.514, Merchant Taylors' Hall

McGrath, Patrick, ed., 1955, *Merchants and Merchandise in Seventeenth-Century Bristol*, Bristol Record Society

McKinley, Richard, 1988, *The Surnames of Sussex*, Leopards Head Press

Medieval Britain, Medieval Carpenter, https://medievalbritain.com

Memorials of the Guild of Merchant Taylors, 1875, pub. Harrison, London

Mercer, Eric, 1975, *English Vernacular Houses: A Study of Traditional Farmhouses and Cottages*, Royal Commission on Historical Monuments: p.95, At Tickeridge in West Hoathly, the crown-posts stand upon base crucks or upon inclined principals or raised crucks

Michell, Thomas of Worth, Gent., Will dated 6 June 1551: "to Alyce Benke 3 keen" (cows), *SAC* 53, 1910, p.115

Mid Sussex District Council Planning Department, 11 Feb.2009, 09/00436/FUL: proposed extension to Tickeridge House

Mid Sussex District Council Planning Department, 1980–2016: particularly application 09/00437/LBC, 2009: "In the 18th C the house was converted to two cottages and extensions to the northern end were added. Converted back to a single residence in the late 1940s."

Milles, Robert, Yeoman of West Hoathly, Will dated 8 May 1641, ESBHRO U1/306, m/f XA26/26: wife Elizabeth, sons Allan, Robert, William; witnesses include John and Allen Browne. Proved 5 June 1641

Mills, Robert, 25 June 1636, Indenture to grant tenancy to John Cheesman, ESBHRO SAS D/300

Nairn, Ian & Pevsner, Nikolaus, 1965, *The Buildings of England: Sussex*, Penguin Books, pp.54 & 628

N/A, 1612, Tendringe v. Clopton, Bill of Complaint, N/A C2/JasI/T6/60, re Bonds, Demurrer and answer of Hannah Lovell, widow, one of the defendants in this Bill, concerning Samuell Banke and his debts

N/A, 1621-1625, C3/365/33-001, Lovell v. Bankes, Plaintiff, Hannah Lovell, widow; Defendant, Samuel Bankes, re property in West Hoathly. Dispute over Tickeridge and Slany's purchase

N/A, 1621-1625, C3/365/33-002, Lovell v. Bankes, re property in West Hoathly. The several answers of John Slany

N/A, 31 January 1924/5, C2/JasI/L4/31, Lovell v. Slany, the final answer of John Slany

Newman, Edward I., 'Medieval sheep-corn farming: how much grain yield could each sheep support?' p.165

Page, William, ed., 1912, *Victoria County History of Hampshire*, Vol.5, parish of Freshwater, Isle of Wight, pp.240-246

Parish, W.D., 1957, *A Dictionary of the Sussex Dialect*, augmented by Helena Hall: meaning of 'Wapple Way'

Payne, Edward, Carpenter of East Grinstead, Will dated 2 April 1688, proved 4 May 1688, ESBHRO A38.120, m/f XA26/48

Pearse, Michael T., 1994, *Between Known Men and Visible Saints: A Study in Sixteenth-century English Dissent*, University Press, London, pp.45-46, John Kempe of Freshwater

Pelham, R.A., 1934, *The Distribution of Sheep in Sussex, Early 14th Century*, SAC 75, pp.129-135

Penn, Roger, 1981, *Portrait of the River Medway*, Robert Hale Ltd.

Pepper, W.R., 1885, *East Grinstead and its Environs*, p.15, mentions the scent of the hop

Pevsner, Nikolaus & Nairn, Ian, 1965, *The Buildings of England: Sussex*, Penguin Books, pp.54 & 628

Plumpton Boscage, 1555, Exemplification of Common Recovery, EDBHRO SAS/A27

Plumpton Boscage, 1592/3, Lands, ESBHRO AddMss 2711

Plumpton Boscage, 1621, Rents, ESBHRO AMS 2684

Plumpton Boscage, 1623, Manor Court Books, ESBHRO A2327/1/6/1-3

Post Office Directory, 1855, p.909, West Hoathly: 'Tickrage'; Henry and James Longley, timber dealers

Power, Eileen, 1941, 'The Wool Trade in English Medieval History', The Ford Lectures, Lecture II, Sheep Farming and Wool Production. Includes information on historic prices paid for wool; p.30, number of sheep per holding

Renshaw, W.C., Saltzmann, L.F. & Deedes, C., eds., 1905, A Poll for Election of Members of Parliament for the County of Sussex, taken at Lewes 24 May 1705, *SRS* vol.4: pp.48-49, William Hamlin of W.H., Stephen Dungate, and Edward Paine of E.G.

Renshaw, Walter C., 1916, 'The Hundred of Buttinghill', *SAC* 58, pp.6-20

Rentapeasant.co.uk, 'Salving'

Richardson, John, 2000, *The Annals of London, A year by year Record of a Thousand Years of History*, Cassell & Co.: maps on pp.94, 95, 146,147, 182, 183

Ridley, Ursula, 1939, 'A List of Church Marks at West Hoathly', *SNQ* 7, pp.19-21: p.21, Francis Hamlin, Tickeridge, for 24ft of the church wall on the east side

Ridley, Ursula, 1955, Letter to John Chapman at Tickeridge, enclosing details of her study of the house, including the table, "with reversible board, at least 4ft. wide", her comparison of Tickeridge with 'Wilmington' in East Grinstead, and her conviction that the north wing "almost certainly replaced a medieval solar wing."

Ridley, Ursula, 1971, *The Story of a Forest Village: West Hoathly*, pub. Friends of the Priest House

Robinson, et al, eds., *The Welde Lute Book*

Rose, George A., 2008, *Cod, The Ecological History of the North Atlantic Fisheries*: p.218-220, Early settlements in Newfoundland

SAC vol.20, 1868, 'Notes on East Grinstead', by J.C. Stenning; pp.151-152, mentions Tickeridge and its fireback

SAC vol.48, 1905, Notes and Queries, p.159: Valuation of Stock at Ticaridge, East Grinstead, in 1781

SAC vol.66, 1925, p.233: grant of land to West Hoathly church witnessed by William de Teggeherugge, mid-13th century

SAC vol.112, 1974, Ralph Hogge's Ironworks Accounts, 1576-81, by D.W. Crossley, p.55, "6 Aprell 1578, payd to Bankes on fful satysf' of all hys due wch is xx cordes cuttyn, 8s."

L.F. Saltzman, ed., 1940, *VCH*, Sussex, Vol.7, p.128, Bolney Farm, Ardingly: pp.166-7, Tickeridge House

Sellens, Barbara, 1 Jan. 1984, 'Wealden Firebacks, Sussex History', Vol.2, No.8, *The Journal of the Federation of Sussex Local History Societies*

Sevenoaks Chronicle and Kentish Advertiser, Friday 17 September 1937, p.5. Marriage of Herbert Leslie Simmonds, son of Mr. and Mrs. Simmonds of Tickeridge Farm

Sharp, J.E.E.S. & Stamp, A.E., 1909, *Calendar of Inquisitions Post Mortem*, vol.7, Edw.III, HMSO, London, files 17 & 18, no.243, IPM 29 Jan. 4 Edw.III (1330) Thomas Bardolf. "Plumpton. The Manor, including a messuage, 88a land and 40a wood and heath in Hodleigh". And in 1331, …"The manor (of Plumpton) including a custom of reaping called 'Gavelrip' etc. a messuage and garden at Westhodleghe …"

Shaw, Andrew, Policy Manager of High Weald, 2009, Data on Tickeridge Farm: Of medieval origins, with a basic plan type of a dispersed multiyard layout including a Loose Courtyard on two sides. An attached building around the house, with alterations

Shelford, W.H. & Bloom, J.H., 1934–1936, The Shelford-Bloom Archive: p.70, 1329, Inquisition after the death of Thomas Bardolf, who died "seized of a messuage, 88 acres of land and 40 acres of wood and heath in Hodlegh," manor of Plumpton. p.56, 1340/1, *Inquisitiones Nonarum*, pub. Record Commission, 1807: p.379 (a tithe of one ninth value of sheaves, wool and lambs), in West Hoathly one ninth of sheaves worth £7.16s.8d., of wool, 2s.0d., of lambs, 16d. Indexed by Kim Bayne in 2018

Shelley, Jean, 1999, *The Timber Framed Houses of Ardingly*: pp.14, Bolney Farmhouse; p.16, Brook Cottage; p.22, Avins Farm

Shipping & Mercantile Gazette, 23 May 1874, p.2, 'Schooner for sale, apply John Lee'

Slaney, Henry, of The Staple, Bruges, Will dated 21 June 1578, N/A PROB 11/60/530: wife English, and daughter Katheryn

Slaney, Stephen of St Helens, Worcester, Will dated 1624, N/A PROB 11/143/140: wife Elizabeth; sons John, Stephen, Richard and William; brothers John and Moses; sister Mary

Slany, John, 19 September 1611, Grant to John Slany of the benefit of the recusancy of John Halsey. N/A Signet Office, SO 3/5

Slany, John, October 1612, Grant to John Slany to build ships, N/A Signet Office, SO 3/5

Slany, John, 1 September 1615, WSRO EPI/336. With signature of John Slany

Slany, John, 1618, Built a school and almshouses in Barrow, Shropshire. Shropshire Archies

Slany, John, 1618, Great and Lesser messuages built at Pansanger, Hertfordshire. Hertfordshire Archives and Local Studies, ref. DE/P/T3230-318

Slany, John, Merchant Taylor of London, Will dated 17 August 1631, N/A PROB 11/161/478: sisters Mary, Margaret, Judith, and Elizabeth married to Eaton; brothers Humphrie and Richard; godson John Banckes son of Symon Bankes in Sussex; housekeeper Ann Eaton and her son Symon; John and Richard Slany sons of brother Richard; and numerous other relations

Slany, John, 1632, Inquisition Post Mortem, N/A C 142/483/77_001. See also

Slanye, Margaret, widow of St Swithin, London, Will dated 20 July 1618, N/A PROB 11/133/578. Widow of Sir Stephen Slany; mentions daughters Mary and Elizabeth; siblings Thomas and Katherine Phesant; "cozens" John and Humfrey Slanye to be overseers. Will proved 24 May 1619

Slanye, Richard, Gentleman of Hem, Shrops., Will dated 6 May 1620, PROB 11/136/62, mentions children Moses, Edward, Stephen, Richard and Marye; brothers John and Humfrey; "my sister Eaton and brother Eaton"

Slanye or Slany, Sir Stephen, Alderman of London, Will dated 2 Aug.1598, PROB 11/113/3, mentions wife Margaret; son Stephen (dec'd); dau. Mary wife of Humfrey Welde, dau. Elizabeth wife of Samuel Lennard and dau. Anne wife of Thomas Colepepper; John Slanye son of my brother Henry; brother William. Will proved 3 January 1609/10

Smith, Rhonda, 1983, *Longleys of Crawley: A pictorial history of James Longley & Co.*, pub. James Longley & Co. Ltd., Crawley

SNQ Vol.3, 1930, The Sussex Manors of Francis Carewe: p.175, Rents of the Freeholders of the Bedelwyk of Plompton Buskage in 1575, Thomas Benke "one yard of lande and all those lands called Sykridge in West hoytlygeh late holden by copy of Court Roll and now be granted by Dede payenge yerely 12s.6d."

SNQ Vol.7, A List of Church Marks at West Hoathly, 1752, p.21, Francis Hamlin owner & Wm Mason occupier of Tickeridge – 24ft on the east side

Spufford, Margaret, 1995, *The World of Rural Dissenters, 1520–1725*, CUP

Stenning J.C., 1868, 'Notes on East Grinstead', *SAC* Vol.20: pp.151-2: description of fireback at Tickeridge; p.167-174, East Grinstead Subsidies, 1296, 1327, 1333, 1524, 1620, 1628

Stenton, Doris M., *English Society in the Early Middle Ages, 1066–1307*, Pelican History of England No.3, pp.126-127

Stow, John, 1633, *The Survey of London*

Straker, Ernest, ed., 1933, 'The Buckhurst Terrier, 1597–1598', *SRS* vol.39: p.7, John Hasleden holds lands called Hasleden by Knight's service, rent 4s.8d. p.48, John Haselden the younger's Bankes land. p.47, fo.214v, Freeholders in the parish of EG:- John Haselden the younger holds land called Yawley, bounds include John Haselden's Sellers on the south. The same John holds land called Benkes als Bankes, 9ac, bounds are Thomas a Burley N., the river from Bishe's mill to Yawley bridge on the west, John Haselden the elder's copyhold called Milshott on the east, and Queens highway Tilkherst Gate to Yarley bridge S; p 48, fo.210, John Haselden the elder holds customary land called Sellers. John Bishe holds land called Morehall, parcel of the tenement at Fenne, 42ac. p.52, John Haselden the elder holds by copy land called Midwaies, parcel of Sellers, 33ac, rent 2s.9d.;

Strype, John, 1720, *A Survey of the Cities of London and Westminster*, Book 1

Strype, John, 1720, *A Survey of the Cities of London and Westminster*, Book 2, Ch.13, p.191, Memorial to Sir Stephen Slanie (full text available on www.dhi.ac.uk)

Strype, John, 1821, *The Life and Acts of Matthew Parker*, Vol.II, Clarendon Press, Oxford, pp.381-385, re Bartholomew Tassell

Sussex Agricultural Express, 12 July 1875, p.2, Death of Henry Longley, timber merchant

Sussex Agricultural Express, 30 Sept.1843, p.4, Death at Paris of W.F. Hick esq.

Sussex Daily News, Tuesday, 22 February 1916, p.7. Harold T. Elwes fined for his bright lights

Sussex Parish Churches online, The church of St Michael, South Malling

Sussex Subsidy of 1332, Rape of Lewes, British History online, p.17, Villat' de Lyndefeld, Rico de Thegheregge, Agn' le Benek; p.18, Rico le Beneke

Tassell, Bartholomew, of Balsham, Cambridgeshire, Will dated 24 February 1576/7. Diocese of Ely, Cambridgeshire Record Office. Mentions his daughter, Ann

Tassell, William, Yeoman of Balsham, Will dated 11 July 1574, proved 29 May 1575. N/A PROB 11/57. Mentions Anne, a daughter of his eldest son, Bartholomew

Tassell, William, Mercer of London, Will dated 20 October 1626, proved 19 June 1629. N/A PROB 11/156/54. Mentions his sister Anne Eaton

Taylor, Arnold J., 1940, Records of the Barony and Honour of the Rape of Lewes, SRS vol.44: Court Rolls, 1265-6,: p.39 – Simonem le Teghere, Thomam Teghere; p.44 – Simonem le Teyere; p.76-77, 6 Jan.1289/90, inquest re land of William Bardolf who died seized of a tenement in West Hoathly of the manor of Plumtone, held in chief of John de Warrenn'. Hugh Bardolf, son of William, is next heir. (see Hudson, SRS 10)

The Law Times, 1876, Tickeridge Farm, freehold, sold for £6,000

Thomas, Edward, 'The Gypsy'

Thomas, R. George, ed., 1978, *The Collected Poems of Edward Thomas*, Clarendon Press

Tickeridge House: for details of its construction, see the following references:- N/A, C3/365/33, dated 1621–1625, Lovell v. Bankes; Mercer, 1975; *SAC* 82, 1942, pp.65-72 ; *SAC* 83, 1943, p.19; *SAC* 95, 1957, pp.72-91; *SNQ* 95, 1957, pp.72-74; *VCH* of Sussex VII, p.166; Wealden Buildings Study Group report, 2002; Nairn & Pevsner, 1965; Mason, 1955; 1964, 1969, 1973 and 1975; Coutin, 2005; Ridley, 1971; *Country Life Magazine*, 5 Oct.2000, p.106

Toulson, Shirley, 1980, *The Drovers*, p.26

Trevelyan, G.M., *Illustrated English Social History*, Longmans, Vol.1, 1949; Vol.2, 1950

Tully v. Page, 1687, N/A C 10/276/60, John Tully v. Richard Page. A set of 11 documents compiled re will of Francis Tully of Tickeridge Farm, comprising detailed lists of farm produce, purchases and sales, and household items

Tully(e), Francis, Yeoman of West Hoathly, Will dated 22 Aug.1686, ESRO A37.186, no.20, m/f XA26/48, wife Ann, sons William and Benjamin, daughter Frances, father John of Ardingly, brother James

Tully, John, Yeoman of Ardingly, Will dated 1701, mentioned in 'The Place Names of Ardingly' by Mary S. Holgate. Sons John, James and Thomas

Turner, E., 'The College of Benedictine Canons at South Malling', *SAC* vol.5, pp.127-142

University of West of England, Bristol, 'Traditional Timber Framing – A Brief Introduction'

Vanderzee, George, ed., 1807, *Inquisitiones Nonarum temp. Edw.III, Inquests of the subsidy of ninths at the time of Edw.III (1327–1377)*, Record Commission. And see *SAC* Vol.20, pp.170-171

VCH, 1978, 'A History of the County of Cambridgeshire and the Isle of Ely', Vol.6. pp.127-135, Balsham

VCH, Essex, Vol.7, 1978, W.R. Powell, ed.: Parsonage and Rainham, re Slany

VCH, Shropshire, Vol.10, 1998, Currie et al. pp.221-233, John Slaney built almshouses and a school on Barrow Hill in 1618

VCH, Sussex, Vol.2: 1907, William Page, ed.: descriptions of locals and farmers in the 18th century.

VCH, Sussex, Vol.7, 1940, L.F.Saltzman, ed.: p.128, Bolney Farm, Ardingly: pp.166-7, Tickeridge House

Venables, Sara of London, Will dated 23 July 1606, N/A PROB 11/112/110: brothers William, Thomas and John Browne; my "brother" John Slany and my sister Elizabeth; "cosen" Mr. Thomas Lovell, Minister, and Titus his son "now dwelling with me". Will proved 25 June 1608

Venables/Venneibles, Richard, Citizen and Merchant Taylor of London, Will dated 28 July 1598, N/A PROB 11/92/118, mentions wife Sara; brothers Nicholas and Edward; sister Allice; brother-in-law John Slany, Merchant Taylor. Will proved 10 August 1598

Venn, A.C., Great Waldingfield Register, III, 108: Thomas Lovell, Rector, 1582–1610

Venn, John, 2011, Alumni Cantabrigienses: A Biographical List of all known students, graduates and holders of offices at the University of Cambridge from the Earliest Times to 1900, p.5, Caleb Kempe

Vince, John, 1992, Wells and Pumps, Surbus County Books, 'The water ram', 29; pp.24-5 Iron pumps

Virginia Magazine of History & Biography, Jan.1900, Vol.7, No.3, p.320, mentions John Harvey/Harby, Skinner and Merchant Adventurer (bc 1544)

Wadmore, J.F., 'History of the Skinners Company: Some Account of the Worshipful Company of Skinners of London, being the guild or fraternity of Corpus Christi'

Walt Disney Pictures, 2007, *Squanto: A Warrior's Tale*, DVD/video

Warner, Henry, Lt.Col. to Maj.Gen. Crawford, Will dated 20 Aug.1644, N/A PROB 11/193/291, mentions father Thomas and mother Anne; siblings Anne, Susan, Rose and Edward; daughters Dorothie and Rose; loving friend Mrs. Anne Eaton; executors Chichester Phillipps and Symon Eaton

Warner, Thomas, Minister of the church of Balsham, Will dated 25 March 1657, N/A PROB 11/254/606, mentions wife Anne; children Henry, Thomas, Edward, Rose, Anne and Susan, wife of Symon Eaton; brother Henry; Lt.Col. Symon Eaton; "my free land which I purchased of Mr. Symon Eaton"

Watson, Hewett C., 1837, The New Botanists' Guide to the Localities of the Rarer Plants of Britain, Vol.II: p.573, Spotted Hawkweed found in the wood between Tickeridge Farm and Selsfield Common

Wealden Buildings Study Group, July 2002, Site notes on visit to Tickeridge

Weeld/Welde, Humphrey, Alderman, Will dated 1 May 1610, N/A PROB 11/116/577, mentions Richard Bradgate, wife Mary's late husband; siblings Anne, Richard, Robert, Elizabeth, Johane, John and several more sisters; daughter Anne, Lady Slanye, mother-in-law. Will proved 3 December 1610

Welde, Mary, widow of London, Will dated 12 February 1622, N/A PROB 11/141/405, mentions uncle Thomas Phesant; "cozens" John and Humfrey Slaney; uncle Henry Slany; "cosen" Marten Bradgate; nephew Sir John Culpepper

West Hoathly parish council, 1977, 'West Hoathly Past and Present' 5th edn., p.9, Gravetye; p.10, Tickeridge

West Sussex Gazette, Thursday, 21 March 1935, p.4. Suicide of Alfred Ansfield

Wikipedia, 'Guinea Company (London)', est.1618

Wikipedia, 'John Slany'

Wikipedia, 'Little Ice Age', 13th & 14th centuries

Wikipedia, 'Stephen Slaney'

Willatts, R.M., 1982, 'Iron Slabs in St Swithun's Church, East Grinstead', *BEGS* no.32: p.5-6, re: vine-leaf decoration on firebacks

Willatts, Rosalind M., 1987, 'Iron Graveslabs: A sideline of the early Iron Industry', *SAC* 125, pp.99-113

Winbolt, S.E., May 1928, 'The Selsfield-Hassocks Roman Road', *SNQ* II, no.2: pp.35-38, includes map of the route

Winthrop, Adam, 1871, 'The Winthrop Papers 1498–1628', Massachusetts Historical Society, Vol.1, 5th series: pp.243-4, Thomas Lovell

Witney, K.P., 1976, *The Jutish Forest: A Study of the Weald of Kent from 450 to 1380 AD*, University of London Athlone Press: droves and settlement in the Weald, esp. pp.139, 154, 162-3

Wolseley, Viscountess, 1930, *Some Sussex Byways*, pub. Medici Society, with drawings by Garnet R. Wolseley, ARWA: p.14, Tickeridge

Wood, P.D., Spring 1996, 'East Grinstead in the Domesday Survey', *BEGS* No.58, p.20, Discussion of locally identified holdings

Woodman, Charles, Yeoman of Haselden, East Grinstead, Will dated 20 Nov.1778, N/A PROB 11/1077/129, son James, dau. Sarah

WSRO, AddMss 47836, miscellaneous farm plans and estate maps of Tickeridge

WSRO, Ep I/336, 1 Sept.1615, mentions John Slanye and Simonis Bankes (in Latin), has signature of John Slany

WSRO, Ep-I-6-355, 1616, mentions Simon Bankes (in Latin and difficult to read)

WSRO, Add MSS 48,841/g, 11 October 1811, Valuation of Woodland at Tickeridge

WSRO, SP 2560, 12 July 1876, Sales particulars, including a map

WSRO, Add MSS 28,161, 25 October 1876, Indenture re sale of Tickeridge by John Woodman, Farmer of East Grinstead, to Henry Longley, Timber Merchant of West Hoathly, listing the fields in the parish of East Grinstead

WSRO, Add MSS 47,771, 25 October 1876, Indenture re sale of Tickeridge by John Woodman to Henry Longley, including a map, listing the fields in the parishes of West Hoathly and East Grinstead

WSRO, Add MSS 47,773, 28 February 1878, Release of Seignory of Tickeridge, by Charles Hubert Husey, Lord of the Manor of Plumpton Boscage, to Henry Longley

WSRO, Add MSS 47,771, 23 August 1879, Indenture re sale of Tickeridge Mead by Henry Longley to James Kennedy Esdaile

WSRO, Add MSS 47,771, 10 June 1880, Additional note on main document dated 1876: Indenture re sale of 10+ acres of land by Henry Longley to the Lewes and East Grinstead Railway Co.

WSRO, Add MSS 47,774, 10 June 1880, Indenture re sale of 10+ acres of land by Henry Longley to the Lewes and East Grinstead Railway Co.

WSRO, Add MSS 47,771, 21 October 1880, Additional note on main document dated 1876: Indenture re sale of land by Henry Longley to Edward Easton

WSRO, Add MSS 47,772, 18 December 1881, Indenture re sale of 51+ acres woodland (Holstein and Mine Pit Woods) by William John Langdale to Henry Longley for £1,054. Includes a map

WSRO, Add MSS 47836, Undated, Map of Tickeridge Estate

WSRO, Add MSS 47,772, 12 May 1900, Indenture re sale of 23+ acres of land by Henry Longley to William Robinson of Gravetye

WSRO, Add MSS 47,771, 12 May 1900. Additional note on main document dated 1876: Indenture re sale of 29+ acres of land by Henry Longley to William Robinson of Gravetye

WSRO, Add MSS 47,771, 11 June 1907, Additional note on main document dated 1876: Indenture/Conveyance re Oak Lodge (lately erected), approx. ½ acre, from Henry Longley to his son Frank Longley

WSRO, Add MSS 28,162, Conveyance of Tickeridge Farm, Henry Longley to his sons, Henry junior and Frank. Includes a map

Young, Rev. Arthur, 1808, General View of the Agriculture of the County of Sussex, Drawn up for the Board of Agriculture and Internal Improvement, Richard Phillips, London. Page 417 describes the condition of roads in the Weald

Zell, Michael, 1994, *Industry in the Countryside; Wealden Society in the Sixteenth Century*, Cambridge University Press

Appendix 1

Will of John Kempe

Dated 15 July 1579, Proved 24 April 1587

IN THE NAME OF GOD AMEN the fifteenth
July anno 1579 I John Kempe parson of ffreshwater in the Isle of Wight and the
servant of God through the mouth of Jesus Christ my Lord and only Saviour in whom
it hath pleased him to accept me for his use and by the assistance of his holy spirit my
comforter I do crave as in all things use so now in the making of this my last will and testament
renouncing all other wills whatsoever shall be found As touching my soul I yield up to God
my only creator and to Jesus Christ perfect god and man my only redeemer and saviour And to
God the holy ghost my sanctifier comforter and instifyer My body I do commit to the earth to be
buried where it shall please Almighty God in sure and certain hope that in the last day God will
raise it up again for his own mercy and promise late made to me and to all men that be in
Christ Jesus and so joining both my body and soul together I shall enter with his son Christ
Jesus my only saviour by his *** and clothed with his righteousness into that immortal glory
and felicity which he hath prepared for all that believe in him there to reign with him for
ever As touching any doctrine that ever I did hold and teach the same of it short
followeth that is to say repentance towards God faith in our Lord Jesus and obedience to
his word Any doctrine contrary to this I did never hold nor teach whatsoever hath been
said of me to the contrary I call this day heaven and earth to witness to my soul against
them if they do not repent But truly such as hath been given more to doubtful questions
than to learn the truth yea more curious than wise more given to seek knowledge to contend
than by love to edify and amend more in contention to continue than to walk in virtue I could
never away with But yet as God is my witness I walked not with them in malice I speak
as a man may speak having infirmities although they have from time to time much abused me
    (page 2)
but this I do confess that I have many times dissembled at their malice and laughed at their
folly for this always *** did assure me that they should never overthrow the truth in me neither
before the world prevail against me in such wise as they looked for and hoped to do and for
further knowledge of such doctrine as I did teach as well in Queen Mary's time as all the time
*** to this day I have put the effect of it whatsoever I did and do hold unto certain
Articles the which are in diverse men's hands to be seen And they are also by Mr. Foxe put into
The third or last setting forth of the Book of Acts and moment in which book they are
With other things to be seen under my name ITEM I do give …

His will goes on to mention:
The poor of Freshwater, Gatcombe, Isle of Wight; his wife Annys; lands in Surrey; house and land in the parish of Godstone, Surrey formerly owned by Tobias Kemp; sons Tobias, John and Caleb; granddaughter Mercy Kemp; daughter Hannah's children; Thomas Banks; brothers Richard and Edward.
It is finally signed on 23 January 1586/7, and proved on 24 April 1587

National Archives ref: PROB 11/70/212

Appendix 2
Waldingfield Family Tree

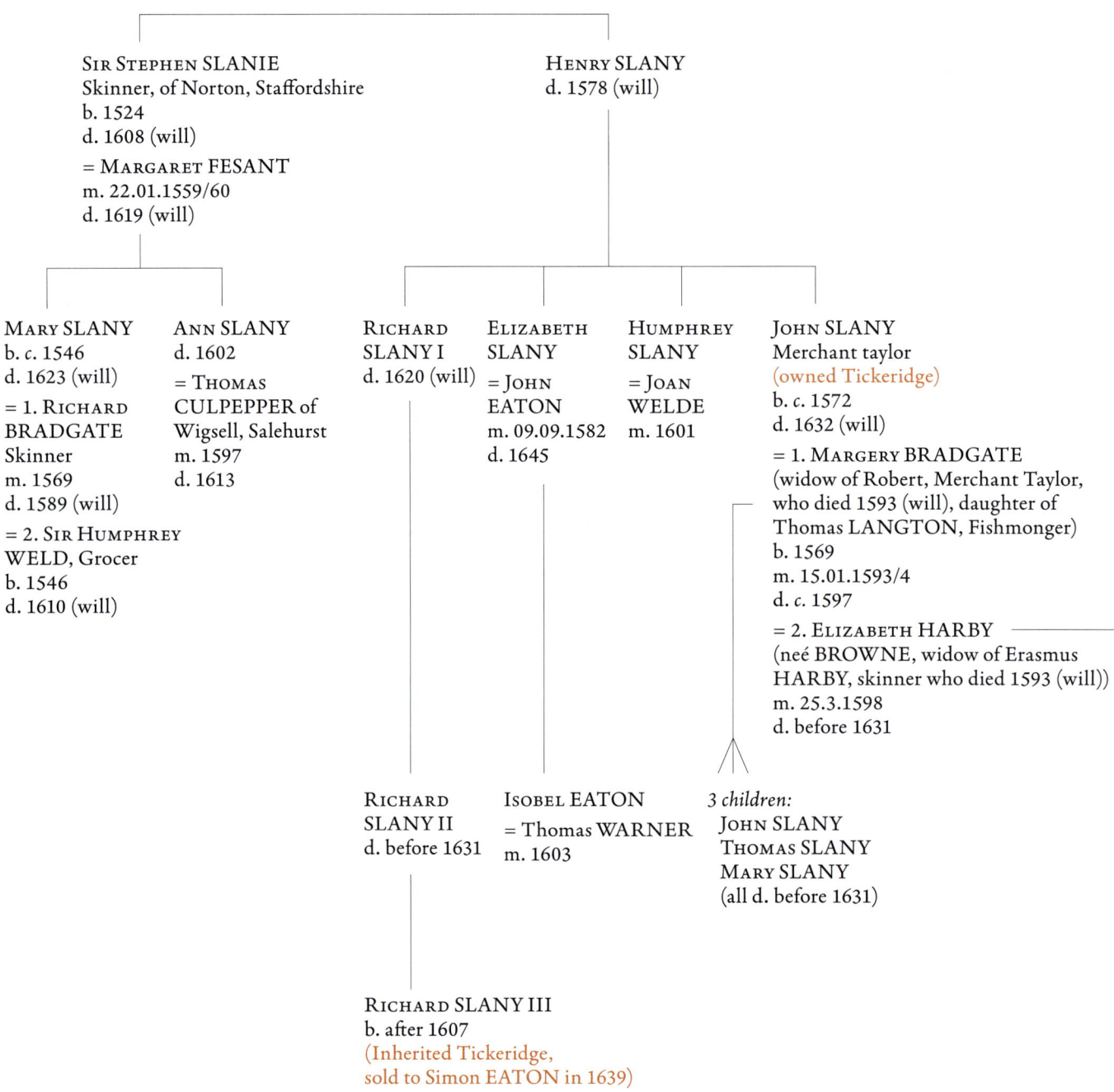

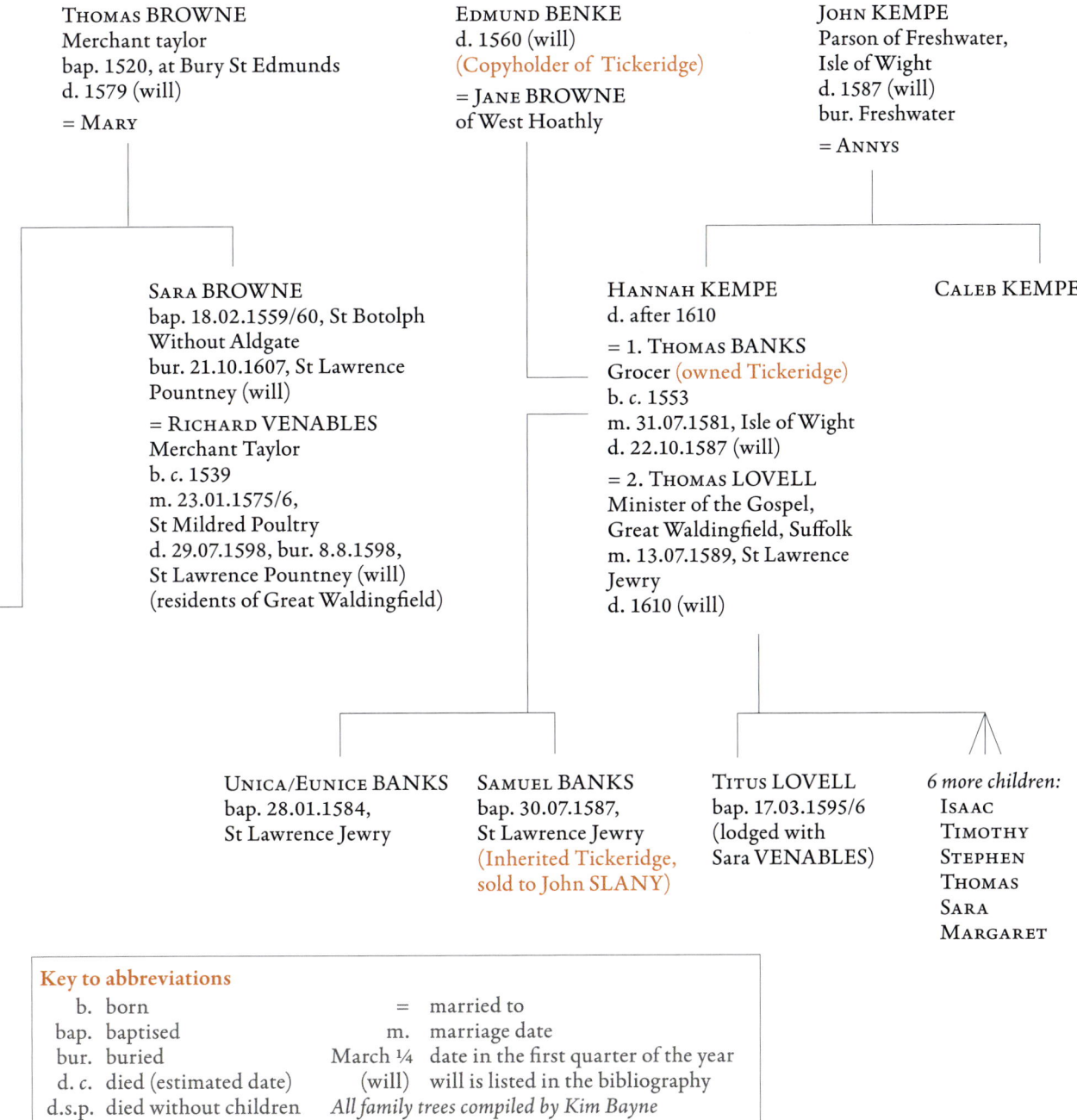

WALDINGFIELD FAMILY TREE

Appendix 3
Hamlin Family Tree

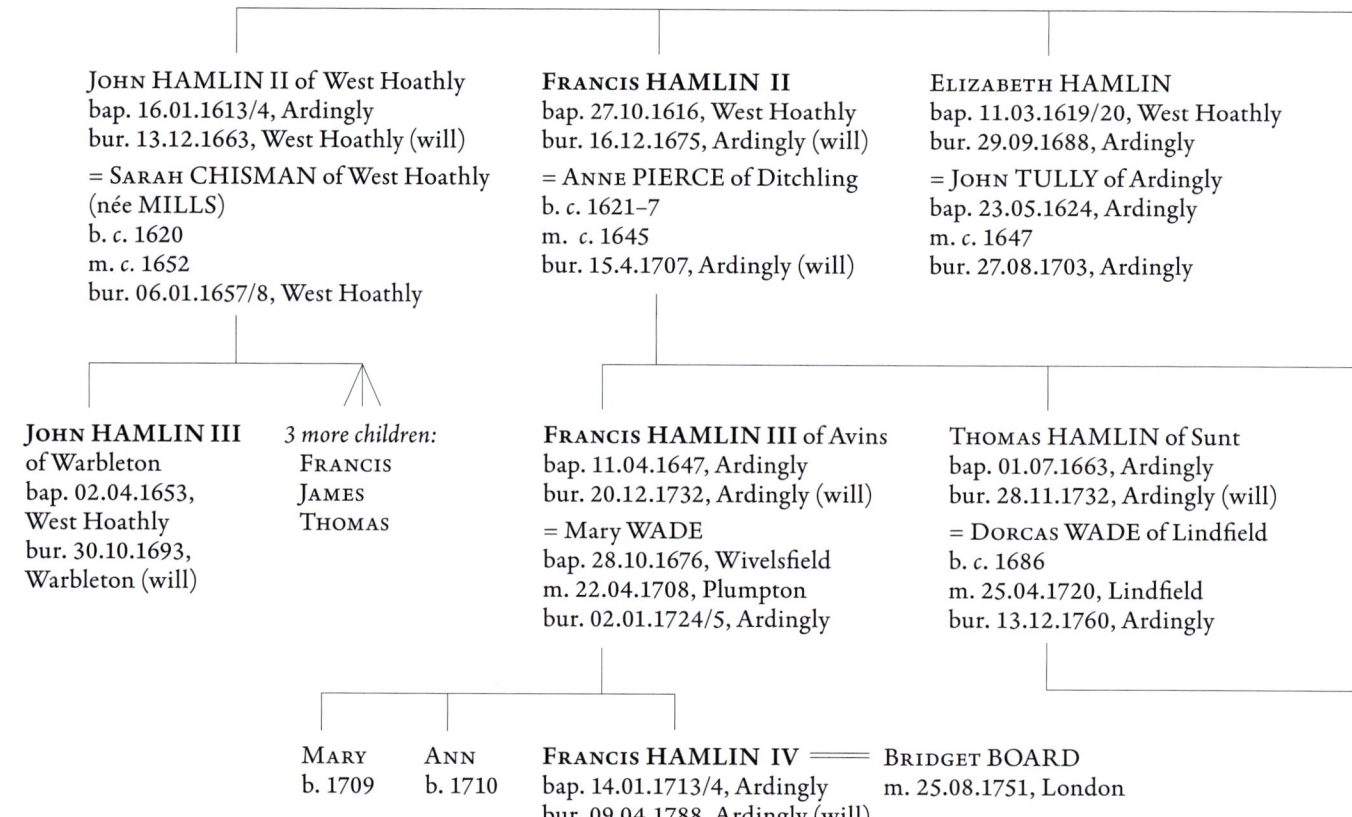

Key to abbreviations

b.	born	=	married to
bap.	baptised	m.	marriage date
bur.	buried	March ¼	date in the first quarter of the year
d. c.	died (estimated date)	(will)	will is listed in the bibliography
d.s.p.	died without children		*All family trees compiled by Kim Bayne*

Hamlin Family Tree

John HAMLIN I
of Maresfield, Sussex
m. 05.02.1584/5, Lindfield

= **Margaret WILLARD**
(née INFIELD, widow of Richard WILLARD)
d. before 1610

---

1. **Elizabeth NEWNAM**
bap. 25.02.1592/3, Ardingly
m. 24.11.1612, Maresfield
bur. 17.04.1630, Ardingly

= **Francis HAMLIN I**
Husbandman of Maresfield,
Yeoman of Ardingly and West Hoathly,
lived at Bolney Farm, Ardingly
b. c. 1588
bur. 27.2.1667/8, Ardingly (will)

= 2. **Elizabeth**
m. c.1631
bur. 22.08.1664, Ardingly

William HAMLIN of Hailsham
bap. 02.03.1622/3, West Hoathly
bur. 29.04.1662, Maresfield (will)
= **Elizabeth KENCHLEY**
bap. 25.10.1635, Westham, Sussex
m. 21.07.1657, Willingdon
d. 1663

Mary HAMLIN
bap. 10.04.1630, Ardingly
= **John HASELDEN**
m. 03.07.1657, Lewes

5 more children:
Elizabeth, 1616
Richard, 1624
Edward, 1626
Sara, 1627
Thomas

6 children:
Frances, 1632
James, 1637
Mercie, 1639
Joseph, 1641
Edyffe
Joshua, 1644

---

2 more children:
John of Ardingly
b. 1650,
d. 1732 (will)
Anne = Allen Mills
d. 1683

William HAMLIN
of Brookhouse, West Hoathly
b. 1663
d. 1743 (will)
= 1. **Mary BROWNE** of West Hoathly
= 2. **Anne FAULCONER** of Balcombe

Elizabeth HAMLIN
b. c. 1600
= **John FAULCONER** of Balcombe
m. 1691

John HAMLIN
of Sunt
b. c. 1721
d. 26.05.1774,
Lindfield (will)

= **Ann WADE**
b. c. 1730
m. 09.07.1763,
Lindfield
d. 20.03.1771,
Lindfield

William
b. c. 1728
d. 1766

Thomas HAMLIN
Vicar of Waldron, mentioned
in the Diary of Thomas Turner;
Rector of Hever, Kent
b. before 1732
bur. 23.07.1762

= **Elizabeth STONE**
m. 11.06.1754, Framfield
d. 1781

Ann HAMLIN
bap. 27.09.1764, Lindfield
d. 1847
= 1. **John BORRER** m. 1785
= 2. **John DENNETT** m. 1799

Mary HAMLIN
bap. 03.03.1767 Lindfield
bur. 10.11.1847, Lewes

= **William Franklyn HICK** of Lewes
b. c. 1764
m. 22.08.1796, Henfield
bur. 22.09.1843, Ile-de-France, Paris (will)

Appendix 4

Slany Family Tree

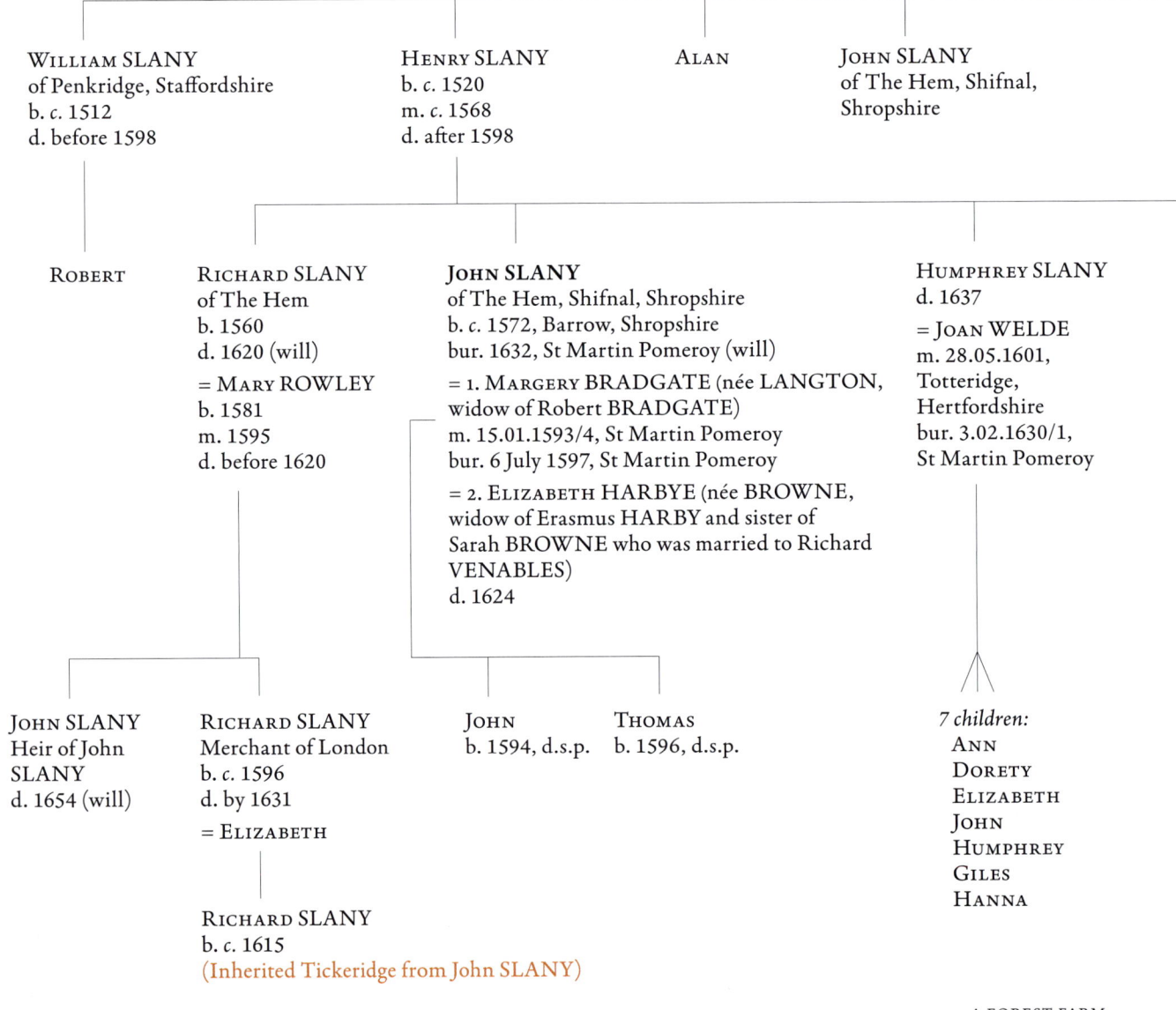

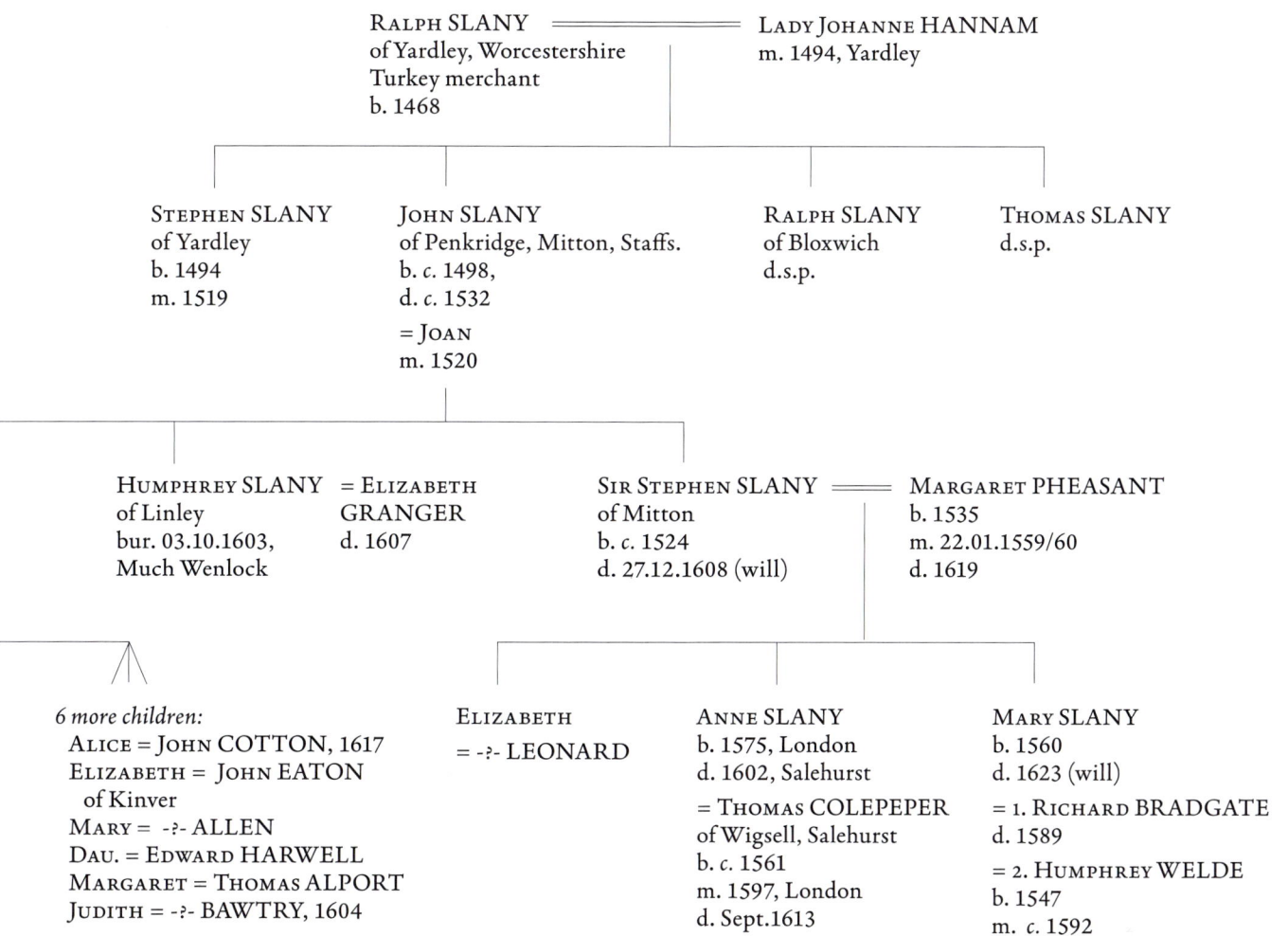

Key to abbreviations

b.	born	=	married to
bap.	baptised	m.	marriage date
bur.	buried	March ¼	date in the first quarter of the year
d. c.	died (estimated date)	(will)	will is listed in the bibliography
d.s.p.	died without children		*All family trees compiled by Kim Bayne*

Sir Stephen SLANY
d. 27.12.1608

Henry SLANY
of Willey, Shropshire
b. *c.* 1525
d. after 1598
(See SLANY family tree)

William EATON
d. 1647, Kinver,
Staffordshire
(Business partner of
Humphrey SLANY)

John EATON/ETON ══ **Elizabeth SLANYE**
b. *c.* 1560   b. *c.* 1560
bur. 03.01.1643/4 Kinver   m. 09.09.1582, Kinver
                                d. after 1631

Humphrey SLANY
d. 1637
= **Johane WILDE**
m. 28.05.1601
bur. 03.02.1630/1

5 more children:
 William, bap. 1583, Kinver
 Agnes, bap. 1585, Kinver
 Elizabeth, bap. 10.09.1587, Kinver
 Marie, bap. 17.8.1589, Kinver
 Alice, bap. 1592, Kinver

1. **Isabell EATON** ══ **Thomas WARNER**, son of John
bap. 22.11.1584,   b. 13.01.1579/80, Frocester, Gloucs.
St Martin Ludgate   d. 04.04.1657, Balsham (will)
m. 23.11.1603,
St Dunstan, Stepney
d. *c.* 1606

Henry WARNER
Lieutenant colonel
bap. 20.04.1606, St Dunstan
d. 29.03.1644/5
= **Elizabeth HAROLD**
(née PHILLIPS)
bur. 02.08.1638, Balsham

5 more children:
 Thomas, b. 1612
 Elizabeth, b. 1619
 Rose, b. 1622
 Thomas, b. 1625
 Frances, b. 1626

Dorothy WARNER
bap. 07.09.1637, Balsham

Key to abbreviations
 b. born
 bap. baptised
 bur. buried
 d. *c.* died (estimated date)
 d.s.p. died without children
 = married to
 m. marriage date
 March ¼ date in the first quarter of the year
 (will) will is listed in the bibliography

All family trees compiled by Kim Bayne

Appendix 5
Warner and Eaton Family Tree

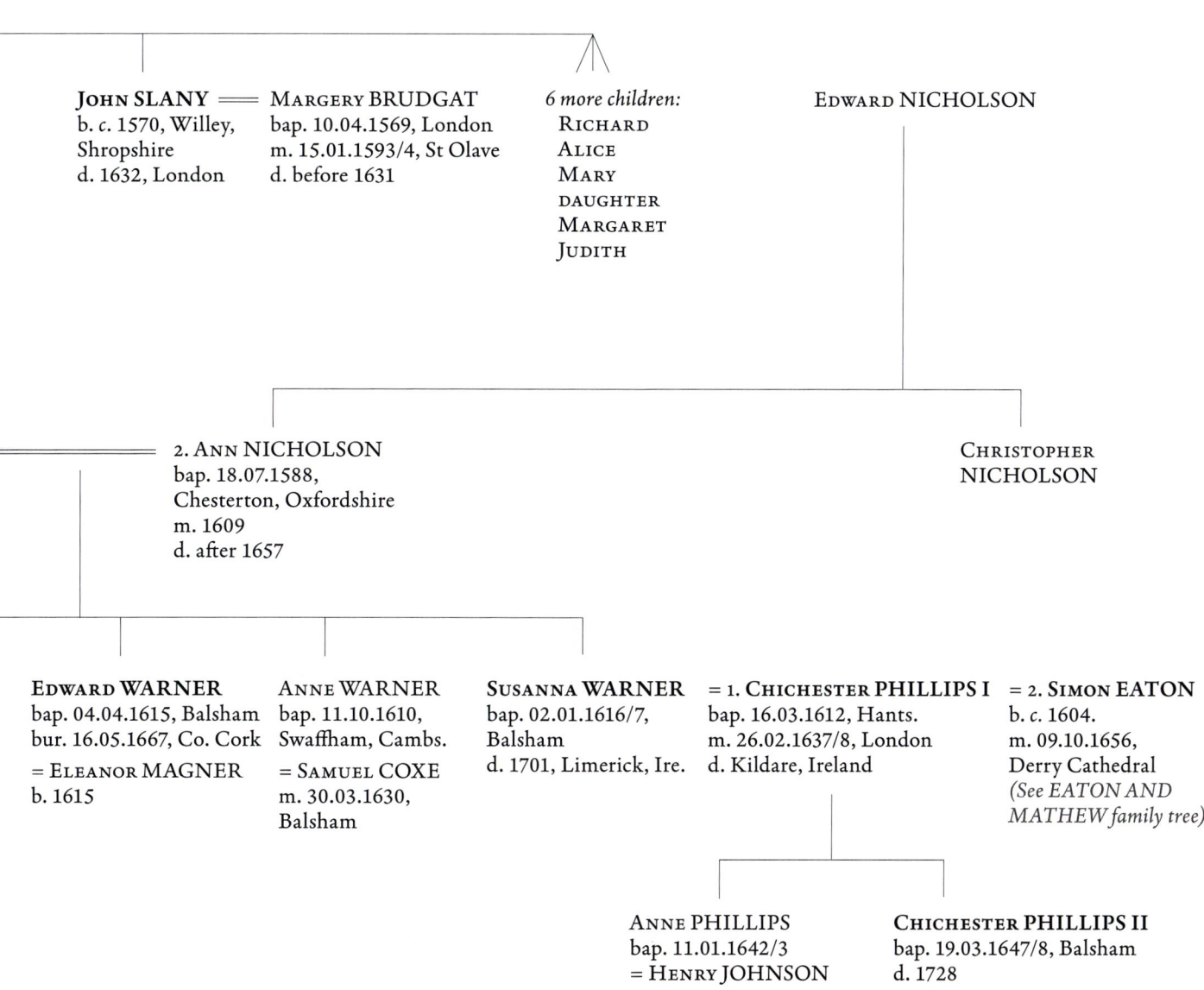

WARNER AND EATON FAMILY TREE

Christopher NICHOLSON

2. Ann NICHOLSON
bap. 18.07.1588,
Chesterton, Oxfordshire
m. 1609
d. after 1657

═ **Thomas WARNER** son of John
b. 13.01.1579/80, Frocester, Gloucestershire
d. 04.04.1657, Balsham (will)

Henry WARNER
Lieutenant colonel
bap. 20.04.1606, St Dunstan
d. 29.03.1644/5

= **Elizabeth HAROLD**
(née PHILLIPS)
bur. 02.08.1638, Balsham

Anne WARNER
bap. 11.10.1610,
Swaffham, Cambs.

= **Samuel COXE**
m. 30.03.1630,
Balsham

Edward WARNER
bap. 04.04.1615, Balsham
bur. 16.05.1667, Co. Cork

= **Eleanor MAGNER**
b. 1615

Dorothy WARNER
bap. 07.09.1637, Balsham

Key to abbreviations			
b.	born	=	married to
bap.	baptised	m.	marriage date
bur.	buried	March ¼	date in the first quarter of the year
d. *c.*	died (estimated date)	(will)	will is listed in the bibliography
d.s.p.	died without children	*All family trees compiled by Kim Bayne*	

Appendix 6
Eaton and Mathew Family Tree

1. ISABELL EATON
bap. 22.11.1584,
St Martin Ludgate
m. 23.11.1603,
St Dunstan, Stepney
d. *c.* 1606

5 more children:
WILLIAM, bap. 1583, Kinver, Staffordshire
AGNES, bap. 1585, Kinver
ELIZABETH, bap. 10.09.1587, Kinver
MARIE, bap. 17.08.1589, Kinver
ALICE, bap. 1592, Kinver

ANNE TASSELL
born 20.06.1568,
Balsham, Cambridgeshire
= - ? - EATON
(*See* TASSELL AND EATON *family tree*)

5 more children:
THOMAS, b. 1612
ELIZABETH, b. 1619
ROSE, b. 1622
THOMAS, b. 1625
FRANCES, b. 1626

1. CHICHESTER PHILLIPS I
bap. 16.03.1612, Hampshire
m. 26.02.1637/8, London
d. Kildare, Ireland

SUSANNA WARNER
bap. 02.01.1616/7,
Balsham
d. 1701, Limerick,
Ireland

2. SIMON EATON
b. *c.* 1604.
m. 09.10.1656,
Derry Cathedral, N. Ireland

ANNE PHILLIPS
bap. 11.01.1642/3
= HENRY JOHNSON

CHICHESTER PHILLIPS II
bap. 19.03.1647/8, Balsham
d. 1728
= SARAH HANDCOCK

1. SIMON EATON
b. 1660
m. 06.06.1678, Cork
d. 19.11.1684, Ireland

MARY ALDWORTH

2. GEORGE MATHEW
m. 16.10.1686
d. 07.12.1735

ALDWORTH EATON

MARTHA EATON
b. *c.* 1682
m. 1609

GEORGE MATHEW

EATON AND MATHEW FAMILY TREE

Appendix 7
Tassell and Eaton Family Tree

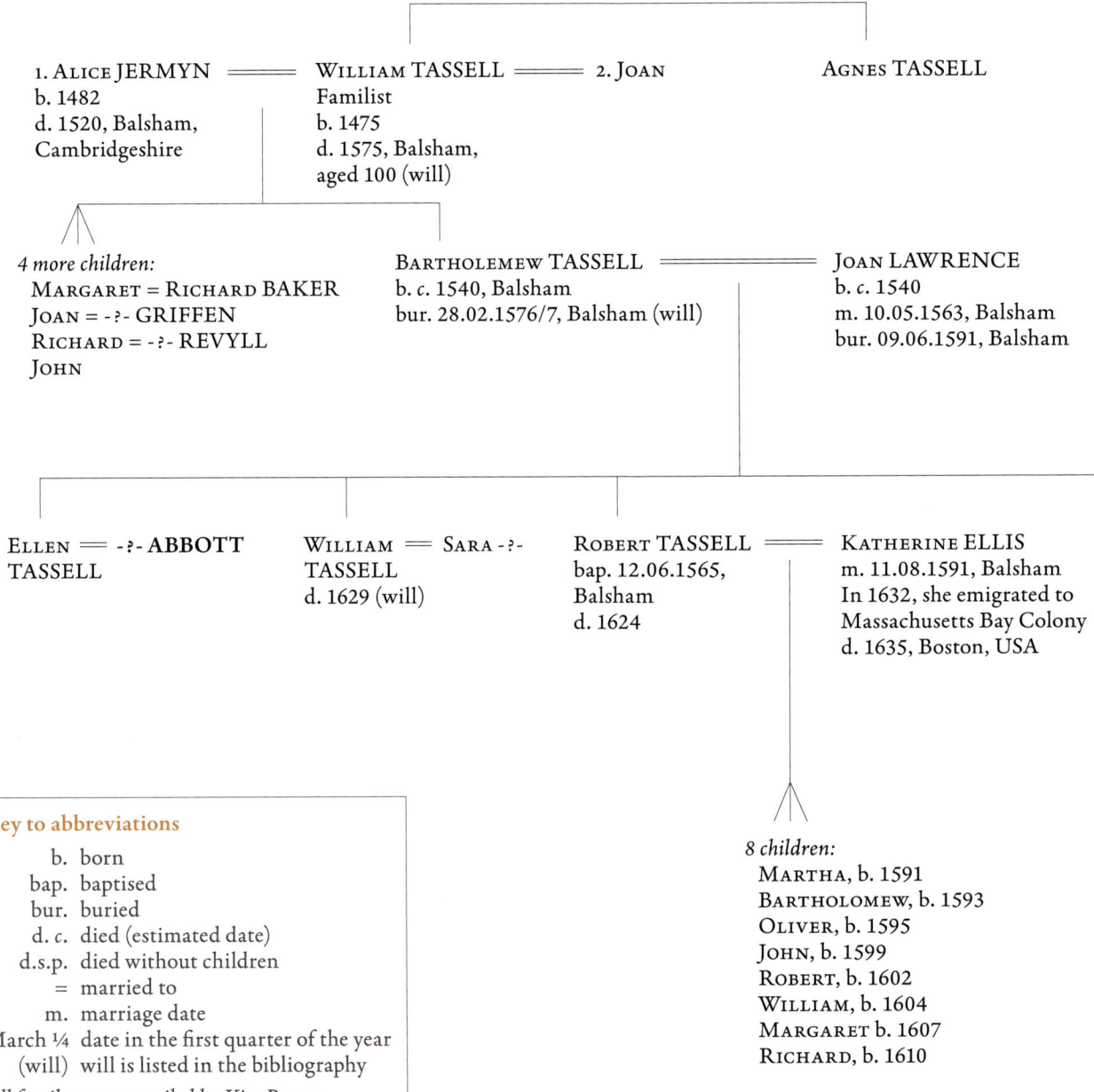

Key to abbreviations
- b. born
- bap. baptised
- bur. buried
- d. *c.* died (estimated date)
- d.s.p. died without children
- = married to
- m. marriage date
- March ¼ date in the first quarter of the year
- (will) will is listed in the bibliography

All family trees compiled by Kim Bayne

ANNE TASSELL ══ **- ? - EATON**
bap. 20.06.1568,   d. before 1631
Balsham

3 more children:
MARGRET
JOAN, bap. 03.10.1572
ALICE, bap. 19.02.1575/6

SIMON EATON ══ SUSANNA WARNER
b. *c.* 1604   bap. 02.01.1616/7, Balsham
d. 10.12.1697, London   m. 09.10.1656, Derry Cathedral, N.Ireland
                    d. 1701, Dunmoylan Castle, Co. Limerick, Ireland

TASSELL AND EATON FAMILY TREE

Appendix 8

Boakes, Gilbert and Still Family Tree

Robert STILL
Agricultural labourer
bap. 11.12.1825, Hartfield
bur. 04.07.1908, Cowden
═══
Jemima COLE
b. 13.01.1839, Withyham
m. 17.11.1855, Hartfield
bur. 15.11.1919, Cowden

Frances COMBES
Sick nurse
b. *c.* 1837, Ashurst Wood, Sussex
m. June ¼ 1857, Sevenoaks reg.
d. March ¼ 1913, East Grinstead reg.
═══
Thomas BOAKES/BOKES
Agricultural labourer
bap. 27.05.1932, Cowden
d. before 1901

13 more children:
b. 1857–1884, Cowden

Harriet Mary STILL
Domestic servant
b. June ¼ 1869, Sevenoaks reg.
m. 16.04.1906, Cowden
bur. 18.09.1943, East Grinstead
═══
Horace BOAKES
Sawyer
b. Dec. ¼ 1870, Cowden
bur. 30.12.1952, East Grinstead

7 more children:
b. 1860–1874, Cowden

Edith Mabel Annie STILL
b. 02.02.1892, Old Kent Road, Deptford
d. Sept. ¼ 1979, Thirsk reg., Yorkshire
═══
Horace GILBERT
Farmer of Hernhill, Kent
b. Sept. ¼ 1888, Hernhill, Faversham reg.
m. Dec. ¼ 1915, E.Grinstead reg.
d. Dec. ¼ 1959, Ashford reg.

1. **Teresa E. RICE**
b. March ¼ 1916, South Shields
d. *c.* 1998
═══
Robin GILBERT
Headmaster
b. 01.08.1916, Whitstable, Kent
d. 24.10.2003, Clifton Moor, Yorkshire
═══
2. **Patricia**

```
                SAMUEL BOAKES         ══════        MARY ALLCOCK
                Agricultural labourer                bap. 14.05.1797, East Grinstead
                bap. 19.03.1797, Sevenoaks           m. 10.11.1817, Pembury
```

MICHAEL BOAKES ═══════ HARRIET SPITAL/SPITTLE   *5 more children:*   THOMAS HART STILL
bap. 13.03.1836, Cowden   b. *c.* 1839, Cowden   b. 1818–1829,
d. June ¼ 1909, Sevenoaks m. Dec. ¼ 1862, Sevenoaks reg.   Chiddingstone
                           d. June ¼ 1905, Sevenoaks

5 more children: EMILY BOAKES   ═══════   GEORGE SYLVESTER STILL
b. 1864–1880   b. June ¼ 1872, Sevenoaks reg.   Agricultural labourer
                          d. 1935, Tonbridge reg.   b. *c.* 1867, Cowden
                                                             m. 18.10.1890, Markbeech, Kent
                                                             d. June ¼ 1942, Tonbridge reg.

Key to abbreviations

b.	born	=	married to
bap.	baptised	m.	marriage date
bur.	buried	March ¼	date in the first quarter of the year
d. *c.*	died (estimated date)	(will)	will is listed in the bibliography
d.s.p.	died without children		*All family trees compiled by Kim Bayne*

BOAKES, GILBERT AND STILL FAMILY TREE

Appendix 9

Tully Documents, 1687–8
Table of Contents of Documents 1–6

DOCUMENT 1

Document delivered to Richard Paige, 22 February 1687	£.s.d
For a pen & spent all	
For held to round	
All churches & fairs	
Chimney money (ie Hearth Tax)	16s./ year
Alfrey for farriering & smiths work	6s.
..... came for milk & butter	
8 lbs of beef	1s.6d.
For washing and shearing sheep	1s.6d.
John ffairehall for threshing	12s.6d.
Spent at Buxted fair with bullocks	6d.
Paid John Nin for wages	12s.
Pocknell & Picks wifes wages in harvest	6s.
For setting of a new shoe	4d.
For 100 nails	6d.
For a hog pen and spent	2s.
For	1s.
For mending a cutter	6d.
John ffairhall wages	£1.10s.
For curing a hide	2s.
For chipping of a plow	1s.
For setting 2 new shoes	8d.
For tobacco stalks to wash sheep	4d.
For 5 stone of beef	6s.
For nursing of Ben Turley to hearle	£1
Edward Ridley for	10s.
Ffrancis Pocknell for work	10s.
Trendell for 12 bushells of Oats	15s.
Thomas Sherman for 3 quarters of Oats	£1.10s.
John ffairehall for wages	15s.
Ffrancis Pocknell for work	16s.6d.
To Wickings a poore tax in Grinstead	3s.
John ffairehall for wages	12s.
Picks boy in harvest	3s.
For meat	1s.
For shooing of horses	£1
For a gallon of Oatmell	6d.
Spent at selling 2 Oxen	6d.
John Tully paid Chimney Money (ie Hearth Tax), 4s.	
For shooing horses	1s.
5 stones of beef	6s.
For reaping and mowing	£4.11s.
For 200 nails	1s.
For mowing & haying grass	£7.4s.6d.
John Mergum for meat	10s.
For drinking of horses	2s.
Will Tulley wages	£9

Additional items in the personal estate of ffrancis Tulley, now in the possession of his widow Anne

Some ducks	1 girdle	1 colt in the hands of William Seale, appraised at £1.15s.	1 feather bed 2 bolsters
Some geese	1 pair of gloves	1 farme at Mr. Willetts	1 worsted rug & 2 pillows
Some poultry	Some cravatts	1 .... Debt due from Nicho.....	
Some stalls of bees	Handkerchifes		
Some bottles	1 cradle		

Document 1 continued

People mentioned	Details of payments made to them by John Tully	£.s.d
Will Hearle	Paid for work	
William Simand(s)	Paid for work	
Will Tulley	Paid for board, Wages	
John Nim	Wages	5s.
ffrancis Pocknall	Paid for work	6s.
Alfrey	Farrier and Smith	6s.
Payne	Paid for board	£1.11s.6d.
Mr. Pawwell	Tithes	4s.
John Haisilden	Paid	10s.
John ffairehall	Wages, and threshing	2s.6d.
Edward Ridley	Paid	10s.
Trendell	Paid for Oats	
Thomas Sherman	Paid for Oats	
Wickings	Poore Tax in E. Grinstead	
Pocknell and Ticks wives	Wages in harvest	
John Mer..um	Paid for meat	
William Maynard	Document witness	
Thomas Pilbeame	Document witness	
William Seale	(?) Horse breaker	
Mr. Willett		

Document 2

People mentioned	Details of payments made to them by John Tully	£. s. d.
John Duny....	Paid	
Richard P....	Paid	
Nathaniell Browne's daughter	Paid tithes	£1.10s.
Mr. Stevens	Paid tithe	9s.
John Steere	Paid for a tubb	10s.
William Hamlin	Due on a bond	£21.10s.
Ann Hamlin	Due on a bond	£89
John Bankes	Paid for a plow	10s.
Ann Willitt	Paid for tanning a hide	5s.
Mr. Cullpeper	Paid for keeping sheep	£1.4s.
Richard Bridgyes	Smith	£1.11s.
John Browne	Tithes in Hoadley	

National Archives ref: C 10/276/60 ly 1579, Proved 24 April 1587

Document 3

People mentioned	Details of payments made to them by John Tully	£. s. d.
Edward Jarvis	Paid for 46lb of beef	5s.3d.
Hearle	Paid for nursing Ben Tulley	15s.
Will Realfe	Paid for 9 stone of Oats	
Edward Muddle	Paid for "setting hops"	5s.2d.
James Baxshell	Paid for hop plants and work	14s.
Goody Wald…	Paid for nursing Ben Tulley	£1.5s.
Thomas Vinoll	Poore Tax in Hoadley	£1.10s.
Mrs. Mathew	Paid for physick	4s.
Goody Pocknall	Paid for haying	10s.
… Pocknall	Paid for mowing Oats	6s.
Thomas Selkner	Paid for keeping 2 steers	10s.
Joseph …	Paid for thatching	15s.6d.
Swaine	Paid for weaving	4s.
Edward Jarvis	Paid for 42 lb of beef	4s.6d.
John ffairhall	Wages	£3.4s.6d.
Nickolde the weaver	Paid for work	9s.6d.
John Bankes	Paid for a coffin with plates	10s.6d.
The Registrar	Re death of son, ffrancis	18s.6d.
Hackman	For trying the seale	1s.
Winter	Paid for the writing	1s.6d.
Walter	For writing the other seale	1s.6d.
Mr. Suwell	Paid 6 years tithes	£1.4s.10d.
Mr. Vernol	Paid tithes	9s.
ffrancis Hamlin	Paid	£73
John Mathew	Paid for shop goods	
James Lindfield	Paid	£6
Alfry the Smith	Paid	13s.
Doosons the Doctor	Paid	£1
Mr. Willett	Paid	£2.4s.
Cornish	Paid for lock and sack	10s.6d.
Nicholas …	Paid for candles	6s.6d.
John Weller	Paid for phisick	7s.
Mr. Abbott	Paid for rent, for 1687	£75
Thomas Davi	Paid	£1.10s.
James Lindfield	Paid for tithes, Oct.1687	£1.5s.
Edward James	Paid	
Mr. Vernoll	Paid	£1.10s.
John Dungate	? Tanner/Farrier	10s.
Richard P….	Paid	
Nathaniell Brownes daughter	Paid for tithes	£1.10s.
Mr. Stevens	Paid for tithes	9s.
William Hamlin	Due on bond	£21.10s.
Anne Hamlin	Due on bond	

Document 4

Items mentioned	Value or Payment Rec'd
1 brass spoon	1s.
1 little table	5s.
1 pair brandirons fire panne & tongs	6s.
1 warming pan	5s.
1 tradle rug	1s.6d.
1 wicker chair	5s.
1 trundle bedstedle cord & matt	6s.
2 pewter dishes weighing 6lb.2oz	4s.
1 flock bed & 1 bolster	12s.
3 blankets	4s.
1 riding coat	18s.
1 standing stoole	2s.6d.
1 hog weighing 22 stone & 6lbs	£1.14s.
1 sow weighing 18 stone & 5lbs	£1.17s.11¼d.
1 half a hog weighing 10 stone	15s.
1 small piece of "linty woolry"	3s.
1 dressed hide	12s.
22 lbs of wool	14s.8d.
1 coat	4s.
1 heifer & calf	£3.10s.
1 colt	£1
2 sheep	14s.6d.
1 yearly stoore	£1.10s.
Funeral charges for ffrancis Tully	£2.14s.

People mentioned	details of payments made to them by John Tully	£.s.d.
Edward Paine & John Browning	Paid for the Lease on Tickeridge Farm	£80
Mr. Barrett	For proving ffrancis Tully's will	£1.2s.10d.

Document 5

Household & Personal items

1 butter tub sold to Thomas Stoner, valued at 2s.6d.
11 yards of cloth
1 desk with writing
1 bedstedle matt cord & buckerum
1 sillybut pot
2 coats
1 old petticoat
2 old pairs of breeches
1 hatt
1 table
1 frame
11 joyned stools
1 small cupboard
3 brandirons
1 iron pot
1 fire pan and tongs
1 iron fender
1 plate
1 settle
1 gun
1 bedstedle curtains, valance matt cord
1 feather bed
1 feather bolster
2 chaff bolsters
1 blanket
1 rug
1 chest of drawers
3 chests
1 box
2 boards
2 pieces of homespun cloth
3 pewter dishes
1 pair of gridirons
1 old bedstead
1 bedsteadle mat and cord
8 pairs of cowan sheets
11 table cloths
3 pieces of coarse linen
4 pairs of fine sheets
3 dozen napkins
5 pillow coats
9lb tyre
1 pair roasting irons

Produce from Tickeridge Farm sold by John Tully	
Oats, 66 bushells	£4.14s.4d
Wheat, 15 bushells	£1.11s.4d.
Peas, 5 bushells	15s.1d.
Hops, 3 lb	4s.6d.
Apples, 40 bushells sold to John Hamlin	£1
Beans, 2 gallons	1s.
1 fat sheep sold to John Budgin	7s.
8lb wood	5s.
2lb black wool	2s.
Butter and cheese	9s.
Feathers sold to Dawes	-
16 rabbits	9s.4d.
6 sucking pigs	7s.6d.
A mow of wheat unthreshed	£15
A stack of hay & part of a stack	£10
1 mare	£8
1 old wool pack	1s.

In the Brewhouse	
1 furnace	*In the Cellar*
1 bucking tub	2 milk heads
1 hog tub	2 little tubs
1 cooler	1 long cooler
1 other tub	1 3-legged cooler
	Some fence boards
In the Bakehouse	2 crocks
2 forms	1 pair of slings
2 coolers	6 small drinking vessels
2 old tubs	1 pair of blades
6 crocks	

Document 6

In the Personal Estate of ffrancis Tully	Details: Sold to	Sold for
3 heifers	William Relfs	£11.1s.
Ewes	Thomas Wickersham	
Half of 1 hog, 10 stone	-	15s.
2 fat oxen	John Budgen	£15.15s.
1 hog, 23 stone	-	£1.14s.
Tubs staves	Edward Muddle	7s.6d.
1 round table	George Dawes	11s.
2 oxen	At Rotherfield Fair	£11.10s.
28 lambs	Thomas Wickersham	£10
A field of grass	John Hasleden	£4
5 calves	-	£5
6 loads of straw	Edward Hasleden	£2
24 bushells Oats	John Budgen	£1.10s.
Sheep	Thomas Wickersham	£4.6s.7d.
1 load of Wheat	Richard Smith	£7.10s.
1 cow	William Hamlin at Cuckfield Fair	£3.10s.
3 sheep	John Hasleden	18s.
2 oxen & 2 steers	John Reynolds	£19
2 oxen	Edward Payne	£10.10s.
2 rabbits	Thomas Hamlin	1s.2¾d.
1 bull & 1 heifer	Mr. Hallatt at Cuckfield Fair	£5.1s.
3 bushells of Oats & teares	-	3s.9d.
8 bushells of Oats	John Cooke	10s.
For Rearing 3 colts	Richard Binall	4s.
800 faggots	Widow Bur..or	£2
1 chest	Thomas Wincorbott...	£1.12s.6d.
4 bushells Peas	Thomas Nash	10s.
378 bushells of Barley	John Wiggons	£14.4s.6d.
20 quarters Oats	Henry Waller	£10
..... & hoggs sold at Grinstead Fair		£8
Several goods	Sowall Plows	£71.7s.2d.
2 horse hides		2s.
1 colt skin		6d.
..... pigs		£2.17s.
2 bushells of Wheat		7s.
2½ bushels of Peas		8s.
1 bushell of Wheat		3s.9d.
4 bushells of Wheat		14s.8d.
A lost bullocks hide		6s.
2 lost sheep skins		2s.
9 bushells of Oats		12s.6d.
4 bushells of Wheat		14s.
8 bushells of Oats		12s.
2 bushells of Oats		3s.
8 bushells of Wheat		£1.9s.6d.
..... bushels of Wheat		15s.
1 young		2s.6d.
1 bushell of Oats		1s.6d.
1 bushell of Wheat		3s.
1 bushell of Oats		1s.8d.
8 bushells of Wheat		£1.8s.6d.
2 bushells of Wheat		7s.
1 bushell of Oats		1s.4d.
3 bushells of Wheat		10s.6d.
8 bushells of Wheat		£1.10s.
3 bushells of Wheat		9s.6d.
4 bushells of Oats & Teares		5s.6d.
2 bushells of Oats		3s.6d.
3 bushells of Wheat		9s.6d.
40 bushells of Wheat		£6.17s.
4 bushells of Wheat		12s.
6 bushells of Wheat		18s.
4 bushells of Oats		5s.3d.
2 bushells of Oats & Teares		3s.
The list continues but is unreadable		

Appendix 10

The Gypsy
Edward Thomas, 1878–1917

A Fortnight before Christmas Gypsies were everywhere:
Vans were drawn up on wastes, women trailed to the fair.
'My gentleman,' said one, 'you've got a lucky face.'
'And you've a luckier,' I thought, 'if such grace
And impudence in rags are lucky.' 'Give a penny
For the poor baby's sake.' 'Indeed I have not any
Unless you can give change for a sovereign, my dear.'
'Then just half a pipeful of tobacco can you spare?'
I gave it. With that much victory she laughed content.
I should have given more, but off and away she went
With her baby and her pink sham flowers to rejoin
The rest before I could translate to its proper coin
Gratitude for her grace. And I paid nothing then,
As I pay nothing now with the dipping of my pen
For her brother's music when he drummed the tambourine
And stamped his feet, which made the workmen passing grin,
While his mouth-organ changed to a rascally Bacchanal dance
'Over the hills and far away.' This and his glance
Outlasted all the fair, farmer, and auctioneer,
Cheap-jack, balloon-man, drover with crooked stick, and steer,
Pig, turkey, goose, and duck, Christmas corpses to be.
Not even the kneeling ox had eyes like the Romany.
That night he peopled for me the hollow wooded land,
More dark and wild than the stormiest heavens, that I searched and scanned
Like a ghost new-arrived. The gradations of the dark
Were like an underworld of death, but for the spark
In the Gypsy boy's black eyes as he played and stamped his tune,
'Over the hills and far away,' and a crescent moon.

Index

ill refers to an illustration; *n* to a note; *port* to a portrait

A

Abergavenny, Lord George 77
Ackerley, Captain Eric and Winifred 117, 119–20, 122
Ackerley, Joan (later Aske) 117
acorn harvesting 15*ill*
Aldworth, Mary (later Eaton) 63–4
All Saints Church, Lindfield 56*ill*
America, colonising of 50–1
Amherst House, East Grinstead 30
Amos, Michael and Maggie 143
animals 151
Anne of Cleves 38
Ansfield, Alfred 113
Ardingly Sandstone 9, 27
Aske, Sir Robert John Brigham 119
Avins House, Ardingly 76*ill*
Aylward, Mary (later Buckman) 98

B

Baesh, Sir Edward 49
Balsham village 57, 59
Banks, Bartholomew 41
Banks, Samuel 42–3
Banks family 41
Bardolf, Hugh 23, 24, 28
Bardolf, Thomas (son of Hugh) 24, 28
Bardolf, William 23
Barkhamridge Kennels 124
Barrett, Edward, Lord Newburgh 49
Barrow 1618 C of E Free School 51
Barrow Hill almshouses, Willey 51
Bass, Ethel Dorothy 124
Battle of Marston Moor (1644) 60
Bayne, John and Jean 119–20, 136–9
Benek family 29, 33
Benke, Edmund 33, 34–5, 37, 40
Benke, Jane 35
Benke, John 36
Benke, Thomas 33, 40–1, 43
Benke family 33–6, 39
Bennett, Nobbie (William Charles) 109

Bevin, Thomas and Willliam 77
Big-upon-Little, West Hoathly 9
Billings, Edwin 98
Billings, Henry and Harriett 98
birds 151
Black Death 30
Blitz (film) 150
Boakes, Horace and Harriette Mary Still 104, 108
  marriage certificate of 104*ill*
Boakes, Thomas 104
Boakes family tree 174–5
Bolney farmhouse, Ardingly 55*ill*, 56
Borrer, John and Ann 78
Bowers, Arthur 117, 126
Bradgate, Robert and Margery 47–8
Breakspear, Rose (later Reed) 132
British National Vegetation Classification 11
Broadley clothing store, East Grinstead 30, 35
Brookwood Memorial to the Missing 114*ill*
Browne, Elizabeth and Sara 48
Browne, John and Thomas 35–6
Browne family 35
Browning, John 72–5
Buckman, Daisy (later Pelling) 101, 105*n*
Buckman, Edward and Elizabeth 98
Buckman, Frederick and Margaret 98–100, 103–4
  grave 103*ill*
Buckman, Thomas (father of Frederick) 98
Buckman family 98–100
Burberry, Amelia (later Turner) 92, 96

C

Carewe, Francis 34
Carewe family 34
carpenters 22*ill*, 25, 32
Chalk Croft 67, 132
Chapman, John and Elsie 122, 130, 143
  letter from R.T. Mason 127*ill*
charcoal production 33, 34*ill*
Chatham Dockyard 46

Chisman (Cheseman), John and Sara 54–5, 62
Church Army Mission Room 108*map*
Church of the Holy Trinity, Balsham 58*ill*
Combes, Frances (later Boakes) 104
Crawford, Major General Lawrence 60
Creasy, Nineon 76
Cromwell, Oliver 60–1
  house in Ely 60*ill*
Cromwell, Thomas 33, 33*port*
Cuper's Cove colony 50, 50*ill*, 51*ill*

D

Dallingridge Mead 77
drovers' huts 15*ill*
drovers' route 14*map*, 15–17
du Maurier, Daphne 9
Dungate, Thomas 35
Dunlop, Jack 139–40
Dunmoylan Castle, Ireland 61
Dutch elm disease (1970s) 137

E

East Grinstead 20, 23, 30, 30*ill*, 39
East Grinstead Fair 101*ill*
East Grinstead High Street 30–1, 31*ill*
East India Company 49
  coat of arms 49*ill*
East Surrey Staghounds 82
Eaton, Ann (mother of Simon) 57, 59
Eaton, Martha (later Mathew) 64–5
Eaton, Simon (later Sir) 54–65, 72–3
  coat of arms 63*ill*
  move to Ireland 61
  letter of purchase to Francis Hamlin III 74*ill*
Eaton, Simon (son of Simon) 63–4
Eaton family tree 169–72
Elizabeth I, Queen 35, 35*port*
Ellis, Vivian Locke 101
Elwes, Harold Theodore 103
English Civil War 54, 60–1
Eton, Isobel 58
Eton, John 57
Everest, Ernest Alfred and Daisy Emma 108

F

Fairhall, Joseph 78
Falconer, Henry of Gravetye 55, 67
Family of Love (Familists) 57
Faulkner, Henry of Gravetye 62
Filtness, Henry William 126
flax 34, 34*ill*, 70, 70*ill*
Fleming, Kenneth and Susan 143
flowers 12
Forman, John 35
Foster, Charles and Charlotte 113–5, 115*port*
Francis, John 88

G

Gibb, William 97
Gilbert family tree 174–5
Gladman, William George and Josefine 120
Going, Amelia 80
Gravetye 115–6
Gravetye family 29
Great Rebuilding movement 39
Great Storm (1987) 144
Great Waldingfield Church 42
Gunpower Plot (1605) 42*n*
Guy, John 50
gypsies 103
Gypsy Caravan at Ringland Hills (Munnings) 103*ill*

H

Haire, Thomas 79
Hamlin, Ann (later Borrer) 78
Hamlin, Elizabeth (later Tully and Page) 68–70
Hamlin, Francis I 56, 62, 66–7
Hamlin, Francis II 67, 72
Hamlin, Francis III 68, 72–4, 76–7
  letter of purchase from Simon Eaton 74*ill*
Hamlin, Francis IV 76–8
Hamlin, John I and Margaret 56
Hamlin, John II 55, 56, 62, 66 CHECK
Hamlin, John III 67, 72 CHECK
Hamlin, John IV and Ann, tomb of 78*ill*
Hamlin, Mary (later Hick) 78
Hamlin, Thomas 67
Hamlin, Thomas III 78
Hamlin family 55–6, 66–7
  family tree 164–5
Harberfield, Edward 73
Harby, Elizabeth 48
Harvo, John 38
Harwoods Farm, East Grinstead 114
Haselden, John 33, 41, 67
Hazelden, John 41
Head, George and Elizabeth 106*n*
Hendry, Charles W.R. 136
Henley, Joseph 110–1

Hick, William Franklin and Mary 78–9
  signature of 79*ill*
Hodgkinson, Jeremy 38
Hogge, Ralph 40
Holmes Wood 52*ill*, 66
Holstein Wood 12, 96, 98
hops cultivation 80, 82*ill*
Hounsome, John 77
Hundred of Streat 10, 17, 24, 29
hunting 82–4, 82*ill*
Hurley Farm 115
Hyder, Kathleen Minnie (later Filtness) 126

I

Imberhorne Manor 10
Infield, Richard of Gravetye 33, 36, 39
Irish people, prejudice against 44
Irish Rebellion 61, 64
iron production 18, 33, 37, 66

J

Jenkins Mead 33, 40, 41, 67
Jenkyne, Edmund 33, 40
Jenner, John and Thomas 42

K

Kean, Herbert and Magdalena 143
Kemp, Hanna (later Benke and Lovell) 40–3
Kemp(e), John 40
  will of 43, 161
Kemp, William 97
Kempe, Caleb 41, 43
Kingscote 102*map*, 105, 107*map*, 107*ill*, 115
Kingscote Station 95, 116, 119, 120, 121*ill*, 123, 150
Knight, Ann (later Longley) 91

L

Lambarde, William 21
Lancaster Great Park 13
Le Hunt, Colonel Richard 61
Lee, John and Robert 91–2
Leppard, Frank (son of Willliam) 100
Leppard, William 99–100
Lewes and East Grinstead Railway 94, 119
Lewes Priory 33
Linton, Duncan and Joey 119, 120*port*
Longley, Charles and Caroline 88, 90*port*
  tomb of 90*ill*
Longley, Frank and Selina 99–100, 111, 116
  grave 100*ill*
Longley, Henry and Ann 88, 90
  gravestone 111*ill*
Longley, Henry II 88, 91, 95, 98, 109, 110*port*, 111

Longley, James 88
Longley, Kate (daughter of Henry) 95
Loog, Hermann 99
Lovell, Thomas 42
Lovell, Titus (son of Thomas) 42
lute 46*ill*

M

Manners, Sir George, Earl of Rutland 49
Margary, Ivan 13–14, 18, 18*n*
Marshall, Ernest and Marjorie 123–4
Mary Tudor, Queen 34–5, 35*port*
Mascall, John 34
Mason, George 96
Mason, R.T. 30, 105*n*
  letter to John Chapman 127*ill*
Mason, William and Sarah 77
  grave of 77*ill*
Mathew, George 64–5
Mathew family tree 171
meadows 20–1, 21*ill*
McQueen, Steve (film director) 150
Middle English language 19–21
Mighall, Mabel (later Kemp) 97
Mill Place 33, 36, 115, 116*ill*
Mills, John 55–6
Mills, Robert 53–4, 56
Mills, Sara 56
Mills family 53–4
Mine Pit Wood 12, 78, 96, 98
Moon, James Edward 116–7, 116*port*
  business advertisement for 117*ill*
Moon, Robin 117*port*
Muggridge, James 117

N

neolithic era, farming techniques in 13
Newfoundland 51*map*
Newfoundland Company 50–1
Newnham, Elizabeth (later Hamlin) 56
Nicholson, Ann (later Warner) 59

O

Ouse Navigation Canal 88

P

Page, Richard 69–70
Pain, George 88
Paine, Edward 72
Pansanger, Hertfordshire 48, 59
Parker, Margaret (later Buckman) 98–9
Pelling, John 101, 105*n*
Penfold, Hugh 98
Phillips, Chichester 62, 64–5
Plumpton Boscage Manor 10, 17, 24, 34, 41
Pounsley furnace, Framfield 38
Priest House, West Hoathly 35, 36*ill*

R

railway 95–6, 95*map*
Rape of Lewes 10, 23, 29
Rapley, Thomas and Elizabeth 97
Reed, Gilbert Ernest 130, 132, 132*port*, 135
Reynolds, Caroline Ida (later Longley) 88
Reynolds, Robert 80, 87, 88
Rice, Doris 117
Ridley, Ursula 29, 105*n*
roasting jacks 79, 79*ill*
Robinson, William of Gravetye 98
Roman era 18
Rowfant POW camp 21

S

St Giles Church, Barrow 52*ill*
St John the Baptist Church, Willey 47*ill*
St Lawrence Church, Great Waldingfield 48*ill*
St Margaret's Church, West Hoathly 35
St Mildred Church, Poultry 48*ill*
St Pancras Priory, Lewes 20
St Paul's Cathedral (1658) 52*ill*
St Peter Parish Church, Kinver 58*ill*
Sargent, Heather 122, 122*port*, 123–4
Schooling, Christopher 144
Scales, Prunella 150
Seale, Anne (later Tully and Page) 69–70
Seale, William 70
Selden family 106*n*
Selsfield Common 18
Selsfield Place 110, 111*ill*
sheep husbandry 19–20, 20*ill*, 23
shipbuilding 49–50, 49*ill*, 91
Shopland, Phil and John 149
Shoreham Harbour (Nash) 92*ill*
Siege of Limerick (1690) 61
Simmonds, Arthur James 109
Simmonds, Herbert Leslie and Hilary 113, 113*port*
Simmonds, Jo and Lucy 116
Simmonds, Thomas and Bertha 108–9, 113, 116
Simmonds family 108–9
Simmons, Henry 98
Simmons, Herbert 113
Simmons, Joseph and Daisy 113
Slane of Ireland coat of arms 44*ill*
Slaney, Henry 46–7
Slaney, Ralph 44
  coat of arms 44*ill*
Slaney, Richard III 52, 54
Slaney, Sir Stephen Slaney Stephen 44–6, 45*port*
  will of 46
Slany, Humphrey 49, 50
Slany, Elizabeth (later Eaton) 47, 52, 57–8
Slany, John I 43–4, 56, 59
  signature of 43*ill*
Slany, John III 47–52
  will of 51–2
Slany family 44–52
  family tree 166–7
Sloughe, Humphrey 40
Smith, Elizabeth (later Hamlin) 67
Spyer, Richard 98
Squanto: a Warrior's Tale (film) 51
Station Jim (film) 150, 150*ill*
Stenning, Sir Alexander Rose 106*n*
Still, Edith Mabel Annie (later Gilbert) 104–5
  memoir 105–6, 106*n*
Still, Harriette Mary (later Boakes) 104
Still family tree 174–5
Sturt, John 78
Styles, Mary Louise (later Henley) 110
Sunte House, Haywards Heath 76*ill*
Sussex Historical Search Society 149
Sussex Subsidy 24, 29
Swan with Two Necks Inn, London 59*ill*

T

Tassell, Ann (later Eaton) 59
Tassell, Bartholomew 57
Tassell, William 57
Tassell family tree 172–3
Teague (surname) 23
Teggeherugge, William de 22
Thegheregg, Simon de 24–5, 28
Thegheregge, Richard de 29
Thomas, Edward 101, 103*port*
  'The Gypsy' (poem) 181
Tickeridge 10, 131*map*
  origin of name of 19–20
Tickeridge Barn 66–7
Tickeridge Farm 9–10, 70–1, 81*map*, 91*map*, 127*map*, 131*ill*, 133*map*, 136*ill*, 151*ill*
  alterations to 136–40
  archaeological finds 18*ill*, 97*ill*, 100*ill*, 110*ill*, 111*ill*, 115*ill*, 149, 149*ill*
  buildings 84–5, 84*ill*, 85*ill*, 130, 130*ill*, 137*ill*, 139*ill*
  catalogue of cattle for sale 112*ill*
  dairy farming 124–6, 125*ill*, 126*ill*, 132, 137, 142*ill*
  equipment 86*ill*, 87*ill*, 137–40, 140*ill*, 141*ill*, 147*ill*
  granary 80, 83, 83*ill*
  location of 14*map*
  pump house 84–6, 85*ill*, 93*ill*, 94*ill*
  sale catalogue 135*ill*
Tickeridge Farm House 25–9, 25*ill*, 28*ill*, 99*ill*, 102*map*, 118–9*ill*, 121*ill*, 122–3, 123*ill*, 129*ill*, 134*ill*, 143*ill*, 144*map*, 145*ill*, 146*ill*
  advertisement for sale of 128*ill*
  fireplaces 37–8, 38*ill*, 105, 105*n*
  outside lavatory 119*ill*
  renovations to 37–9, 122, 143–50, 148*ill*
  solar bay 26
  stained-glass windows 37*ill*
  Wendy House 117, 119*ill*
timber industry 86–8, 96*ill*
Tisquantum (Squanto), slave 51, 51*port*
Townsend, Jane (later Reynolds) 80, 88
Tree, Ann 35
trees 11–12, 11*ill*, 12*ill*, 30, 32
Tritton, Veronica 136, 138
Tully, Francis 68–71
Tully, John and Elizabeth 68–9
Turner, John and Joseph 92, 94

V

Venables, Richard 48
Vowels Lane 16*ill*, 25, 82, 95–6, 98, 113, 120, 123, 124, 143*ill*

W

Waldingfield family tree 162–3
Warner, Henry 60, 63
Warner, Dorothie 61
Warner, Susanna (later Phillips and Eaton) 59, 62–5, 73
Warner, Thomas 58–9, 62–3
Warner family tree 169–70
Warrenne, John de, Earl of Surrey 24
Wealden Buildings Study Group 25, 144
Welde, Dorothy *The Welde Lute Book* 45
Welde, Humphrey 45
Welde, John 45
West Hoathly 9, 20, 23, 24, 29, 33, 35, 38, 77, 82
Willoughby, Sir Percival 49
Wilmington House, East Grinstead 30
Wimhurst, Elizabeth (later Rapley) 97
Wolseley, Viscountess Frances Garnet 113
Woodman, Caroline (later Reynolds) 80, 88
Woodman, James 78
Woodman, John and Elizabeth 89, 90
Woodman, William 79–80, 87–9
World War II 21, 115–6
Worshipful Company of Grocers coat of arms 40, 40*ill*
Worshipful Company of Merchant Taylors 47, 48, 52
  coat of arms 47*ill*
Worshipful Company of Skinners coat of arms 45*ill*